The Common Ground
of Psychoanalysis

Commentary

"*The Common Ground of Psychoanalysis* is an amazing document about the current status of psychoanalysis as a science, a discipline, and a clinical practice. It deals with fundamental, hotly debated issues that are of considerable interest to all mental health professionals who care about the scientific and ideological underpinnings of their clinical work. . . . Wallerstein's work is a courageous scientific effort and a statesman-like achievement."

—Paul Ornstein, M.D.

"The publication of Robert S. Wallerstein's volume, *The Common Ground of Psychoanalysis,* represents a major event in the current national and international psychoanalytic worlds. His courageous contribution has already proved to be a peaceful disturber of the psychoanalytic peace within organized psychoanalysis; its reverberations should lead to considerable psychoanalytic soul-searching and a multitude of crucial—even respectfully irreverent—questions. What else can we ask of an author?"

—Edward M. Weinshel, M.D.

"Robert Wallerstein, one of the foremost psychoanalytic researchers, has tackled the problem of the essential differences and similarities among various psychoanalytic approaches. He has assembled a splendid group of contributions, held firmly together by his two introductory and two concluding chapters. This book presents the question of whether there is one psychoanalysis or many, and the debate contained within it, presented extremely clearly, will fascinate all those interested in the relation between psychoanalytic theory and practice—not only psychoanalytic practice, but all those clinical areas in which psychoanalysis is applied. It will certainly take its place as a most important work, highly relevant to current major concerns in the psychoanalytic world."

—Joseph Sandler, M.D.

The Common Ground
of Psychoanalysis

edited by
Robert S. Wallerstein, M.D.

JASON ARONSON INC.
Northvale, New Jersey
London

The editor and publisher gratefully acknowledge the following for permission to reprint material found in this book.

The International Journal of Psycho-Analysis, which previously published the papers, and the individual authors. Copyright © Institute of Psycho-Analysis, London.

Harcourt, Brace Jovanovich, Inc. and Faber and Faber Ltd for excerpts from "Burnt Norton" and "East Coker" in *Four Quartets,* copyright © 1943 by T. S. Eliot and renewed 1971 by Esme Valerie Eliot.

Production editor and interior designer: *Gloria L. Jordan*
Editorial director: *Muriel Jorgensen*

This book was set in 12 point Galliard by Lind Graphics of Upper Saddle River, New Jersey, and was printed and bound by Haddon Craftsmen of Scranton, Pennsylvania.

Library of Congress Cataloging-in-Publication Data

The common ground of psychoanalysis / edited by Robert S. Wallerstein.
    p. cm.
  Includes bibliographical references and index.
  ISBN 0-87668-555-6
  1. Psychoanalysis—Philosophy—History. I. Wallerstein, Robert
S.
  [DNLM: 1. Psychoanalysis. 2. Psychoanalytic Theory. WM 460
C7345]
RC506.C619 1991
616.89'17—dc20
DNLM/DLC
for Library of Congress   91-18035

Manufactured in the United States of America. Jason Aronson Inc. offers books and cassettes. For information and catalog write to Jason Aronson Inc., 230 Livingston Street, Northvale, New Jersey 07647.

Contents

PART I
PSYCHOANALYTIC PLURALISM

PART II
SEARCH FOR THE COMMON GROUND

PART III
SHARED UNDERSTANDING

Acknowledgment

This book does not have the customary preface since the first chapter comprehensively sets the scientific and historic context of its guiding theme. However, acknowledgment should be duly rendered here to those who have contributed variously to its production. First, it was Jason Aronson who suggested to me that the theme of the quest for the common ground of psychoanalysis elaborated in my two presidential addresses to the Congresses of the International Psycho-Analytical Association in Montreal in 1987 and in Rome in 1989, together with the highlights of the far-ranging responses that those talks evoked, both in qualified agreement and in vigorous question and dissent, should be developed into a book. Together we agreed on the present format, placing first my original presentation of the issue in my Montreal address, *One Psychoanalysis or Many?* to be followed by the six prepublished papers for the succeeding Rome Congress on the *Common Ground of Psychoanalysis*. The two main published Congress plenary clinical presentations on this theme come next and are followed by my Rome address, *Psychoanalysis: The Common Ground*, a response to this array of presentations. I agreed to write the first and final chapters, the first setting the context of the issue, and the last assessing its current status. And when Richards's overview of the Rome Congress, reviewing the dialogue on the Congress theme, appeared in print, it was invited (in a somewhat edited form) as another chapter in this book.

The necessary typing and secretarial work in my office was accomplished by Kira Tiedgens with her usual high competence. Editorial and production help in the publisher's office was given generously by Muriel Jorgensen, Anne Patota, Norma Pomerantz, and especially Gloria Jordan. Responsibility for the content and organization of the final product, with its inevitable shortcoming and omissions, remains mine.

Contributors

Samuel Abrams, M.D., is a member of the Psychoanalytic Association of New York.

Gottfried Appy, M.D., (deceased) was a member and president of the German Psychoanalytical Association.

Carlos Mario Aslan, M.D., is a member of the Argentine Psychoanalytic Association and a former vice-president of the International Psycho-Analytical Association.

Michael Feldman, M.D., is a member of the British Psychoanalytical Society.

Arnold Goldberg, M.D., is a member of the Chicago Psychoanalytic Society.

Max A. Hernández, M.D., is a member of the Peru Psychoanalytic Society and a former vice-president of the International Psycho-Analytical Association.

Claude Le Guen, M.D., is a member of the Paris Psychoanalytical Society.

Eustachio Portella Nunes, M.D., is a member of the Rio de Janeiro Psychoanalytic Society.

Arnold D. Richards, M.D., is a member of the New York Psychoanalytic Society.

Robert S. Wallerstein, M.D., is a member of the San Francisco Psychoanalytic Society, a former president of both the American Psychoanalytic Association and the International Psycho-Analytical Association.

Part I

PSYCHO-ANALYTIC PLURALISM

1

The Context
of the Issue

Robert S. Wallerstein, M.D.

A recent major phenomenon in psychoanalysis has been the ongoing accommodation to our increasing theoretical diversity, or what has come to be called our psychoanalytic pluralism. This increasing pluralism—of theoretical perspectives and of regional, cultural, and linguistic emphases—is not actually itself of recent origin; rather, we have collectively come quite recently to experience it as a major problematic within psychoanalysis as a science and as a discipline, and we have barely begun to explore its scientific and professional implications.

Freud made a valiant and lifelong effort to hold psychoanalysis together as a unified theoretical enterprise solidly built upon his own unique lifetime achievement in creating almost singlehandedly the essential fabric of a fully operating scientific and professional activity. However, Kleinian analysis, the first alternative theoretical perspective that successfully resisted the expulsive pressures that had led to the departure of the very early deviants (like Adler and Stekel and Jung, and then Rank) from its ranks, actually had its roots still during Freud's active lifetime, as far back as the

1920s, when Melanie Klein accepted Jones's invitation to move from Berlin to London in order to develop her new psychoanalytic thinking within the receptive framework of the then-new British Psychoanalytical Society. And it is of course in Great Britain, with its polarization over the decades of the 1930s and 1940s into the (Anna) Freudian and the Kleinian viewpoints, with then the rise, in between, of the so-called Middle or Independent group, that a large body of distinctive and distinguished contributors evolved who chose not to align themselves with the partisan and adversarial positions of the two rival factions. Instead, this group developed a loose commonality of viewpoints that came to be designated the British Object Relations school, and it was in this setting that the earliest overt clashes of theoretical perspectives and struggles for intellectual hegemony took place, leading ultimately to the so-called Controversial Discussions of 1943 and 1944, with the compromise resolution then of those fractious intellectual and political struggles via the so-called gentleman's agreement signed by three women, Anna Freud, Sylvia Payne, and Melanie Klein, each on behalf of her respective group.

A first widely attended account (in the sense of worldwide psychoanalytic focus and attention) of these "controversial discussions" was published by Riccardo Steiner in 1985. King, the official archivist of the British Psychoanalytical Society, has together with Riccardo Steiner recently published an extraordinarily detailed account of these events, including the almost verbatim texts of all of the scientific presentations, formal discussions, and scientific and business meetings that marked their course (1991). In the almost half century since those "controversial discussions" and their resolution, the British Society has lived under one administrative roof, containing three major and widely differing theoretical perspectives, each with its staunch adherents. These three perspectives maintain three separate training tracks, albeit with significant cross-fertilizations built in (in accord with the terms of the "gentleman's agreement"), and the ongoing enforced scientific dialogue among these three viewpoints has over the years actually become more tolerant and understanding, with more mutual accommodations to the discerned insights and clinical and theoretical values of the other theoretical perspectives. The British Society has therefore been living almost since its inception with a more or less harmonious accommodation to this close confrontation of viewpoints that the rest of us are coming much more recently to face.

The history has been different in the rest of the psychoanalytic world, however. For a long while, the British experience was not factored into significant psychoanalytic awareness in other areas. This has largely been a reflection of the insularity that seems to have marked psychoanalytic historical development in most places of the world—this despite the existence, from 1908 on, of the International Psychoanalytical Association, with its biannual International Congresses at which psychoanalysts from around the world have faithfully and regularly come together for scientific exchange. Nonetheless, developments in psychoanalysis in most places have been constrained by particular intellectual and cultural conventions that have given quite distinctive, and at the same time reasonably homogeneous, casts to the psychoanalysis of each place. All of this has been abetted by our language differences worldwide, so that those in each country have been most familiar with the literature in their own national language journal, and the great bulk of the literature published in other countries has been varyingly inaccessible. Another reason perhaps for the relatively small influence of the pluralistic British experience upon psychoanalytic development elsewhere until quite recently may have to do with the fact that the most intensive controversy, the "controversial discussions" themselves, and the structural and intellectual resolutions then arrived at, took place during the enforced national scientific isolationism of the World War II period, when the International Psychoanalytical Association itself had an 11-year hiatus in its customary biannual Congresses between the Paris Congress in 1938 and the next Zurich Congress in 1949.

What has been much more typical of worldwide psychoanalytic development within national borders has been the experience in the United States, which, since World War II, has indeed been the largest and the most dominant component of organized psychoanalysis worldwide. Psychoanalysis, of course, was established in the Central European heartland, and its first major centers were in Vienna, Zurich, Budapest, and Berlin—largely the German-speaking world. Soon there were extensions to Holland and England, and in the 1920s psychoanalysis began to be established in the United States, partly by immigrant analysts and partly by pilgrimages of varying length by American aspirants to Vienna and Zurich, and later to Berlin. By 1925, 16 percent of the International's 210 regular members were in the United States, and by 1931, 22 percent of the now 307 members were Americans.[1] But this minority situation was totally reversed by the tide of emigrant analyst

---

[1] These figures are from Knight's history of psychoanalysis in the United States from its pre-1911, preorganizational beginnings until 1952, presented in his 1952 presidential address to the American Psychoanalytic Association. See his article (1953) for an account of those first four decades of American psychoanalysis.

refugees, who fled Central Europe in the 1930s to escape Nazi persecution and went overwhelmingly to America. A significant minority, including the Freud family, went to England instead, and a handful even went elsewhere, to Latin America. By 1952, the International membership stood at 762, with 64 percent in the United States—a two-thirds majority in the world.

And in contrast to that in Great Britain, psychoanalytic development in the United States, in the immediate aftermath of World War II the dominant voice and therefore the dominant mode in the world, developed in accord with Freud's own devout hope for a centrally unified and coherent theoretical development. This occurred, of course, in the form of the ego psychological metapsychology paradigm as articulated especially by Hartmann, Kris, and Loewenstein, as well as a host of distinguished collaborators, mostly in New York (which then comprised 40 percent of the total U.S. membership), and mostly among refugees from Central Europe, many of whom had had close personal contact with Freud and others of the first-generation pioneering psychoanalysts surrounding Freud. The ego psychology theoretical developmental line took as its point of origin Freud's creation of his "structural model" (called in some places the second structural model) as proposed in the *Ego and the Id* (1923) and *Symptoms, Inhibitions, and Anxiety* (1926) (appearing in English translation in 1927 and 1936 respectively). It was subsequently added to by Anna Freud's *The Ego and the Mechanisms of Defence* (1936), the elaboration of the defensive aspects of ego functioning, and by Hartmann's *Ego Psychology and the Problem of Adaptation* (1939), the contrapuntal elaboration of the adaptive aspects of ego functioning (these appearing in English translation in 1946 and 1958 respectively). And

9

it came to its fullest delineation in the many papers published in America by Hartmann, Kris, and Loewenstein, singly or in various combinations (Hartmann 1964, Hartmann et al. 1964)—amplified and extended then by many other of their European refugee colleagues, including Jacobson, Annie Reich, and so on. It was Rapaport, another refugee from Hungary, who became the great systematizer of the ego psychology metapsychological edifice being created by this galaxy of contributors. This ambitious, systematizing agenda was established with Rapaport's first monumental book, a compendium of articles translated and painstakingly commented upon by himself, published in 1951. It was furthered by his full English translation of Hartmann's path-breaking 1939 book in 1958, and further added to by his effort to place Erikson's pioneering studies on *Identity and the Life Cycle* (1959) into juxtaposition with the ego psychological contributions of Hartmann and his collaborators as a complementary psychosocial theory of the epigenesis of the ego (Introduction to Erikson's monograph, pp. 14–16). And it came to its fullest flowering with the posthumous and lovingly edited *Collected Papers of David Rapaport* (Gill 1967). A project left unfinished by Rapaport's untimely death in 1960, to which he had devoted his last years at the Austen Riggs Center, was the elaboration (both theoretically and experimentally) of a psychoanalytic learning theory, the only major piece he felt to be still missing from the total fabric of the ego psychological metapsychology model of psychoanalysis as a complete general psychology, encompassing all the phenomena of normal and abnormal mental functioning.

It was within this comprehensive intellectual structure of (American) ego psychology that all the leadership generations of American psychoanalysis have been trained for the past four decades. During my own psychoanalytic training in the 1950s, it was *the* expression of proper psychoanalysis in an unbroken line from Freud and the first-generation analysts constellated into the brotherhood of the seven famed ring-holders, through the pivotal elaborations of Anna Freud and Heinz Hartmann, still in Europe and written in German, and then opening into the prevailing ideology of the American dominance of the psychoanalytic world in the first post–World War II decades. In my own training, this tradition constituted the totality of the literature that was prescribed in our clinical and theoretical course work, drawn mainly—after reading Freud and the early Freudians, Abraham, Ferenczi, Jones, Sharpe, and the like—from the *Psychoanalytic Quarterly,* the newly established official *Journal of the American Psychoanalytic Association,* the Anglo-American *Psychoanalytic Study of the Child* (with the English contributors drawn overwhelmingly from the Freudian group of the British Society, mainly those clustered around Anna Freud's Hampstead Clinic), and those articles from the British-published *International Journal of Psycho-Analysis* that served as conceptual building blocks in the evolution of the ego psychological edifice, contributions by Nunberg, Glover, Sterba, Strachey, Heiman, Annie Reich, and so on.

We knew, of course, that there was a large Kleinian literature in the pages of the same *International Journal,* but it was not assigned and was not read; we were essentially under the sway of the thinking embodied in Rapaport's dismissive footnote in his introduction to the Erikson monograph (1959, p. 11) that "the 'theory' of object relations evolved by Melanie Klein and her followers is not an ego psychology but an id mythology." Nor were the burgeoning writings of the evolving British object relations school, Fairbairn, Guntrip, Balint, Bowlby, Winnicott, etc., really read. Some of these were not read at all; Bowlby's attachment theory concepts were known but usually dismissed as deviant from proper psychoanalysis, and Winnicott was very sparsely read—his "Hate in the Countertransference" (1949) and his "Transitional Object" (1953) papers, for example—but mostly he was dismissed as an untheoretical and unsystematic writer whose elusive and often ambiguous conceptions could not easily fit into our available theoretic schemas. Occasionally, American psychoanalytic institutes during that era gave single, elective courses on Other Schools of Psychoanalysis, or Deviant Psychoanalytic Schools, and these purported to introduce Kleinian or object relational perspectives via a rapid scanning of a superficial array of some classical articles from prominent representatives of these viewpoints. And, of course, almost none of the literature in the other major psychoanalytic languages, French, German, and Spanish, with all the developments of French Lacanian thinking, of German language phenomenological-existential perspectives, subsequently of the Franco-German hermeneutic conceptions, and of the Latin American variants of Kleinian thought, was almost none of it translated during that time, and it was thus almost entirely unavailable to the American majority psychoanalytic audience.

This hegemony of the prevailing ego psychological metapsychology paradigm was of course never really as absolute in the United States as we perceived it to be. There had actually been, early in the history of American analysis, in the 1930s and 1940s, the defection of many of those who espoused the culturalist and the interpersonal perspectives associated with the names of Horney, Fromm, Sullivan, and Fromm-Reichmann. This led to a cluster of new psychoanalytic institutes, mostly in New York, but they were clearly outside the framework of the American Psychoanalytic Association; they developed their own journals (including the *American Journal of Psychoanalysis*), and there was scant scientific interaction or influence either way. Similar disaffection existed in the Washington area, with the creation of the Washington School of Psychiatry, but more of the followers of this Interpersonal School did remain within the official structure of the American in the Washington Psychoanalytic Society, which was thus somewhat more "interpersonally oriented" than the dominant ego psychological perspective (and tended to be represented more in the journal *Psychiatry,* the official publication of the Washington School of Psychiatry).

And across the decades of the 1960s and 1970s, there was a burgeoning interest in Kleinian thought in Los Angeles. Bion was invited there in 1968 and remained for just over a decade; a few other British Kleinian analysts either emigrated to Los Angeles or visited for extended periods of time. But just as the Washington-area Sullivanian (or interpersonal) emphasis was a restricted phenomenon, much of it clustered around work with the severely ill and hospitalized at centers like the Sheppard and Enoch Pratt Hospital and at the Chestnut Lodge, so the espousal of Kleinian views continued as a local Los Angeles phenomenon. It spilled into the politics of the American and the International, however, when, in 1975, a group of Los Angeles analysts appealed to the International Congress in London, over the heads of the American, claiming that they were being discriminated against in achieving training-analyst status because of their Kleinian leanings.

The first real opening in the monolithic American hegemony of the ego psychology paradigm and its structural theory was the unexpectedly rapid rise and spread of Heinz Kohut's new self psychology, with its shift in conceptual focus from psychoanalysis's classical "guilty man," the product of conflict and compromise, to self psychology's "tragic man," the product of deficit and its repair (Kohut 1971, 1977, 1984). To most "classical" (American) analysts, this was an effort at a fundamental alteration of the essential structure of psychoanalysis from a theory based on intrapsychic conflict and its resolution to a theory based on (infantile) deprivation and deficit and its repair, carried out via sharply modified technical approaches, built on empathic immersion in narcissistic (later called selfobject) transferences and the countertransferences that they characteristically evoke. At first propounded as a new theoretical and clinical approach to a particular segment of the psychopathological spectrum, the narcissistic character disorders, in whom these particular transference configurations are most salient, the self-psychological approach was rapidly extended as a putatively more useful therapeutic approach across the entire array of psychopathology. The tripartite structure of id-ego-superego came to be replaced by a supraordinate bi-polar self that was claimed to be more encompassing. Within a very short span of time, the new self psychology spread far beyond its Chicago origins with Kohut and his colleagues, and found new adherents in Cincinnati, New York, Denver, Boston, and Los Angeles, to identify some of the more prominent.[2]

---

[2]For a critical comparative discussion of self psychology vis-à-vis "classical" ego psychological psychoanalytic theory—written from a "friendly-critical" perspective—see the sequence of three articles by Wallerstein (1981, 1983, 1985). The first two of these articles were presented at conferences in dialogue with Heinz Kohut and were in turn discussed critically by him. The last was presented at a Self Psychology Conference in Toronto in 1984 after Kohut's death.

Kohut was quite self-conscious of the particular role that he and the theoretical development he originated were to play in the historical evolution of psychoanalysis in America. In a rare self-revelatory moment at the Self Psychology Conference in Boston in 1980, at which both he and I presented papers, he told me that he wasn't at all sure about how widespread and lasting an alteration he had brought about in psychoanalytic theory and practice in America. But, he said, I certainly had to admit that he had shaken up the "establishment" as no one else had before him. Of course, self psychology has survived Kohut's death and has crystallized into a distinct movement within American psychoanalysis. It has its own society, its own journals, and its own conferences, while remaining at the same time solidly within the organizational and scientific structure of the American Psychoanalytic Association.

What somehow became more visible at the same time as this Kohutian, or self psychological, perspective assumed an increasingly prominent (and controversial) place in American analysis, was that the unifying hegemony of the seemingly monolithic "classical" ego psychological perspective in America had been itself fraying if not yet actually crumbling (although it has had and continues to have its very prominent and staunch proponents; witness the books by Charles Brenner [1976, 1982] and Leo Rangell [two volumes, 1990]). This began with the concerted repudiation of the structure of ego psychology and the claims of ego psychology to have made psychoanalysis into a fully comprehensive general psychology—repudiation by a whole group of the most influential former colleagues and students of Rapaport, Gill (1976), Schafer (1976), George Klein (1976), and Holt (1976, 1989), all in their own very individual ways. George Klein proposed what he called a "theorectomy" to separate and expunge the "general theory" or the ego psychological metapsychology from psychoanalysis as an unnecessary and mischievous theoretical encumbrance, in the service of disentangling and freeing psychoanalysis for the better development of its more experience-near and proper "clinical theory." A major aspect of the reaction against the ego psychology metapsychological paradigm was the turning away from the natural science framework and biological orientation within which it was cast, with its heavy focus on the adaptive aspects of ego functioning, the conflict-free sphere of the ego, and the maturational unfolding of the evolutionarily determined preadapted ego capacities toward a more hermeneutic model of the psychoanalytic enterprise (Schafer 1976, Spence 1982, 1987). Today, even within so-called mainstream American psychoanalysis, many speak of the post–ego psychology era.

Alongside this rise and fall of the ego psychological metapsychology, there has been a steadily growing interest in the British object-relational approaches, including the Kleinian as one kind of object-relations theory,[3] although this direction was for long the work of but a few individuals and was mostly seen as a supplement to and modification of ego psychology rather than as the offering of an alternative theoretical paradigm. Zetzel, trained in England, very early introduced "British approaches" into juxtaposition with American structural ego psychology thinking (1955, 1956, 1970); Edith Jacobson (1964) put "the *Self* and the *Object World*" into her book title and the center of her thinking;

---

[3]See Greenberg and Mitchell (1983) for a persuasive argument about why Kleinian theory, in its language the most grounded in the body, should nonetheless properly be placed as an object-relational rather than a drive-structural psychoanalytic model, in fact the earliest departure from Freud's drive-structural theory toward an object-relational theory.

Mahler (1975) developed her object relational–based concepts of separation and individuation; and Kernberg (1975, 1976, 1980), acknowledging his solid anchoring in the contributions of Jacobson and Mahler, created his particular amalgam of ego-structural and object relations concepts, with his conception of the internal units of self representations and object representations and the emotional valences that link them as the primary and primitive structural building blocks of the gradually evolving tripartite structural apparatus.[4] Today it is largely the work of Kernberg as well as of Modell (1968, 1984) that is looked at as the particularly American expression of the object relations viewpoint or influence to be put alongside the currently burgeoning interest in America in the British School, in Winnicott particularly, but also in Balint, and even in Fairbairn and Guntrip.[5] And even such major luminaries within the American psychoanalytic "mainstream" as Loewald (1980) and Stone (1961) either can be read as softening and humanizing the sharp contours of the very austere model of the psychoanalytic situation, and of psychoanalysis as a therapy, that was propagated so successfully by Eissler (1953), or can be read more boldly as affirming an object-relational emphasis within analytic work without departing from the language and structure of classical ego psychology.

---

[4]See Greenberg and Mitchell (1983) for a fundamentally dissenting view. Kernberg's theorizing is toward an amalgam of drive-structural and self and object representational perspectives into one overarching theory. Greenberg and Mitchell hold the drive-structural and the object-relational models to be antithetical and irreconcilable.

[5]Bowlby has always been a steady center of major interest and influence in America, but more in academic psychology and child development circles (cf. the work of Main, Ainsworth, Sroufe, etc.) than in psychoanalysis proper.

And in the most recent years, the increasing ecumenicism within American psychoanalysis has extended to a growing curiosity about the schools of Lacan and of Melanie Klein. Lacan, who had long enjoyed a reputation for his baffling and inscrutable prose, established his first beachheads in America in the French and English departments of major universities. But soon the Lacanian visitors from France began to address mental health professional and strictly psychoanalytic audiences as well. Two of his major books appeared in English translation (1977, 1978). Writings "explaining" Lacan also began to be published, including some by American authors (Schneiderman 1980, 1983, Smith and Kerrigan 1983) who had gone to France for analytic study with Lacan, like Schneiderman, or who, from within American analysis, became interested in the Lacanian perspective, like Leavy (1977, 1983a, 1983b). When, in 1984, the journal *Psychoanalytic Inquiry* devoted an issue to commentaries on Gill's *Analysis of Transference* (1982), it was considered *de rigueur* to include a Lacanian perspective (Nasio 1984) as well as a Kleinian one. It was also, however, not considered out of bounds for Gill (1984), in his own very detailed and meticulous response to the entire array of commentaries, to devote only a half dozen lines to the Lacanian view, including "I cannot claim to have made a strenuous effort to understand that perspective, but I do not understand it. I cannot therefore comment any further on Nasio's contribution" (p. 513).

And the Kleinians, long the isolated purveyors of their particular brand of "id mythology" within their quarantined Los Angeles enclave, have of course also burst those bounds. Actually, Racker's book (1968), translated from the Spanish, was the first book by a major South American Kleinian author to win a wide and critical hearing in

America, apart from the special interest of our child analysis colleagues in the writings of Melanie Klein (1948, 1949) as part of their study of the polarized Anna Freudian–Kleinian theoretical and technical concepts in the psychoanalytic understanding and treatment of children. Today, however, American analysts more readily read the Kleinian papers in the *International Journal* and the *International Review,* and leading Kleinian clinicians and theoreticians like Segal and Joseph are regularly invited to make presentations and participate in comparative panels at American psychoanalytic societies. More recently, Segal participated as a counterpart to Weinshel at an all-day panel comparing and contrasting Kleinian and "Freudian" analysis at the May 1990 meeting of the American Psychoanalytic Association in New York.

All this brings us to the present state of analysis in America. Alongside the still-dominant American drive-structural or ego psychological or post–ego psychological metapsychology, we now have a broad panoply. There is the thriving self psychology (no longer just Kohutian) enterprise, which has long since transcended its original restricted focus on the narcissistic personality disorders, that it purported to understand more comprehensively, and now has its own diverse array of theoretical progeny. There is as well the developmental focus innovated by Mahler with its particular bailiwick in, but not limited to, workers in child analysis. There is further the blend of ego psychological and object relational perspectives offered first by Kernberg as a better road to the understanding and treatment of the borderline personality organizations, but also now broadened into a supraordinate across-the-board amalgam of the drive structural and the object-relational models in relation to the entire psychopathological spec-

19

trum. There is the interpersonal approach of the current intellectual heirs of Sullivan (Levenson 1972, 1983) now rejoining into dialogue with the American psychoanalytic intellectual mainstream. And then there is the "action language" language-centered idiom of Schafer (1976), and the hermeneutic approach of Spence (1982, 1987), and, very oppositely, the cybernetic, systems and information-theory, psychoanalytic models offered by Peterfreund (1971) and Rosenblatt and Thickstun (1977). These are, of course, all relatively indigenous American products. This is not to speak of the current burgeoning interest in America in the writings of the British and Latin American Kleinians, in the British object relations school (Kohon 1986), in the French Lacanians, and in the many efforts at comparison across schools and perspectives (Bacal and Newman 1990, Greenberg and Mitchell 1983). It is this growing interest across theoretical perspectives that led Schafer (1985) to propose that Freud's (1910) original phrase "wild analysis" had outlived its once-clear meaning and usefulness, for what is now one person's proper analysis is another's wild analysis. Schafer proposed its replacement by the phrase, more suitable to present circumstance, "comparative analysis" (p. 276).

The broadening development in the intellectual centers of American analysis chronicled to this point is, of course, that most familiar to the American audience. In addition, it has, by weight of numbers, exerted the most powerful and visible pressures within the worldwide psychoanalytic community. But comparable developments have taken place in the other regions of the psychoanalytic world, each shaped by the particular historical trajectory of psychoanalysis within that area. I cannot even begin to state them in comparable detail; I can only indicate their scope. In

Holland, Scandinavia, and Germany, the dominant perspective has been "traditional" Freudian analysis—that is, the drive-structural model—and there has been a major flowering of empirical psychoanalytic therapy research within this framework, centered at the University of Ulm in Germany; at the same time there has been in Germany, and in other northern countries, a very significant philosophical and psychoanalytic hermeneutic emphasis identified with such names as Habermas, Gadamer, Lorenzer, and Lesche.[6] France has been the center of the explosive growth of Lacanian thought, with spillover to other romance-language countries, as well as to Latin America. But there has also been an equal flowering of non-Lacanian, albeit distinctively francophone, psychoanalytic perspectives. [See in this connection the book edited by Lebovici and Wid-

---

[6]In this connection see, for example "The Psychoanalytic Scene in Sweden," by Norman (1990). A few quotations telescope the argument: "Twenty years ago it was fairly easy to describe the theoretical orientation of Swedish psychoanalysis, and this was probably the case in many other countries. Swedish psychoanalysis lay within the mainstream of traditional Freudian thought with a strong bent towards ego psychology and a rejection of, for example, Klein.

Specific to Swedish psychoanalysis during the seventies was the marked preoccupation with philosophical questions and discussions on the philosophy of science. Carl Lesche, psychoanalyst and philosopher, developed a metascience of psychoanalysis based on phenomenology and on hermeneutics, the science of interpretation" (p. 8).

And "the breakaway from . . . dogmatic orthodoxy has dominated the eighties, but has not led away from Freud; on the contrary. . . . [But] the field has broadened and now, after a period of time, it has become acceptable to interest oneself in Winnicott, Klein, Bion, even Lacan. But not everyone encompassed everything, and there was no longer a mainstream as before; rather there seemed to be *many psychoanalyses*" (p. 9).

löcher (1980) and the journal issue edited by Poland and Major (1984)]. France has also been home to the combined energetic-hermeneutic perspective of Ricoeur (1970). And Latin America, so long regarded as a monolithically uniform bastion of Kleinian thought, has seen over the decades successive waves of involvement in the Bionian modifications and extensions of Kleinian analysis, then in Lacanian analysis, and now in Kohut's self psychology. All along there has also been representation by the North American ego psychology perspective, especially in Mexico and now in various other places, including in the largest center of Latin American analysis, the Argentine Association. In fact, many Latin American analysts take as a point of pride and as one explanation of the current rapid expansion of psychoanalysis on their continent—at present the most rapidly growing region of psychoanalysis worldwide—what they call their receptivity to all major currents of psychoanalytic thinking and to the challenging and invigorating clash of theoretical and clinical views that marks their psychoanalytic scientific life.

It is this story that has posed the issue to which this volume is devoted. We now live, in America and all over, in a world of self-conscious psychoanalytic diversity, or pluralism. This is now everywhere an accepted part of our psychoanalytic scientific life, and we all individually experience it, with varying degrees of comfort or disquiet, and with varying views about what it means to our status as a science and what it portends for the historical evolution and the future of our discipline. Those of us involved in the organized institutional life of psychoanalysis are confronted more sharply by all the varying political, professional, and scientific expressions of that pluralism as they are played out and shaped by the various intellectual and scientific histories and cultural and language contexts of the various centers of psychoanalytic activity around the world.

It is the overall awareness of the issues spelled out in this chapter that configured my own thinking when presented with the task and the opportunity, as president, to give an opening day plenary session address to the 35th International Psychoanalytical Association Congress in Montreal, Canada, in July 1987. The topic that I chose under the title "One Psychoanalysis or Many?", a topic that I felt to be of central importance to our worldwide psychoanalytic community, was what, in the face of this diversity, this pluralism, nonetheless still held us together as common adherents of a shared psychoanalytic science and profession. That 1987 address is the next chapter in this volume.

2

One Psychoanalysis or Many?

Robert S. Wallerstein, M.D.

The privilege, as president, of addressing the International Psychoanalytical Association (IPA) Congress is tempered by the corresponding obligation to select a topic of sufficient importance to the worldwide psychoanalytic community, in the hope that a dialogue about it initiated or furthered here can enhance our shared psychoanalytic understanding and commitment. Such a topic, I think, is the one I have selected today, that of our increasing psychoanalytic diversity, or pluralism, as we have come to call it—a pluralism of theoretical perspectives, of linguistic and thought conventions, of distinctive regional, cultural, and language emphases; and what it is, in view of this increasing diversity, that still holds us together as common adherents of a shared psychoanalytic science and profession.

Psychoanalysis was not always characterized by this pluralism; in fact, quite the opposite. Perhaps more than any other branch of human knowledge, psychoanalysis has been uniquely the singular product of the creative genius of one man, Sigmund Freud. His lifetime of productive work was extraordinarily prodigious, and if the totality of psychoanalysis consisted of nothing more than the corpus of Freud's *die Gesammelte Werke,* I think we could readily agree that all the fundamental principles and the essential fabric of a fully operating scientific and professional activity would be available to us as students and as practitioners.

And Freud made strenuous efforts throughout his lifetime to define the parameters of his new science of the mind, and to hold it together as a unified enterprise against both destructive or diluting pressures or seductions from without and also against fractious human divisivenesses from within. To him psychoanalysis was not only a science and a profession, but also a Movement, with all the calls to a dedicated and disciplined allegiance that that word connotes. When divergent tendencies threatened to splinter the unified edifice that Freud was trying to build, he created the famous Committee of the seven ring holders to try to guarantee the stability of his central psychoanalytic doctrines. And we all know the story, which Freud chronicled in 1914, in "On the History of the Psycho-analytic Movement," of how that first wave of close co-workers who began to differ with him in major ways, Adler and Stekel and Jung, each found it necessary to leave psychoanalysis over the three-year span from 1910 to 1913.

Freud from his side declared the psychological deviations of these dissidents to be totally incompatible with the fundamental postulates of psychoanalysis as he had established them to that point, and when they left the Movement over these differences, he professed himself to be satisfied that they should pursue any psychological and psychotherapeutic bent that they wished so long as they did not claim it to be psychoanalysis. Two of them did establish schools or movements of their own; Adler called his "Individual Psychology" and Jung took the name "Analytical Psychology.'' Of these two new theoretical systems Freud felt Adler's to be the more important (p. 60) and potentially the more enduring and in this his prediction proved to be faulty. It is the Jungian movement, which has more recently even reappropriated for itself the designation psychoanalysis, which has endured worldwide as an alternative therapeutic system—and I will return later to its potential current relationship to the psychoanalysis represented within the ranks of the IPA.

Freud did declare that both Adler and Jung had brought valuable new contributions to analysis, Adler to the psychology of the ego and its role in adaptation and to the recognition of the importance of the aggressive drives in mental life, and Jung to tracing the way infantile impulses are used to serve our highest ethical and religious interests. But Freud felt that each of these two in his own way had at the same time abandoned the central psychoanalytic concepts of the unconscious and repression, of resistance and transference, and that they had therefore placed themselves outside the definitional statement that Freud made for psychoanalysis in this selfsame history of his movement—actually the first, the most succinct, and the best known of the several such statements that Freud enunciated over the long span of his writings. As we all know so well, he said there, ''the facts of transference and of resistance. Any line of investigation which recognizes these two facts and takes them as the starting-point of its work has a right to call itself psycho-analysis, even though it arrives at results other than my own. But anyone who takes up other sides of the problem while avoiding these two hypotheses will hardly escape a charge of misappropriation of property by attempted impersonation, if he persists in calling himself a psycho-analyst'' (1914a, p. 16). Of course we must add here that the key words *transference* and *resistance* also imply the concepts of the unconscious, of psychic conflict, and of defence, the key building stones of our shared psychoanalytic edifice.[1] Since then, of course, several of Adler's central conceptions—like those of the ego and adaptation or of the motive power of aggression—have been actively re-incorporated into the main body of psychoanalysis, first by Freud and then by others who came after, like Hartmann, and perhaps that is related to the near collapse of Adlerian psychology as a separate therapeutic enterprise. There have been lesser but nonetheless still substantial reincorporations also from Jungian psychology, or at least cognate developments within the psychoanalytic framework, like Erikson's life span focus, with its shift in emphases to the coequal concern with the second half of the life span, or like our focus on unconscious fantasy systems as guides to understanding motivation and behavior—albeit in a different way than the Jungians—and this somewhat lesser reappropriation of concepts from Jung's theoretical system may relate to its continuing greater vigor as a separate psychology and therapy than its Adlerian counterpart.

Within another decade, after the departures of Adler and Stekel and Jung, psychoanalysis was threatened with new deviations, those of Ferenczi and of Rank, partly linked

---

[1]Freud earlier made this same point as my addendum quite explicit further along in his "History." He said at this further point, "The first task confronting psycho-analysis was to explain the neuroses; it used the two facts of resistance and transference as starting-points, and, taking into consideration the third fact of amnesia, accounted for them with its theories of repression, of the sexual motive forces in neurosis and of the unconscious" (1914a, p. 50). He just does not specifically mention the word *conflict* but it is totally inherent; the concepts mentioned don't hang together otherwise.

together in their monograph, *The Development of Psycho-analysis* (1924), and partly developing in differing, albeit related, directions, Ferenczi in his Active Therapy and Rank later in his Will Therapy. Actually, despite the severe strains aroused by these theoretical and technical developments, Ferenczi never left psychoanalysis, though Rank ultimately did and developed a new school in America more influential in social work than within psychoanalysis, the so-called functional school of social work, but that Rankian deviation and outgrowth has, like Adler's psychology, mostly now faded into history.

But that same decade of the twenties also saw the origin of the first major new theoretical direction within psycho-analysis that at the same time fought fiercely to maintain its sense of direct descent from the psychoanalysis of Freud, that indeed in some respects, like its unswerving acceptance of Freud's most problematic and controversial theorizing—the introduction of the death instinct theory in "Beyond the Pleasure Principle" in 1920—and the making of it a central building block in its own theoretical conceptual development, that in this it could even claim a closer adherence to the persona and the mind of Freud than those of the Viennese school who while closer to Freud personally yet split sharply on the value to psychoanalysis of this particular theoretical turn of Freud's. I refer here, of course, to Melanie Klein and the development of Kleinian analysis.

Riccardo Steiner, in his recently published review (1985) of the British society's so-called "Controversial Discus-sions" of 1943 and 1944, traces clearly the political history of the Kleinian theoretical development in England; the original invitation to Melanie Klein to come from Berlin to London to lecture on her new ideas about theory and technique that had developed out of her work with children, the interest aroused by these ideas in the British group, the invitation then to come permanently to London, and the early support and adherence to the Kleinian views by Jones and a distinguished group of the first generation British analysts, and the adversarial letters around this between Jones and Freud with Jones supporting Melanie Klein and Freud supporting his daughter Anna in the growing controversy over the proper theoretical and technical development of child psychoanalysis seen as an unhappy divergence between Kleinian and Anna Freudian views or between what was called the London and Vienna positions, representing at that time the two main centers of psychoanalytic influence in Europe and actually in the world.

The fundamental difference here, however, was that the Kleinian development did not lead to a split and departure from the organized body of institutional analysis, the IPA. Rather, the Kleinians insisted, as I have stated, on their even more impeccable psychoanalytic credentials, and their movement remained within the British organizational framework and therefore within the IPA, although the exact terms under which the British Society would henceforth operate with a Kleinian group and a Freudian group, and in between, an independent or middle group, were not settled until the year-long Controversial Discussions, which took place four to five years after Freud's death.

My point here is that the Kleinian development, still within Freud's lifetime and when his personal leadership in psychoanalysis was, of course, unquestioned, nonetheless represented the beginnings of the gradual transition of psychoanalysis from being—at least in appearance—a thoroughly unified theoretical structure evolved around the creative intellectual corpus of its founding genius, Sigmund

Freud, a gradual transition from that into the present-day worldwide theoretical diversity. Today we have existing side by side the American ego psychological (and by now post-ego psychological) school, the Kleinian, the Bionian, the British object-relational sometimes narrowed down to the Winnicottian, the Lacanian (largely outside but to a considerable extent in Europe and in Latin America inside our official ranks), and even in the United States, so long the stronghold of the unquestioning monolithic hegemony of the ego psychological metapsychology paradigm of Hartmann and Rapaport, we now have recently witnessed the rise of Kohut's self psychology as a major alternative psychoanalytical theoretical perspective, and, to a lesser extent as new schools, Mahler's developmental approach and Schafer's new voice or new idiom for psychoanalysis.

Of course, these varying *theoretical* perspectives do not exhaust the diverging conceptual developments within our field. We have all the advocates of our traditional natural science approach to the nature of the psychoanalytic enterprise with its requirements ultimately for evidence and validation in our inferential and predictive processes in accord with the canons of empirical science, albeit, of course, in ways fully consonant with the subjectivistic nature of our primary data, the transactional exchanges in our consulting rooms. We have all this as against those who see psychoanalysis as a social or historical science that is somehow different in the logic of its theory, in its epistemological base, and in its methods of discovery and validation, a different *kind* of science, in Harrison's (1970) words, "our science" meaning our "peculiar" science. And at the other extreme we have those who see psychoanalysis as not any kind of science at all but rather as a hermeneutical discipline like literary criticism or the biblical exegetical interpretation from which the term *hermeneutics* derived in the first place, a psychology that is based only on reasons, on the "why" of human behavior, and not at all like a science that is based on causes, on the "how" of human behavior. Although the natural science perspective has its main strongholds in America and in Britain and the hermeneutical perspective, with such names as Gadamer (1975), Habermas (1968), and Ricoeur (1970), is centered in Germany and France, there are indeed passionate advocates of each of these polar opposed positions everywhere, and within the hermeneutic camp there are all varieties of hermeneutic, phenomenological, exclusively subjectivistic, and/or linguistically based conceptualizations of our field. All these issues of the *nature* of psychoanalysis as a discipline I have dealt with at length in my Freud Anniversary Lecture in New York (Wallerstein 1986) and need not elaborate further for my purpose here.

But I do want to call attention in this context to yet another array of distinctivenesses that characterizes organized psychoanalysis worldwide. I am referring to all the regional and cultural and language emphases that make French (or francophone) analysis, quite aside from Lacan, into a different analytic "voice" than Anglo-American (or anglophone) analysis. This is what Bergeret in France has in mind when he calls for an official scientific council under the auspices of the IPA that would extend the contending conceptions about the nature of our discipline as a science beyond the "English-language cultural model" with its particular linguistic and thought conventions that can tend to constrain analysis into one predominant mold, not responsive to what he calls *"all* the currents of thought existing in the psychoanalytic world" (1986). It is also what the meetings between French and American analysts—the first was in Paris in 1983—have been about—to give the Americans present a "sampling of the range of ideas of French analytic thought" (Poland and Major 1984, p. 145), and of course vice versa, and hopefully in ways that would enable each side to the dialogue to transcend the prevailing stereotypes concerning the other. These differences that were explored are not just stylistic but also perspectival and therefore value laden with, for example, the differential allegiances, as values, to fluid and expressive freedom of discourse by metaphor and poetic allusion as against precision of meaning with careful denotation of explicit thought boundaries. All of this, of course, underlines what Steiner (1984) said in his review of the English language book *Psychoanalysis in France* (1980), edited by Lebovici and Widlöcher, that, "Despite the universality of the process of the unconscious, psychoanalysis is considerably influenced by the historical, cultural and social context in which it is developing. This can be regarded as a negative or as a positive phenomenon according to one's point of view, but it is a reality which cannot be easily refuted" (p. 233).

It should not be thought, however, that this transition from the theoretical unity of psychoanalysis that Freud tried to embody and enforce in his conception of a shared intellectual movement built around the intellectual charisma of his leadership, from that to the broad theoretical diversity with which we are today variously easily or uneasily content, was a smooth or uneventful journey. The interpolated momentous event for psychoanalysis, given the nature of our discipline and its origins, was the death of Freud and the burden thereupon thrust on analysts to carry their field beyond the consummate genius of one man who had so adventurously and single-handedly brought it into being, to what had to become a discipline and a science, that, true, built on its past, but rested on the from-now-on independent work of its collectivity.

This was for psychoanalysis a truly wrenching task. Freud's name and work had come to mean so much, and not just to psychoanalysts. As the literary critic Alfred Kazin (1957) expressed it in his assessment of the Freudian revolution:

> His name is no longer the name of a man; like "Darwin," it is now synonymous with a part of nature. This is the very greatest influence that a man can have. It means that people use his name to signify something in the world of nature which, they believe, actually exists. Every hour of every day . . . there are people who cannot forget a name, or make a slip of the tongue, or feel depressed; who cannot begin a love affair, or end a marriage, without wondering what the "Freudian" reason may be. [p. 15]

It is perhaps then small wonder that although Freud died in 1939, more than half a century ago, we have not yet fully come to terms with his transience and his death (Wallerstein 1983a). We still use his monumental contributions as the benchmarks against which to measure our progress. For so many of us, Sigmund Freud still remains our lost object, our unreachable genius, whose passing we have perhaps never properly mourned, at least not in the emotional fullness that leads to intellective accommodation. Knight (1953) put it thus: "Perhaps we are still standing too much in the shadow of that giant, Sigmund Freud, to permit ourselves to view psychoanalysis as a science of the mind rather than as the doctrine of a founder" (p. 211). Gombaroff, in a paper on our training issues, has called Freud the "father who does not die" (unpublished manuscript). What this persisting feeling, of course, adds up to is that, unlike other sciences, psychoanalysis has not yet been able really to accept Whitehead's famous dictum: "A science that hesitates to forget its founders is lost." Witness our common habit, established by Freud's first followers, of clinching our arguments by reciting a relevant passage from his papers; witness the curricula of our institutes built so centrally around the corpus of Freud's writings, usually studied chronologically. And we all know well the galvanizing impact of Lacan's battle cry, "back to Freud," as the rallying point of the Lacanian movement, the point of pride in differentiating themselves from all the rest of us who by implication have not as fully kept this personal (and personality) faith.[2]

It would be a digression here to try to trace the multiple consequences for our discipline of this unique continuing historic and mythic relationship to our founder as a fantasied continuing presence among us. I want now only to speculate about its relationship to my own central theme in this presentation, the dialectic between the effort to maintain the theoretical unity of psychoanalysis through a process of extrusion of those like Jung and Adler and others in subsequent generations whose new theoretical proposals, whatever their putative value, were, or seemed to be, linked to a major dilution if not a full abandonment of central psychoanalytic concepts, as against the contrapuntal effort

---

[2]Sandler made this identical point well in his prepublished paper for the 1983 IPA Congress in Madrid. "Freud's ideas are seen as the core of existing theory, and acceptable later developments are viewed as amplifications and additions which are consistent—or at least not inconsistent—with Freud's thoughts. Those who think in these terms will, when they disagree with other writers, do so on the grounds that the others have misunderstood, misinterpreted or misapplied Freud, and will turn back to Freud's writings to find supporting evidence for their own ideas" (p. 35).

at accommodation of diverging theoretical perspectives within a more generous and elastic overall definitional framework for psychoanalysis—albeit one that somehow can define what nonetheless we all do share and keeps us together as analysts (and differentiates us from nonanalysts), despite, among ourselves, our diversity in theory, in perspective, and in cultural and language emphasis and thought convention.

The main thrust of our developmental dynamic following upon Freud's death could have tilted in either of these two opposed directions, either of an ever-tighter circle of orthodoxy, or required adherence to one mainstream psychoanalytic doctrine, or of an expanding diversity of theory that could ultimately pose bewildering problems of boundaries, of deviation, of what is then "wild analysis," and of what is altogether beyond analysis, problems that all seemed simpler of resolution in Freud's day. In practice and for a long time after Freud's death—until the 1970s in fact—the tilt was in *both* directions, toward diversity in Europe and by extension also in Latin America, and toward maintained unity within one "mainstream" in the United States.

The philosophy and the justification of the European development toward an acceptance of diversity was spelled out by Isaacs (1943) in response to the discussion of her paper "The Nature and Function of Phantasy" during the British Society's Controversial Discussions in 1943. She said:

Listening to the selective accounts of Freud's theories offered by some of the contributors to this discussion, and noting their dogmatic temper, I cannot help wondering what would have happened to the development of psychoanalytic thought if for any reason Freud's work had not been continued after 1913, before his work on Narcissism and Mourning and Melancholia; or after 1919, before Beyond the Pleasure Principle, and the Ego and the Id. Suppose some other adventurous thinker had arrived at these profound truths and had dared to assert them! I fear that such a one would have been treated as a backslider from the strict path of psychoanalytic doctrine, a heretic whose views were incompatible with those of Freud, and therefore subversive of psychoanalysis. [p. 151]

Certainly Isaacs's heartfelt cry can be read as a Kleinian plea for tolerance of diverse theoretical viewpoints *within* the body of psychoanalysis, each equally sincerely—and perhaps with equally good reason—feeling itself to be in a direct and logical developmental line from the overall corpus of Freud's work, each in emphasis perhaps centering itself more in one than in another of the main theoretical conceptions for the understanding of the human mind offered by Freud over the span of his life's work, and not all of these conceptions easily reconciled with each of the others.

Sparked, then, by the success of this Kleinian development in England even within Freud's lifetime, a success consolidated in the outcome of the so-called Controversial Discussions shortly thereafter, and sparked perhaps also by the natural national and language diversity of the European continent, from rather early on, the psychoanalytic development in Europe was diverse and pluralistic. The Kleinian movement spread to other parts of Europe, and as far away as India and Australia, and most significantly became the dominant theory in the original growth of psychoanalysis all over the South American continent. The role of the British Society, with its powerful Kleinian group as a main training center for so many of the psychoanalytic pioneers in these various countries, has been, of course, a central element in that development.

But the post–World War II decades have also seen the rise and flowering of the differing theoretical work of Lacan and his followers in France, of the extensions of Kleinian thought by Bion in England, and of the whole development of the British independent group of the object relational perspectives in psychoanalysis pioneered by Suttie and Fairbairn and Guntrip and further developed by Balint and Bowlby and Winnicott and a host of others. It is this pluralistic theoretical development, to which can be added in Europe the various other distinctive and differentiating perspectives to which I have already alluded, the natural science versus hermeneutical, as well as the varying cultural and linguistic emphases—it is all this that has, despite our usually professed desire to see psychoanalysis as a body of theory that is expected to be consonant with some unifying perspective on Freud's writings—it is all this that has rather eventuated in our present-day pluralism of perspectives with varyingly inconsistent psychoanalytic theoretical structures to which we differentially adhere, depending mostly, it should be added, not on grounds of inherent appeal, plausibility, or heuristic usefulness, but rather on where and how we were trained, and where we then live and practice. And in a tour that Dr. Weinshel and I made of the various Latin American psychoanalytic societies, it became clear how that whole region, once thought to be a monolithic center of Kleinian analysis, has become home to each and every one of the theoretical developments in analysis emanating from centers in Europe, and from the United States as well.

By contrast to these developments in Europe in the post-war decades, psychoanalysis in the United States for a long time took a different course. With the rise of Hitler, collapse of the main psychoanalytic strongholds in central Europe, the main bulk and intellective power of psychoanalysis was transplanted to the United States though, of course, some went to the periphery of the European continent, to England, and to South America. And in America the post-war historical tilt, different from that elsewhere in the world, was in the direction of a unitary and unifying "mainstream"—the heir in that way of the political-administrative ambitions of Freud, epitomized in his conception of the role of the seven ring holders and expressed in the development and fruition in America of the ego psychology metapsychological paradigm, which under the aegis of Hartmann and Kris and Loewenstein and Rapaport and Jacobson and a host of others for long maintained a monolithic hegemony over the psychoanalytic domain in an arena that contained in those earlier post-war years at least half the world's psychoanalysts.

And when divergent theoretical directions emerged in the United States as they did elsewhere, as early as the forties—and here the names of Horney and Fromm and Thompson and Sullivan as well again of many others come to mind, all associated under the loose rubrics of either the interpersonal or the culturalist schools of psychoanalysis—the resulting controversy led in America just as it had in Freud's day in Vienna to a forced leaving of the affiliation with organized psychoanalysis and the founding of independent schools and training centers, though some like Fromm-Reichmann and Rado and Kardiner did manage to remain within the American Psychoanalytic Association and even to found new institutes and societies within it. But overall, the turmoil and the leavings of the forties in America were indeed reminiscent of the turmoil and the leavings of Adler and Stekel and Jung three decades earlier in Vienna.

However, this uniform character of the defined psychoanalytic mainstream was in the end no better able to survive intact in post–World War II America than in post–World War I Europe. The ego psychological metapsychology edifice has itself, though it is still the main focal strength of American psychoanalysis, nonetheless been gradually transformed into what some today call the post–ego psychological age, and object relations perspectives have been varyingly incorporated into it by such workers as Zetzel and Modell and Kernberg. The natural science model of psychoanalysis has been vigorously attacked including by some of its once staunchest adherents with a variety of hermeneutical, phenomenological, totally subjectivistic, and/or linguistically based perspectives like those offered by George Klein and Gill and Schafer and Spence. And, of course, aside from the decades-long work of Mahler and her followers who have used their child development observations to fashion an explicitly developmental perspective into psychoanalytic theory and praxis—which has never quite become a school of its own, however—there has been the evolution within America starting in the seventies of the self psychology of Kohut and his many followers, a psychology with a distinctive metapsychology of the bipolar self and the vision of Tragic rather than Guilty Man, very much an alternative psychoanalytic theory, and school of its own.

All this has now led to a situation of diverse and diverging developments within American psychoanalysis in recent years that, although it is not yet comparable to the established pluralism of psychoanalysis in Europe and in Latin America is perhaps fast getting there. This indeed led a representative of one of the outside groups in the United

States to comment at a panel of the American Psychoanalytic Association devoted to this current growing diversity of theoretical perspectives within American analysis to say that it would be a fine thing if the split of fifty years ago in America could be healed, so that all American analysts could discuss their different views within a single scientific and professional organization. For, after all, he said, "the differences of Silverberg, Rado, Sullivan, and Horney from orthodox psychoanalytic views are not materially greater—in fact, less so—than those of Kohut and Schafer, both of which, and others, are today comfortably contained within the American Psychoanalytic Association" (Post 1986, p. 21).

Which brings me to the crux of the dilemma, or if not dilemma, the issue that I am proposing for consideration by us all. Psychoanalysis, despite all the efforts of Sigmund Freud, its founding father, and despite the like-minded efforts of many of his most gifted followers, which actually succeeded for so many more years in the United States than anywhere else in the world in maintaining an integrated and overall uniform perspective on psychoanalysis, called (and cherished) as the mainstream, psychoanalysis worldwide today, and all within the organizational framework of the IPA, consists of multiple (and divergent) theories of mental functioning, of development, of pathogenesis, of treatment, and of cure.

If this is so—if we do indeed have several, or even many, psychoanalyses today, and not one—then we are faced with two formidable questions, questions for any discipline, any body of theory, or derivatively, body of praxis, that strives to organize and give meaning to a coherent and discrete segment of human experience. The first question is, what do these diverse theories all have in common that they are all recognizably psychoanalysis in terms of fundamentally shared assumptions? The second question, perhaps the other side of the same coin, is, what differentiates them together from all the other, the unpsychoanalytic theories of mental life, for surely not every psychology of human behavior is psychoanalytic, and there is only intellectual destructiveness in a posture that "anything goes" or that anything, anything mental that is, can somehow be construed as psychoanalytic.

To begin with, what they all *do* have in common are our shared definitional boundaries of psychoanalysis. Here we do, I think properly, revert to Freud and his definitional statement of 1914 on "the facts of transference and of resistance." There are any number of ways to try to capture in a single statement the central conception of Freud's revolutionary way of understanding mental life. Certainly, however, I think we can all agree that Freud's fundamental discovery was that human beings have thoughts and feelings that they don't know they have, and that these constitute an unconscious mental life expressed in unconscious fantasy and unconscious conflict—and that this set of conceptions is not only contained within but is the distinguishing feature of each and every psychoanalytic psychology of mental life. In Ernst Kris's famous aphoristic definition, psychoanalysis is "nothing but" human behavior considered from the point of view of conflict.[3]

---

[3]I include in this conception of who and what is properly psychoanalytic Kohut's self psychology even though it avows itself to be centrally a psychology of the supraordinate self and its developmental struggle for cohesion, with a psychopathology and a therapy based on conceptions of deficit and of restoration rather than primarily of conflict and its resolution. I do this on the basis of my reading of the clinical material presented by Kohut and other self psychologists and my view of the clinical data that are presented as indeed dealing planfully with

Considered in this way, the decision about whose work and whose theoretical views then belong within psychoanalysis is not a political-administrative issue of who remained within the organized institutional psychoanalytic framework of the IPA like Fromm-Reichmann and Alexander and who left it like Fromm and Horney (and, of course, there are Lacanians in significant numbers both inside and outside the IPA). Nor can that decision be based just on whether one claims Freud's heritage, as the adher-.ents of both Melanie Klein and Kohut do, or disavows it, as Jung did in creating his Analytical Psychology. In fact, Jungian analysis is a case in point, as its followers have in recent years reappropriated the label *psychoanalysis*, calling themselves Jungian psychoanalysts and implying that only political and organizational issues, reflections of bygone struggles, keep them in a world apart from the psychoanalysis operating within the IPA. I am myself not in a position to have an adequately informed opinion on the psychoanalytic credentials of Jungian theory. Here I would only quote Goodheart (1984), a Jungian analyst in America, who, in a detailed disquisition on Jung's doctoral dissertation published in 1902, in which Jung's first clinical material and clinical formulations were presented, demonstrates impressively how Jung avoided seeing the interactional dynamic, the evidence of psychic conflict, seeking

---

the interplay of conflicted transferences (and countertransferences); I present my reading of these reported clinical interactions in the several critiques I have published (1981, 1983b, 1985) on self psychology and its relation to American mainstream ego psychology and post–ego psychology. I therefore view self psychology as a new and variant theoretical school of psychoanalysis and not as a species of nonanalytic psychotherapy, which some of its critics have declared it to be (see Wallerstein 1985).

out instead a mechanical (and nonpsychological) explanatory framework of autonomous psychic productions—the autonomous psyche that was ultimately expressed in the collective unconscious existing apart from personal experience or meaning. Goodheart describes how at several points in his dissertation Jung came close to the Freudian notions of conflict but then each time backed away and how finally, "Jung skipped away from his own proposals and inserted the abruptly aborting conclusion that all this 'must remain unanswered.' This is actually the first Freud–Jung split" (p. 12). All this is written by a Jungian analyst and is describing Jung's thinking even before he ever met Freud. Goodheart took it to presage the ultimate actual break with Freud. It is on the basis of evidence of this kind that I would in the end answer for myself whether Jung's psychology is truly a *psychoanalytic* psychology or not; clearly such a perspective as Goodheart's would first have to be substantiated by other thoughtful and knowledgeable students of Jung's scientific corpus.

All this, of course, creates for us another dilemma or issue. Living with the pluralism of psychoanalysis not only creates what Cooper (1984) called "porous boundaries" (p. 255) for our field, but it also makes it much more difficult today than for Freud (1910) to try to define "wild" analysis. Schafer has made just this point in his article entitled "Wild Analysis" (1985). When Freud wrote on the subject in 1910, psychoanalysis was indeed simpler, and it was easier to say what departed from it, what was "wild" analysis. Today, with our pluralistic conceptions, our varying theoretical perspectives and models of the mind, what may be conventional or proper analysis within one perspective may well be wild within another. To deal with this issue, Schafer introduced the phrase "comparative analysis" and said of it, "The appropriate name for my method of reexamining wild analysis is comparative analysis, that is to say, seeing how things look from within the perspective of each system" (p. 276) and he undertook to compare from this point of view the theoretical systems of Melanie Klein, Kohut, and Gill. One can wonder, incidentally, in this connection how much Glover's (1931) conceptions of inexact interpretation, incomplete interpretation, and incomplete analysis would be relevant in this context.

Given the acceptance of these realities, then, of a poly-theoretical psychoanalysis, how can we understand what we all know as a commonplace everyday observation, that we all, adherents of whatever theoretical position within psychoanalysis, all seem to do reasonably comparable clinical work and bring about reasonably comparable clinical change in the (comparable enough) patients that we deal with? An example drawn from Kohut's last book (1984) puts this question as well as anyone has. In that book Kohut gives a detailed account (pp. 92ff) of an interchange with a Kleinian colleague from Latin America who told him how she had responded interpretively to a patient's silent withdrawal from the analytic work in the hour immediately after notification of the planned cancellation of a session in the near future. The interpretation had followed the presumed standard Kleinian format, that the patient's basic perception of the analyst had been abruptly altered by the announcement, that the analyst had shifted from being a good, warm, feeding breast to becoming a bad, cold, withholding one, and that the patient had responded with sadistic rage against the analyst *qua* bad breast, a rage that was defended against through a general inhibition, with a particular inhibition of oral activity, of "biting words."

Kohut, in his account, expressed surprise that this (to him) "farfetched interpretation" albeit given in a "warmly understanding tone of voice" (p. 92) nonetheless elicited a very favorable response from the patient. He went on to say that the analyst could equally have couched an interpretation within ego psychological, conflict-drive-defense terms (i.e., the cancellation experienced as an abandonment by the oedipal mother locking the child-patient out of the parental bedroom), or, for that matter, within Kohutian self-psychological terms (the loss of a self-sustaining selfobject leaving the patient feeling empty and not fully alive). What Kohut made of all this was that the clinical context given by his Kleinian colleague was insufficient to decide which interpretation would be closest to the mark in this instance and so he called all three examples, potentially, of "wild analysis"—until proven otherwise. What I will make of it—as I shall make clear further on—is that the clinical context, by itself, will never determine which interpretation, within which theoretical framework, is closest to the mark, that in fact, put in those terms, the issue is totally miscast.

At this point I want to add only that the lesson that Kohut drew from the patient's favorable response was that, although the (Kleinian) *content* of the interpretation may have been wrong, off the mark (in Kohut's sense), it *was* nevertheless a therapeutically effective "inexact interpretation" in Glover's (1931) sense, since it was "in its essence more right than wrong" (p. 97), since the analyst was conveying (indeed in any of the three alternative interpretive forms presented, could have been conveying) her understanding that the patient was sorely troubled over the announced cancellation and was understandably reacting unhappily to it. Again, my framework for understanding the patient's favorable response will differ significantly from that of Kohut, but here there will also be points of convergence.

To make clear what I have in mind, and how I would understand and interpret the whole sequence outlined by Kohut, I turn now to some fresh perspectives on familiar conceptions proposed by Joseph and Anne-Marie Sandler in their papers on the past unconscious and the present unconscious. As elaborated in this sequence of papers (1983, 1984; J. Sandler, 1986), "the *past unconscious* can be conceived of as containing the whole gamut of immediate, peremptory wishes, impulses, and responses of the individual that have been formed early in his life" (1984, p. 369); these are clearly stated to be "more than instinctual wishes . . . they also include the immediate and spontaneous modes of reacting in any given psychological situation, at any given moment, in any particular set of internal or external circumstances" (1984, p. 369). That is, they "may be instinctual but need not necessarily be so. Thus, for example, solutions to conflict devised or elaborated in early childhood acquire a peremptory quality, as do all sorts of responses aimed at avoiding dangerous situations and preserving safety" (1984, p. 370). In sum total the past unconscious represents the "child within the adult" (1984, p. 370), the totality of the mental life roughly "corresponding, from a developmental point of view, to the first four to six years of life" (1984, p. 371). It is all this that is essentially sealed off by the repression barrier that covers the infantile amnesia and "which is for the most part only reconstructed in analysis, reconstruction which is usually reinforced by those scattered memories that are available from the first years of life, but which memories can only be understood in the light of later reconstruction" (1984, p. 371).

Granted that this "past unconscious is active in the present, and is stimulated by internal or external events occurring in the here-and-now, what . . . [the Sandlers] have termed the *present unconscious* is conceived of as a very different organization. . . . Whereas the past unconscious acts and reacts according to the past, the present unconscious is concerned with maintaining equilibrium in the present and regards the impulse from the past unconscious as intrusive and upsetting" (1984, p. 372). And, "While it is itself . . . the product of the past development of the individual, it [the present unconscious] is orientated, *not to the past, but to the present,* in order to prevent the individual from being overwhelmed by painful and uncontrollable experiences. It constantly creates conflict-solving compromises and adaptations that help to keep an inner balance. Foremost among these is the continual creation or recreation of current *unconscious fantasies and thoughts.* These have a function in the present, are constantly being modified and orientated to the present, although they will, of course, reflect their history in the past" (1986, p. 188). In the clinical situation, the prime example of such fantasies, of course, are the unconscious transference fantasies about the analyst.

It follows from all of this, of course, that the central interpretive work in the analytic situation is with the unconscious transference fantasies that are the direct representations of the activities of the present unconscious. And since "the *present unconscious* contains present-day, here-and-now fantasies and thoughts that are after all current adaptations to the conflicts and anxieties evoked by the contents of the *past unconscious*" (1986, p. 191), it is clear that via the analysis of the fantasies of the present unconscious, centrally the transference fantasies of the present unconscious, we can and do reach an understanding of the originating infantile past—what the Sandlers call the past unconscious. The mechanism of that understanding, they remind us, is a creative act of *reconstruction,* abetted by whatever fragmentary memories have survived the childhood amnesia, but these memories, too, being given meaning only via the act of reconstruction that puts them into coherent context.

All of this stated in this somewhat new language is, of course, recognizable to us as a vivid description of our everyday work of analysis. How does it all relate to my central theme of the *pluralism* of the theoretical frameworks within which we do our *consensually shared* psychoanalytic work and to my case example drawn from Kohut's account as the paradigm illustration of my theme? I would submit that the thrust of the present unconscious in the patient described by Kohut as conveyed in the analyst's transference interpretation (albeit clothed within the analyst's Kleinian theoretical language, which, as Kohut indicated, could have alternatively been equally well embedded in an ego psychological or a Kohutian self-psychological explanatory language), was centered in the meaning—common to all the three possible theoretical explanatory languages presented—that the patient was acutely distressed over the coming cancellation and was reacting unhappily and resentfully to that announcement. Here we are dealing in the actual observables of the analytic interaction, in the clinical data of the consulting room fashioned into the low-level and experience-near "clinical theory" that in George Klein's perspective (1976) is all the theory that psychoanalysis needs and is indeed all the theory that its data can truly sustain and can test.

When we reach beyond the interactions of the analytic consulting room, beyond the elucidation of the present unconscious, beyond, that is, the clinical phenomena captured in and explained by our *clinical* theory, to a more encompassing, more generally explanatory, more causally developmental accounting of mental life from its earliest fathomable origins, we are getting into another realm. This other is the realm George Klein called the unnecessary *general* theory that we should sever and cast out by an action he dubbed "theorectomy," the realm that the Sandlers call the *reconstructed* past unconscious, the realm of our pluralistic theoretical perspectives in psychoanalysis, the ego psychological, the object relational, the Kleinian, the Lacanian, and so on. These, as Kohut illustrated so well with his vignette, can *each* be invoked and each used to explain the same clinical interaction—that is, to put its specific into a framework of general meaning within an overall theoretical context. And each of these theoretical explanatory contexts, the Kleinian, the ego psychological, and the self psychological, will be persuasive indeed to the adherents of that viewpoint, who in fact will look at it as *the* useful and natural way in which to understand the phenomenon, the clinical interaction.

What I am suggesting by all this is that our *data* are the data of the present unconscious and their interpretation that carries real meaning is embedded in our clinical theory, the theory of transference and resistance, of conflict and defence—that is, the original fundamental elements of Freud's 1914 definition of psychoanalysis, with which I began this presentation and which I have underlined as the consensual understanding that unites us all as psychoanalysts. What I am further suggesting is that our pluralism of theoretical perspectives, within which we try to give overall meaning to our clinical data in the present (in the present unconscious) and to *reconstruct* the past out of which the present developed (the past unconscious), represents the various scientific *metaphors* that we have created in order to satisfy our variously conditioned needs for closure and coherence and overall theoretical understanding.

The Sandlers had already approached this same conception in their statement that deep interpretations into the infantile past could be viewed as but metaphoric reconstructions. For example, "It is our firm conviction that so-called 'deep' interpretations can have a good analytic effect only because they provide metaphors that can contain the fantasies and feelings in the second system. The patient learns to understand and accept these metaphors, and if they provide a good fit, both cognitively and affectively, then they will be effective. This view gives us a way of understanding the interpretive approach of some of our colleagues . . ." (1983, p. 424). Or, "In terms of the model we have put forward, we would say that Kleinian interpretations that are affectively and cognitively 'in touch,' when formulated in terms of the most primitive processes and fantasies, provide 'past unconscious' *metaphors* for processes in the present unconscious" (1984, p. 392). I would only broaden and extend this thinking to the conception that all our theoretical perspectives, Kleinian, but also ego psychological, and all the others are but our chosen explanatory *metaphors,* heuristically useful to us, in terms of our varying intellectual value commitments, in explaining the primary clinical data of our consulting rooms, the realm of our present unconscious in the Sandlers' terms, or the realm of our clinical theory, in George Klein's terms. Put most simply, this conceptualization makes all our grand general theory (and all our pluralism of general theory) nothing but our chosen array of metaphor.

In order to make sure that my meanings are not misunderstood as an assault upon the credentials of psychoanalysis as a science, I should at this point state my perspective on the relationship of metaphor to science or, better put, the role of metaphor *in* science. Metaphor is, of course, usually regarded as the province of poetry and art and therefore the antithesis of science. When it finds a place in scientific theorizing, and Freud—along with many others, it should be added—was famous for his use of metaphor, it is characteristically ascribed to the immaturity of the particular scientific undertaking that will in due time be able to replace the metaphor by theory linked operationally to observable phenomena that can be manipulated and studied within an experimental setting or some other of almost equal rigor and with analogous control. And some psychoanalytic theorists, like Schafer, have dedicated themselves to a relentless quest to extirpate metaphor from our theory statements.

Let me here propose a different perspective on metaphor and science. I want to follow here with Wurmser (1977) in his vigorous defense of the place of metaphor in theory formation in psychoanalysis. Wurmser's position is that rather than trying to eschew and uproot metaphor as a tool for theorizing within psychoanalysis, we should unequivocally accept that "No science can operate without metaphors" (p. 472). He quotes the physicist Heinrich Hertz, who tried to derive all the physics of his time from the basic concepts of time, space, and mass. Hertz was particularly explicit about metaphor, declaring, "the basic concepts of *every* science, the means by which it poses its questions and formulates its solutions, appear not as passive copies of a given being, but as self-created intellectual symbols"—that is, metaphors (Wurmser, p. 472, my italics). Wurmser goes on himself to declare that, "What is crucial is that our science, like any other science, is woven of the warp of observations and held together by the intricate woof of symbolism, of many layers of abstractions, of stark and faded metaphors which 'interpret' for us ('explain' to us) the 'direct' facts which, as we know, are never really direct" (pp. 476–477). And even more that, "Metaphors, taken literally are unscientific. But Metaphors, understood as symbols, are the only language of science we possess, unless we resort to mathematical symbols" (p. 483).

In the end, Wurmser comes to the statements: "Metaphors (unless reified . . . and treated as if they were 'substance,' not 'function') are indispensable for scientific generativity. They are not evil and to be shunned; they are to be sought and applied. We do not have too many metaphors in psychoanalysis; we have too few. We should not eliminate parts of our theory because they are too metaphorical; we should respect them as such and enlarge them" (p. 491). Far-ranging as this defense of the vital role of metaphor in our theory formation is, I would still like to extend beyond it, and to develop more explicitly what is only implicit in Wurmser when he states, for example, that "our interest is *whether and in what forms and on what levels we choose symbolic representatives* for the specific experiences gained by the psychoanalytic method and the scientific inquiry based on this method . . ." (p. 482).

What I would like to suggest in my extension of this thinking is that I view the role of metaphor differently (both in its scope and in its developmental place) in regard to what Rapaport and George Klein have designated the clinical theory of psychoanalysis—the clinically near theory of conflict and compromise, of resistance and defense, of transference and countertransference, in which we all of us who are psychoanalysts relate to our patients with common intent and common impact—than I view its role in regard to what they have designated the general theory of psychoanalysis—all the different metapsychologies that distinguish our different theoretical perspectives in psychoanalysis, our theoretical pluralism. In regard to the clinical theory, I view the theory formation, aided though it is in its conceptualizations by the symbolisms of our metaphoric constructions, as nonetheless sufficiently experience-near, anchored directly enough to observables, to the data of our consulting rooms, that it is amenable to the self-same processes of hypothesis formation, testing, and validation as any other scientific enterprise, albeit, of course, by methods adapted to the peculiar subjectivistic nature of the essential data from the psychoanalytic situation. For on this, our whole claim to be a discipline of the mind that is also a science of the mind does—and must—rest, and this, the nature of psychoanalysis as a science, is something on which I have written affirmatively at length elsewhere (1976, 1986).

But in regard to our general theory or theories, our metapsychologies—and here I interpolate a reminder of Freud's metaphoric commentary, our *witch* metapsychology (1937, p. 225)—our different and distinguishing theoretical positions, ego psychological, Kleinian, object relational, and so on, that mark our psychoanalytic pluralism, in regard to all these I see them, at least at this stage of our historic developmental dynamic, as primarily metaphors, our large-scale explanatory metaphors, or symbolisms, which we use to give a sense of coherence and closure to our psychological understandings and therefore to our psychoanalytic interventions. They are therefore the metaphors that we live by, that are our pluralistic psychoanalytic articles of faith, and that I feel in our current developmental stage to be essentially beyond the realm of empirical study and scientific process.[4] This, of course, is not meant to draw

---

[4]Freud (1914b) made much the same point in regard to the relationship between the observational base and the theoretical structure of psychoanalysis in his famous statement in the paper on

an all-or-none line between our clinical theory and our general theory and certainly some aspects of what I call our large-scale explanatory general theories may already be linked enough to observables as to come within the scope of scientific testing. Nor does it preclude that future developments—in psychoanalytic observation and psychoanalytic theorizing—may yet bring us to a much more evolved general theory formation that can pass beyond metaphoric symbolism, but by then we would have witnessed the processes of accommodation and translation that would have brought a coalescence of our current disparate theories and our theoretical pluralism into an overarching consensually accepted general theoretical structure. That day is not yet and at this point looks far away. My current vision of psychoanalysis, then, is of a unitary clinical theory that is empirically testable—a theory that binds and unifies us as psychoanalysts—and of a pluralistic general theory, the explanatory symbols, the metaphors, that embody our intellectual commitments and values and to which we differentially adhere.

That life values are distinctly involved in our choice of theoretical perspectives has been clearly articulated by Gedo (1984), although perhaps not in a form with which we would all agree. He has said on this issue:

> Each of these conceptual schemata [the various psychoanalytic theories] encodes one or another of the primary meanings implicit in human existence—unfortunately, often

---

narcissism: "For these ideas [the theory] are not the foundations of science, upon which everything rests: that foundation is observation alone. They are not the bottom but the top of the whole structure, and they can be replaced and discarded without damaging it" (p. 77). He made very similar statements in "Instincts and their Vicissitudes" (1915, p. 117) and in the "Two Encyclopaedia Articles" (1923, p. 253).

to the exclusion of all other meanings. Thus, the view of man embodied in the libido theory, especially in the form it took prior to 1920, attributed primary significance to the satisfaction of the appetites. By contrast, Melanie Klein's psychoanalytic system teaches the need to make reparation for man's constitutional wickedness. . . . In the 1970s Heinz Kohut promulgated views that give comparable emphasis to the unique healing power of empathy while acknowledging man's entitlement to an affectively gratifying milieu. . . . Let me hasten to add that I am emphatically in agreement with the need to satisfy appetites, to curb human destructiveness, and to provide an affectively gratifying environment for our children. And I am for other desiderata to boot! Isn't everyone? [p. 159][5]

---

[5]This same point, that our theoretical positions in psychoanalysis are inevitably embedded in fundamental social, political, and moral value dispositions, has been strongly made as the closing statement in Greenberg and Mitchell's (1983) book on object relations perspectives in psychoanalysis traced developmentally and historically through critical discussion of the work of the various major object relations theorists starting with such diverse contributors as Melanie Klein, Fairbairn, and Sullivan. The summarizing point that they make at the end of their book is that the drive theory perspective and the relational theory perspective are linked to differing views of the essential nature of human experience: Drive theory is linked philosophically to the positions of Hobbes and Locke, that man is an essentially individual animal and that human satisfaction and goals are fundamentally personal and individual; the role of the state rests on the concept of "negative liberty," that the state adds nothing essential to individual satisfaction as such, but just ensures the possibility of personal fulfilment: Relational theory is linked philosophically to the positions of Rousseau, Hegel, and Marx, that man is an essentially social animal and that human satisfactions and goals are realizable only within a community; the role of the state here rests on the concept of "positive liberty," to provide an indispensable "positive" function by offering its citizens that which they cannot provide for themselves in isolation. Greenberg and Mitchell (1977) state in relation to this that "The drive/structure and the relational/structure

I would like to close with two cautionary implications, one related to issues of therapy and technique, and the other to issues of theory and science, and then with a final general statement. The first caution on the matter of technique is in response to Cooper's (1977) view in regard to the modern-day pluralism of our theories, which he presents as a very welcome transition in the history of analysis. He has said of this, "Because we have more than one mode of conducting psychoanalysis [that is, more than one theoretical framework], it is incumbent upon us to make sufficiently accurate diagnosis to decide which mode is best suited for the given patient" (pp. 20–21). I would disagree with this conclusion since to me *each* theoretical framework essays to be a comprehensively adequate explanatory system within which the whole range of psychoanalytically amenable psychopathology can be understood and treated—and in practice, of course, they all try to do just that. We have different theories, that is, to deal with the *same* patients; our explanatory and therapeutic psychologies do not change with our patients' diagnostic categories.

The second caution on the matter of science is in response to Edelson's (1985) view that since Freudian, Adlerian, and Jungian theorists all claim that the data of the consulting rooms support their hypotheses, this argument in theory can and should be tested by the methods of

---

model embody these two major traditions within Western philosophy in the relatively recently developing intellectual arena of psychoanalytic ideas" (p. 402). And in this context they quote Thomas Kuhn, the well-known philosopher and historian of (natural) science, that "communication between proponents of different theories is inevitably partial. . . . What each takes to be facts depends in part on the theory he espouses, and . . . an individual's transfer of allegiance from theory to theory is often better described as *conversion* than as choice" (p. 338, my italics).

science. He has said of this, "If incompatible inferences about an analysand, based on different theories, are made by different psychoanalysts, then the same kinds of scientific arguments about the relation between rival or alternative hypotheses and evidence I shall describe further on . . . in this paper must be used to decide which inference or hypothesis is to be provisionally accepted over another" (p. 584). Here, too, I would disagree since our general (metapsychological) theories that constitute our pluralism of explanatory frameworks are in my view but our grand and very experience-distant symbolisms or metaphors, and therefore far from the realm of empirical testing which can operate at this point only in the realm of our experience-near clinical theory encompassing the interactional phenomena of our engagements with our patients' present unconsciouses.

My concluding general statement can be understood in either scientific or political terms. Psychoanalysis has developed a pluralism of theoretical perspectives in order preferentially to explain the essence of mental development and human psychology, what I have conceptualized as our variety of symbolisms or metaphors designed to grasp and to give coherence to our own internal unknowables, our past unconsciouses. In that very real sense there are today many psychoanalyses. At the same time, psychoanalysts in their daily work deal with the shared phenomena of our consulting rooms employing interactional techniques built around the dynamic of the transference and the countertransference, as we try empathically to reach our patients' present unconsciouses, the psychic pressures that disturb their current lives and bring them to us. In that equally real sense there is but one discipline of psychoanalysis. I trust that the International Psycho-Analytical Association can represent proudly and well both our diversity of theoretical viewpoint and our unity of clinical purpose and healing endeavor.

Part II

SEARCH FOR THE COMMON GROUND

INTRODUCTION

My presidential address, "One Psychoanalysis or Many?" was delivered at the opening morning plenary session of the Thirty-fifth International Psychoanalytical Association Congress in Montreal in July 1987. Although it did not relate to the overall theme of the Congress, which was the reconsideration after fifty years of Freud's "Analysis Terminable and Interminable," this address was nonetheless referred to and commented upon, informally and very positively, by a considerable variety of speakers during the ensuing Congress week.

When the program committee was appointed for the next, Thirty-sixth Congress, to be held in Rome in July 1989, the decision was arrived at to take this talk and the task set by it, the search for the common ground within the increasing worldwide psychoanalytic theoretical diversity or pluralism, and make it—under the title "Common Ground in Psychoanalysis: Clinical Aims and Process"—the theme of the Rome Congress. To establish the ground for the

Rome dialogue, six statements on this theme were solicited, to be prepublished in the first issue in 1989 of the *International Journal of Psycho-Analysis*. They were to represent the major geographic regions of psychoanalytic work and the major theoretical perspectives guiding that work. From North America, the two selected were Samuel Abrams, of New York, representing the mainstream drive/ structural "classical" Freudian paradigm, and Arnold Goldberg, of Chicago, representing self psychology. From Latin America, the two were Eustachio Portella Nunes, of Rio de Janeiro, representing a strongly Kleinian institute, and Carlos Mario Aslan, of Buenos Aires, representing a more ego psychological viewpoint from a Latin American institute containing the greatest diversity of psychoanalytic theoretical perspectives. From Europe, the two were Gottfried Appy, of Stuttgart, a more North European drive/ structural viewpoint, and Claude Le Guen, of Paris, representing a distinctive francophone psychoanalytic voice. These six statements were published together, in alphabetic sequence, in the *International Journal of Psycho-Analysis* (1989; vol. 70:3–28); they are Chapters 3 to 8 of this book.

The Congress week consists of four full days of scientific meetings. For Rome the plan was to have a plenary session clinical presentation each of the first three mornings on the Congress theme, followed by formal discussants and then discussion from the floor, and after that multiple small-group discussions of the plenary session paper. The three main plenary clinical presentations were given by analysts representing again the three main psychoanalytic regions and three major theoretical perspectives within psychoanalysis. The three were: Max Hernández, of Lima, Peru, trained at the British Institute with the Independent (Object Relations) Group; Anton Kris, of Boston, representing the American ego psychology viewpoint; and Michael Feldman, of London, a British Kleinian. The papers by Hernández and Feldman, published in the *International Journal of Psycho-Analysis* (1990, vol. 71) are Chapters 9 and 10 of this book. In order to safeguard the confidentiality of the patient, the paper by Kris was not published.

On the final day of the Rome Congress, I gave my presidential address, entitled "Psychoanalysis: The Common Ground," in which I reviewed the responses that had appeared in the literature to my address to the Montreal Congress two years earlier, commented on the six prepublished statements from the Rome Congress, and then carefully compared and contrasted the three main Congress clinical presentations, which I had had the opportunity to study before the Congress, from the point of view of my search for the unifying common ground of psychoanalysis within the clinical interactions in the consulting room, the play of transferences and countertransferences, and the experience-near (common) clinical theory within which these interactions are described. (Care was taken to have Kris review my discussion of his paper to ensure that my comments did not inadvertently breach the patient's confidentiality.) That paper was published in the *International Journal of Psycho-Analysis* (1990; vol. 71); it is Chapter 11 in this book.

Arnold Richards wrote a summary of that Rome Congress proceedings built around its theme of the search for common ground. This summary was not published in the *International Journal of Psycho-Analysis* until 1991, as part of a group of papers on the Congress theme. Richards's paper essayed to review the totality of the Rome Congress presentations on the theme of the common ground. Besides presenting a detailed summary and critique of my own plenary address (Chapter 11), Richards covered in detail Anna Ornstein's discussion of Feldman's paper, Schwaber's (1990) discussion of Hernández's paper, and Schafer's (1990) and Lussier's (1991) discussions in response to my address, as well as a very relevant and heuristically valuable paper by Hanly (1990) entitled "The Concept of Truth in Psychoanalysis," in which he relates Hanly's philosophical discussion of correspondence versus coherence theories of truth to the implicit adherence of each of the protagonists in the common ground discussions to one or the other of these philosophical positions. Richards's paper is Chapter 12 in this book.

3

Ambiguity in Excess: An Obstacle to Common Ground

Samuel Abrams, M.D.

In science, an optimal level of ambiguity stimulates productive controversy. Regrettably, in psychoanalysis, at present, some ambiguity borders on chaos; some controversy, on open warfare. Reducing ambiguities to an optimal level should promote the effort to find common ground. I will try to suggest approaches to do so in four intimately linked areas.

In *Development:* By describing a psychoanalytic perspective on human development, differentiating supraordinate organizations and subordinate phases, and distinguishing three "oedipals"—Oedipus complex, oedipal phase, oedipal-age organization.

In *Pathogenesis:* By defining the clinical scope of our work in terms of a classification of disorders that encompasses both the level of achievement in psychological organization and the nature of the pathogens that intrude upon that achievement; and by distinguishing neurosogenic patho-

I wish to thank Drs. Peter B. Neubauer, Vann Spruiell, and Edward Weinshel for suggestions about the form and content of this chapter.

gens, where psychoanalysis is most effective, from other intruders where its effect is more chancy.

In the *Clinical Process,* which is partly shaped by the nature of the disordered development: By distinguishing obstacles in general from resistances in particular, by separating the empirical from the conceptual, and by differentiating three major resistances in order to define the more abiding places where analyses often come to grief.

In the *Operational Sphere,* the therapeutic interaction necessary to actualize the clinical process: By differentiating encumbrances arising from within the patient from those arising from within the analyst so as to define the causes of interruptions and interminability.

Among analysts, some of these concepts constitute old ground, while some of them are new; each, however, is presently burdened by an excess of ambiguity, an obstacle to common ground. A more differentiated view should lighten the burden.

NORMAL DEVELOPMENT

Psychoanalytic concepts of normality provide the foundation for differentiating disorders and designing approaches to their management. Isolating the components of mental development and accounting for how those components are usually brought together ease the task of distinguishing those disorders that are more likely to be responsive to psychoanalysis from those that are less responsive.

The structure of the mind emerges in an expectable sequence of discontinuous steps. During development, an inherent maturationally-determined timetable triggers a series of psychological organizations. The supraordinate organizations bring together the evolving subordinate phases of drives, ego, and the object-interaction system; consequently, every new step is characterized by distinctive ways of feeling, knowing, being, representing, behaving, and getting along. Each succeeding organization is partly shaped by those that have preceded it and, curiously enough, may be further consolidated by those that follow it. Each more-or-less reorganizes antecedents with transformational impact, thereby establishing an enhanced capacity to differentiate stimuli and move toward fresh possibilities.

Organizations often feature conflicts, expressions of one or another of the evolving subordinate phases. Conflicts such as those between good and bad objects, those that appear during separation-individuation, and those inherent in oedipality are critical junctures that often catalyse the pull forward. Of these, the oedipal conflicts, expectable crises immutably linked with drive development, are the best understood and most widely investigated by psychoanalysts. This is true because they play a central role in neurosogenesis and because the ways they are resolved provide a specific impetus for establishing and shaping the foundation of the tripartite mind. To be sure, prior organizations, antecedent drive conflicts, and other stages and phases will have left their influence. Such influence, however, will be felt chiefly in the quality of the building blocks that are made available for that foundation. When little goes wrong with those building blocks or with the expectable oedipal crises, the psychological organization of oedipal-age children conveys within it an effective ground plan for higher-level functioning, for progressive differentiation, and for further developmental transformations.

DISORDERED DEVELOPMENT

But a lot can go wrong.

1. *Organizational Impairment:* The synthesizing and integrating functions necessary to convert maturational potential into developmental organizations may be defective. This creates a variety of worrisome chaotic disorders that are not treatable psychoanalytically.

2. *Disharmonies:* There may be a disparity between the phases of development of ego, object relations, and the drives. The resulting disharmony threatens the usual balance necessary for optimal growth. A psychoanalytically informed series of interventions early in life may reduce the strain. However, psychoanalysis is usually not the treatment of choice for these disorders during childhood, although it may prove useful later in life if the disparities were not too burdensome.

3. *Deficiencies and Excesses:* The stimuli needed for growth to actualize the phase potential may be deficient, excessive, or otherwise aberrant; or the ego equipment needed to perceive and organize what the surround is expected to provide may be inherently defective. One result is impaired or limited psychological structures, reflected in an array of symptoms and personality disturbances. A variety of treatment modalities, including psychoanalysis, offers promise for managing some of the less disruptive sequelae originating from such excesses or deficiencies. When structural integrity or developmental progression have been compromised too much, however, psychoanalysis is not an effective approach.

4. *Unresolved Conflicts:* The expectable conflicts which customarily catalyze phases may prove more than routinely burdensome and may be settled ineffectively. As a conse-

quence, when the maturational clock calls the next step forward, features of the unsettled conflict remain entrapped within earlier organizations and cannot be influenced by the transformational action of the later ones. This may lead to deformations of character and symptoms; or to a continuous shaping of reality offerings by unconscious fantasies; or it may encumber self- and object-representations; or it may compromise the newly emerging adaptive repertoire. Some of these disorders may be responsive to psychoanalytic treatment.

5. *Unresolved Oedipal Conflicts:* When the embedded conflicts derive from or have been pulled into an otherwise competent oedipal-age organization, the resulting disorder is *especially* amenable to psychoanalytic treatment, however disabling the manifest symptoms, however compelling the unconscious fantasies, or however severe the impact on self- and object-representations. The accompanying distress or failure in life make psychoanalysis necessary; the acquisition of this degree of organizational competence makes a successful outcome likely. The treatment provides the opportunity to liberate the entrapped pathogens. Once set free, they are freshly acted upon by the continuous available integrating and reorganizing tendencies of a solidly based mind and pulled forward into more mature psychological structures.

THE PSYCHOANALYTIC PROCESS: HOW THE TREATMENT WORKS

How does the liberation of entrapped pathogens take place?

I conceptualize the treatment process as a sequence of steps that lead to the goal of freeing old pathogens and integrating them into new hierarchies. The steps, organized resistances, are more or less stable way-stations that transiently appear to obstruct the overall task. They are the resistance of character, the resistance of the consolidated transference, and the resistance of the childhood past. Despite the conciseness of the labels, I never think of them appearing in a precisely demarcated fashion or in an orderly sequence. Overlapping and interweaving, coexistence and isolation, shifts forward and backward—styles often shaped by patterns of development—are more the rule than the exception.

This model of process can be used to outline expectable crises within the clinical setting. The tendency to stabilize within each step provides the temptation to bring the treatment to a close prematurely: character traits and defenses may become supported anew, the transference-countertransference relationship may become fixed, or both participants may choose to settle into the patient's childhood interminably.

Resistance of character usually comes first. When a patient is offered a partnership and presented with the analytic task, he is likely to adapt to the work in a highly personal way. For example, a phobic may align himself to his partner and constrict the task, while an obsessional may distance himself from his partner and become preoccupied with details. Traits that have seemed to serve so well for so long are not so readily dispatched. The analyst tries to demonstrate the patient's ways of being and behaving, ways that are so much a part of who the patient is that they often escape attention altogether. As these features are explored, and as the disadvantages of the strategies become increasingly evident to both patient and analyst, the psychological equilibrium afforded by character loses some of its stability.

The infantile pathogenic components that gave rise to the disordered traits are regressively reactivated. The backward sweep is always a wide one—that is, preoedipal, oedipal, and postoedipal on the one hand, drives, ego, and object relations on the other. However, in the more suitable patients, the neurosogenic components characteristic of the oedipal phase are most compelling.

The revived components cluster about the patient's mental representations of the analyst. The resistance of character is overcome but has been supplanted by the resistance of the consolidated transference (preferably centered in neurotic mechanisms), a new threat to the patient's capacity to see the setting for what it is. The therapeutic relationship and task are clouded afresh; the patient tries to convert analysis to a new edition of his own past. This attempt at repetition, especially if it is not clearly recognized by both participants, threatens to place the analytic interaction into an endless loop of aimless searching that conceals an unrecognized childhood bond. After many interpretations, the patient usually succeeds in coming to terms with the distortions; the stabilizing tendency of the transference resistance yields.

The entrapped pathogens have been further loosened but they are still not liberated. This requires the third step, overcoming the resistance associated with the recall and reconstruction of central childhood experiences. While memories of childhood have been part of the prior steps, until now they have functioned to anchor or rationalize the resistances of character or transference. During this third step, childhood memories are more gripping, richer in color, affectively intense. If the patient succeeds in dealing with the memories in ways that reduce their pathogenic features—for example, through greater tolerance, forgiveness, or a less burdensome detachment—the pathogens become sufficiently freed to be available for integration into the more mature organization. The decision to bring the treatment to a close is often the catalyst that facilitates the move toward integration.

The revival of entrapped elements and their placement within a more advanced hierarchy are the most important achievements of an analysis, in essence, its therapeutic action. Such conceptual achievements are often concretely experienced as insights by the patient, a result of the effect of insight-producing integrating tendencies upon the hitherto unavailable elements. This capacity to discover is the hallmark of a successful analysis.

OPERATIONAL: THE ANALYTIC INTERACTION

But how is the process activated, what sustains it in its course, and how is it formally brought to a close?

While the process can be conceptualized as what goes on *within* the mind of the patient, those steps can only be set in motion by the interaction *between* the participants. Analysts treat people, not minds.

The analyst–patient relationship is a partnership with a defined approach designed to achieve a goal too difficult to define with precision at first. Each partner is obliged to assume certain tasks, both usually share some values, and each is expected to bring to the enterprise a specific set of aptitudes.

The patient brings—among other things—psychological mindedness, a capacity for controlled regression, competent integrating and organizing functions, the potential to observe at a distance and experience with immediacy often at the same time, and a reasonably intact psychological foundation arising from a more or less successful oedipal-age organization. This grouping of aptitudes helps define the sources of problematic analyses attributable to the patient by distinguishing obstacles due to faulty ego equipment or limited developmental progression from resistances originating in the dynamic unconscious.

The analyst brings—among other things—a conviction about the wisdom of what he is obligated to do, a frankness tempered with considerateness, a tolerance for being misunderstood and misrepresented, an attunement to the dynamic unconscious, and a willingness to avoid the temptation to renounce or abuse his office no matter how much his patients or some theories urge him to do so. Other tasks he learns in his training: how to integrate art and science, how to sort ambiguities from certainties, how to establish categories for listening, what to say and how to say it, how to actively refrain from speaking, what constitutes an interpretation, and how to permit a patient to acquire possession of his own analysis in order to discover how to discover. He also brings some points of view from his own analysis—most important, a conviction of the value of the long search. This grouping of aptitudes helps define the sources of problematic analyses attributable to the analyst.

At the outset, for example, an analyst bent merely on relieving symptoms may be too zealous in his approach, too ready to offer what he already "knows" to someone who is unprepared to use the knowledge or too prepared to assume a submissive position.

Another analyst may overlook some emerging character resistance especially if he happens to share features of the patient's adaptative patterns. A facile concurrence about politics, religion, the arts, and philosophy may signal future entanglements.

Such encumbrances due to character should be distinguished from countertransference encumbrances, impediments that occur more frequently once the transference consolidation becomes dominant. An analyst's stable tainted traits are a different order of resistance from a set of specific responses to revived infantile desires.

Still another encumbrance originating in the analyst derives from overly forbidding attitudes about childhood wishes, experiences, or objects. Some explanatory theories of pathogenesis seem to encourage accusations rather than suggest causes, and some analysts feel more comfortable with theories that indict rather than explain. Such stances always consolidate rather than loosen the bonds to the past.

I believe that this differentiated view of the therapeutic interaction may reduce that excess of ambiguity that always occurs when the terms *transference* or *countertransference* are used globally.

CONCLUSION

I have tried to focus on several areas intimately linked with clinical work where ambiguities are sufficiently pronounced to disrupt the search for a cohesive framework—a common ground. Those areas include normal development, pathogenesis, the concept of the psychoanalytic process, and the nature of the therapeutic interaction. Analysts need a concept of normality to help sort their data; we need a classification of disorders to specify the domain of our treatment; we need a concept of process to categorize expected encumbrances to the cure; and we need perspectives about the therapeutic relationship to help specify the sources of the encumbrances. An excess of ambiguity in these areas compromises those needs and burdens productive discourse.

4

Where Does the Common Ground among Psychoanalysts End?

Gottfried Appy, M.D.

W allerstein gave a detailed review of the history and present situation of psychoanalysis, in Montreal in 1987. For all the increasing and controversial divergences in theory and technique, it was for him beyond question that there was common ground in analytical thinking and objectives. He felt that, eventually even if not yet today, a uniform overall view of this common ground could be expected. His contribution initiated a dialogue, which is gratifyingly being continued with the subject of the 1989 Rome IPA Congress.

I take it for granted that psychoanalysis begins with the assumption of the existence of the unconscious. This contains the matrix for the unfolding and development of human mental life and is influenced by a wide variety of motivations. This thesis is *the* fundamental prerequisite of psychoanalysis and its applications and distinguishes it from all other, nonanalytical psychologies. Hence psychoanalytic thinking concentrates on a specific method of observation of unconscious phenomena, such as transference and resistance. The method equally specifically determines and conceptualizes the theoretical attempts to explain data of empirical origin. On account of these premises, opponents reject psychoanalysis as dogma and hence discriminate against it as unscientific.

Since its beginnings, psychoanalysis has been characterized principally by the diversity of stories. Individual developmental processes, the course of clinical treatments, social situations and aspects of the critique of civilization were made hermeneutically comprehensible by them. It was only after the event that the stories were made amenable to rational understanding and communication and "scientificized" by the creation of theoretical concepts. An increasingly important verificatory function has in this connection been assumed in recent times by fundamental psychological research.

This chronological discrepancy between experience and incorporation into a conceptual or metaphorical system was attributed by Wallerstein to the antinomy of the "present unconscious" and the "past unconscious" (A-M. and J. Sandler). He thus related the development of psychoanalysis to that of individual mental life, treating the results of analytical activity as derivatives of an unconscious group dynamic common to all analysts.

This thesis is appealing by virtue of the parallels it draws between the reality of analytical work and psychoanalytic theory. However, attractiveness arouses skepticism and compels the professional analyst to ask whether the idea will stand up to critical examination or whether it stems from momentary needs for harmonization. After all, the reality of human systems of thought—including that of psychoanalysis—is determined more by confrontations between pluralistic wishful fantasies about "truth" than by common ground. This pluralism demands an increasing capability for empathy and tolerance, particularly as the unifying trust in an overriding, all-embracing regularity based on immutable laws has crumbled, having proved to be a relic of narcissistic feeling states from early infancy which, although important for survival, is becoming harder and harder to sustain.

Human life is limited and is as a rule overtaken by death before it can achieve retrospective acceptance. "Our life remains unavoidably contingent: it consists of stories and, *nota bene,* the more stories it is allowed to have, the freer it is," writes O. Marquard as a comment on his essay *"Abschied vom Prinzipiellen"* (Farewell to Considerations of Principle) [1981]. The pleasure taken by analysts in sharing in a constant flow of new stories appears to bear him out. This pleasure may be understood as a desire to intensify the finitude of one's own experience and thinking and to extend it (into the infinite). This might explain part of the creative force that has always made the analytical quest for new meaning contexts successful.

In addition, however, the work of analysts is molded by conflicts and divergences. Some analysts concentrate on the diversity of stories that can be experienced and fight against the obligation to allow the finitude of their own feeling and thinking, which can apparently be overcome by way of identifications, to be restricted by considerations of principle and by theoretical structuring work. Others endeavor to secure the boundaries of their rational understanding against regressive misapprehensions of reality by increased fundamental research and try to verify their hypotheses scientifically. Many resort for this purpose to electronic data processing machines, because they distrust the results of evenly suspended attention by itself on the grounds of subjectivity, and attribute higher statistical significance to allegedly more objective programming.

Such polarizations tend to spill over via self-justifications into controversies in which one side appoints itself as the bad conscience of the other, criticizing its antagonist with an undertone of moral devaluation—as if it were more desirable to be the superego for others than to possess a superego. The feuding parties then try to convert each other by warnings either of the irrational unpredictability of the unconscious or of the alienating effects of external reality on analysis. The upshot is a never-ending conflict about what is analytical and what is psychotherapeutic or unanalytical.

Wallerstein considers that the common ground begins with the concentration, shared by all analysts, on the clinical interactions in the consulting room; I would add that this is also the point where they already end and dissociate. As an analogy with the analytical treatment situation, Freud told the story of the insurance agent on his death bed whose family sent in a pastor to convert him. However, the burgeoning hopes of the waiting family were dashed because the pastor eventually went away insured, leaving the dying man unconverted.

Freud told this story from the point of view of the family waiting outside the door, but it is also possible to concentrate directly on the interactions in the sick chamber: the pastor attempts to endow the free-thinking patient with an insurance policy against eternal damnation, while the dying man for his part wants to provide the pastor with an insurance against earthly risks. The desire for immortality prevails, as the dying man sells the survivor an insurance policy, consolidating his own view of his situation by this concretistic success and living on in it. The pastor, too, displaces guilt feelings and loss anxieties of his own on to external risks, assuaging them by the purchase of the policy.

In this way, both have acted contrary to the ideal demand for "ultimate truth"—yet one has allegedly given succor to the other in his need.

In "Observations on Transference Love" (1915), Freud comments on the "dangers" of the psychoanalytic method form the immediate context of this analogy. Freud's courage is tellingly revealed by the fact of his embarking on the investigation of the unconscious in spite of his knowledge of its dangers. The analogy of the conflict between the insurance agent and his pastor, between wanting to live and having to die, was surely not arbitrarily chosen, although Freud still preferred to tell the story from the point of view of those waiting outside the sick chamber rather than entering directly into the "analytical situation." He was more concerned to show that the strict observance of abstinence and the upholding of reality testing were essential conditions for the opening up of the analytical space within which unconscious fantasies and motives could be constituted and verbalized.

However, his pressing injunctions to respect the rule of abstinence and uphold reality testing had the aim not only of safeguarding the objective of treatment for the patient but also, indirectly, of protecting the analyst within the analytical process. The analyst needs a reliable knowledge of his own position in order to be able to empathize with the unconscious fantasies of his patients, to think them through and to name them, and in order not to be overcome by their irrational forces. Temporarily to exchange the certainty of presumed reality for the uncertainties of the unconscious meanings of reality is and remains an endeavor full of risks.

If it is true that all analysts have in common the fact that they work with unconscious processes, then they have also secured for themselves into the bargain the permanent conflict between finitude and infinitude, life and death, renunciation and assertion, transference and countertransference. This conflict becomes more acute the closer it approaches to the sphere of the primary process. Psychogenetic reconstructions and theorizations then often become premature bastions of reality testing, into which the analyst withdraws and protects himself from being overwhelmed. Thus, Freud still considered the psychoanalytic method to be unsuitable for narcissistic disturbances, as such patients were felt to lack the ability to form a transference. Nowadays, the specific transference patterns of narcissistically disturbed patients are better known, and the discussion merely revolves around the appropriate treatment techniques: the classical analytical setting or the introduction of parameters in the sense of the application of psychoanalysis.

Kris (1947) defined psychoanalysis as conflict psychology. His definition means that conflict is inevitably the central common ground of all analysts. The plurality of analytic thinking and action remains indissolubly linked to conflicts and their resolution. As a result, psychoanalysis takes on as many different meanings as there are different analysts with different sensitivities and conflictual patterns, abilities and origins who use it. This gives rise to the constant and probably unalterable challenge of tolerance and understanding for divergent opinions.

This discussion for the time being leaves open the matter of the space or time to be allowed unconscious fantasies so that they can unfold and become perceptible in their manifold ramifications. This technical problem can, of course, not be discussed on the basis of treatment frequency alone, although it is a decisive factor. Whether and how the analytical process takes place depends primarily on the unobstructive and unbiased attention of the analyst and on his empathizing interest. However, patient and analyst need the optimum space and the necessary time to delve deeply into the meanings of transference and countertransference fantasies, to understand each other's specific communications and to integrate them. Analytic work is in a sense comparable with dream work. It demands leisure and is disturbed or even destroyed by haste and discontinuity.

I should like to illustrate these considerations and explain them in detail by means of a clinical vignette.

In a state of acute confusion and utter panic, a 40-year-old female teacher burst in on me without notice and took possession of my time and attention. She was single and had promiscuous relationships. She had had a number of previous disappointments with analysts, and she told me in the early sessions of her analysis, which began a few months later: "We live in an age of duplication. Copies cannot be distinguished from the original. You too want to turn me into a copy of your psychoanalytic technique. But I will use every trick to remain not you but myself [*mich selbst*]."

Her use of the accusative *"mich selbst"* instead of the nominative *"ich selbst"* for "myself" indicated that she was equating being with having. Just as she had at first burst in unannounced on my routine analytical activity, so she went on trying to fill me up with her wishes, ideas and feelings. She wanted to infiltrate herself more and more into me and my life. In this way I was to become a copy of herself—the inevitable consequence being the fear that I might manipulate her as intrusively as she manipulated me. She therefore had to use "every trick" as long as she imagined herself to be taken possession of by me and my words. What I said, and indeed whether I said anything or not, was irrelevant. My mere existence and otherness seemed to provoke rage and to goad her into acting out.

Just as she struggled to keep me at bay, so she defended herself against the envy and hatred in herself, which constantly flared up anew, directed at my "analytical privileges." Obstinately and irreconcilably, she therefore has not only to turn me into a carbon copy of herself but also to devalue me with mordant comments and despise me. After each session, she then suffered from anxious feelings of having offended or wounded me or even cut me into pieces. At the beginning of the next session, she would be perceptibly relieved and sometimes euphoric at finding me unchanged.

She had many ways of ignoring the analytical setting, which she discredited as "male chauvinism" that degraded her as a woman: instead of lying down, she would sit on the couch and stare at me provocatively; or, instead of associating, she would bring along pictures painted by herself or others, books, letters, or newspaper articles that she wanted to discuss; or instead of coming for analysis, she would appear seductively and revealingly dressed, with champagne, glasses, and a candle to celebrate Carnival with me; and so on.

By this stage I was condemned to helplessness; I was virtually paralyzed and, so to speak, robbed of my empathy and creative fantasies to an almost unbearable degree. I felt myself abused and scorned and was constantly at pains to preserve at least my critical ability to think. In such phases, I tended to disengage my attention from the inner processes and to step out of the plane of perception of myself and of the analytical situation. I was now completely distanced and concerned myself only with diagnostic considerations, by means of which I tried to reclassify the patient's troubles theoretically and to categorize her. The longer her acting out went on, the more hopeless I felt the prognosis to be and the more my doubts about the indications for analysis grew. Eventually, I was repeatedly on the point of deciding to give up the analytical setting and convert the analysis into a psychiatric/psychotherapeutic treatment. I wanted to get rid of her as quickly as possible.

She, however, constantly picked up my varying feelings with the sensitivity of a seismograph and immediately initiated reparative measures that frightened and moved me equally: she plunged into pseudo-etymological "do-it-yourself activity" using dictionaries and onomastic works from a few libraries to establish alleged relationships between her name and mine or between words that had been spoken in the previous session. The meaning contexts of the names and words and the relations between them felt intellectual and alienating. However, they were presented by her with the certainty that is reserved for magical evidence: she was convinced that she could divine from this information, for example, my age or the name of my first girlfriend.

The "do-it-yourself activity" represented a helpless but strenuous attempt to restore and rescue the contact with me which was threatening to be lost. She had now taken me and my theorizing abstraction as a blueprint that she desperately copied in order not to be left in the lurch.

She could communicate her dependence on me in no other way than by acting out. She had shown from the beginning how vitally important I was to her by never missing a session and appearing reliably 10 minutes early for each session. Such considerations repeatedly caused the decisions I had previously taken to crumble.

Unfortunately (or fortunately?) for me, I had hardly any biographical information about the patient. She had told me of her rural origins and hinted equivocally that she had lived as a student in an attic room with no heating, with a view of the church to the right and the brothel to the left. I also knew that her mother had suffered from depressions and had hanged herself five years before the beginning of the analysis. I therefore had hardly any solid basis for reconstructions of biographical meaning contexts—a possibility of which she deprived me so as not to become "indoctrinated" by interpretations, with which she was reportedly familiar from previous analysts.

After she had for a long time persecuted—and occasionally alarmed—me with fantasies that I was incurably ill with cancer and would soon die, she for the first time, in the second year of her analysis, showed a willingness to try to understand the unconscious content of her fantasies: with expressions of pain and not without exhibitionistic appeal, she massaged her left breast and told of feelings of discomfort that she said had become concentrated there in the form of an increasingly hard knot, as if a malignant growth were spreading in the tissue. My interpretation that she wanted to take into herself the illness that was gnawing away at me and my foreseeable death in order to rescue me led for the first time to the beginnings of constructive and lasting analytical work.

After this I was no longer blocked, and she was able to moderate her defense and come closer to me step by step: she replaced her impulsive acting out by verbal communications and, in increasing dismay, began to recognize that she had compulsively needed to devalue and then restore both me and other people, so as to fuel an omnipotent-narcissistic delusion of herself as redeemer. This delusion had kept her free of the guilt feelings she had had toward the "dead" mother because of her oral-sadistic incursions and death wishes. In particular, however, she was able to "rescue" the "living" mother by means of delusional total identifications. This had allowed the remobilization and intensification of an infantile megalomania which enabled her to continue the relationship with the early mother autonomously and auto-erotically.

As a result of the experience of clinical interactions in the consulting room, most analysts will have a common understanding of, and share a high degree of agreement on, the contents of this patient's unconscious fantasies, their significance for the transference and the psychodynamics of the unconscious conflict, and their biographical roots. A consensus is still possible on the epicritical assessment of the defensive processes—in particular, projective identifications and introjections—and on diagnosis of a severe narcissistic disturbance in the form of a borderline condition or a prepsychotic state.

The first divergences and contradictions in theoretical conceptions arise when an attempt is made to integrate the phenomena observed into hypothetical or metapsychological conceptual systems. This pluralism is not as a rule experienced as a hostile rivalry between scientific camps, although approaches in terms of instinctual psychology, ego psychology, object-relations psychology, Kleinian theory, and so on, give rise to differences of emphasis in regard to one and the same problem. These differences are felt to be beneficial in the common desire for enlightenment, which not only tolerates but welcomes diversity of opinion.

However, serious and potentially irreconcilable controversies arise with the discussion of analytical technique. This situation is all the more remarkable because it is generally assumed that the way analysts treat patients is taught as a uniform method. The reality contradicts this expectation, as the analytical situation is in fact like the analogy of the insurance agent: the analyst may observe it from the outside, participating indirectly, and comment on it subsequently, or he may walk directly into the sick chamber and expose himself to the unconscious transference processes in which he is temporarily forced to feel and think as the dying man or the pastor. The analytic technique of the analyst varies according to his particular position.

My clinical vignette shows that both analyst and patient can succeed in understanding and discovering only if the unconscious fantasies that unfold are decoded in the transference and countertransference. The fact of naming them affords trusting access to the split-off, needy, and helpless parts of the personality that had formerly been defended against by omnipotent-narcissistic and destructive identifications. This route is risky and leads through numerous and unforeseeable hazards, which can be tolerated only by an indispensable fixing of one's analytic position. All premature theoretical considerations or premature reconstructions of biographical reality are defensive reactions against being overwhelmed by unconscious forces on exactly the same level as partial or total erosions of abstinence. Their aim is to put a quick end to dangerous situations that, however, have not really been overcome until the "soft voice of reason" also has its say and permits insight and renunciation.

Freud was right to warn of the dangers of the analytic method. We shall therefore have to accept that different analysts cope in different ways with the dangers of the unconscious, justifying and championing their individual techniques theoretically in different ways. Our individual differences and those of our patients will persist and the conflicts about the psychoanalytical method will continue. Doubts about the common ground in psychoanalysis will constantly flare up anew and draw us into the turbulent waters of the analytic Scylla and Charybdis, the dilemma of transference and countertransference. The closer we dare to approach this maelstrom, the more consistently our activity serves the psychoanalytic investigation of the unconscious; the less we are prepared to go into it and the more we keep it at a distance, the more we are pursuing psychotherapeutic objectives in our work.

5

Aims and Clinical Process As I See It

Carlos Mario Aslan, M.D.

And the whole earth was of one language, and of one speech. And it came to pass, as they journeyed from the East, that they found a plain in the land of Shinar; and they dwelt there.

And they said one to another, Go to, let us make brick, and burn them thoroughly. And they had brick for stone, and slime had they for mortar.

And they said, Go to, let us build us a city and a tower, whose top may reach unto heaven; and let us make us a name, lest we be scattered abroad upon the face of the whole earth.

And the Lord came down to see the city and the tower, which the children of men builded.

And the Lord said, Behold, the people is one, and they have all one language; and this they begin to do: and now nothing will be restrained from them, which they have imagined to do.

Go to, let us go down, and there confound their language, that they may not understand one another's speech.

So the Lord scattered them abroad from thence upon the face of all the earth: and they left off to build the city.

Therefore is the name of it called Babel; because the Lord did there confound the language of all the earth: and from thence did the Lord scatter them abroad upon the face of all the earth.

The Tower of Babel Genesis 11

THE PSYCHOANALYTIC BABEL

The richness and vitality of current psychoanalysis tells us that we psychoanalysts keep building "our city." The multiplicity of frames of reference constitutes precisely a demonstration of such richness and vitality. Many of them relate widely and deeply enough to the main body of psychoanalytic theory as to (1) go on being psychoanalysis and (2) enrich psychoanalysis at the same time.

As I see it, we must settle what we have in common that allows us to go on working as analysts and establish the possibility of profiting from the clinical and theoretical creativity of the different frames of reference.

One of the obstacles that opposes these aims is the diversity of the languages developed by many schools (language both in its metaphorical sense—that is, the set of proposals—and in its concrete sense—the terms in which these proposals are stated). I shall not go here either into the conscious and unconscious reasons that have determined this state of affairs or into considering whether it would be possible and/or desirable to reach a unified language. What I do believe desirable is to avoid a situation in the development of these languages such that we may "not understand one another's speech."

We find ourselves in a psychoanalytic Babel where (1) the same words name different concepts; (2) the same concepts are named by different words; and (3) there are a number of words only validated within the context of a given frame of reference.

The predominant ways that we psychoanalysts have found, up to the present, to face the multiplicity of schools, may be briefly outlined as follows (even though we must have in mind that the boundaries between one position and another are not always neatly drawn, and that a manifest position may cover a latent one):

1. Opposition among frames of reference. This is a *dogmatic position* and implies that the "owners of the truth" denigrate those who, obviously, do not possess it.

2. "Peaceful" coexistence without interchanges going on. Although appearing to be a rational one, this *skeptical position* implies an attitude similar to the previous one.

3. The *eclectic position* consists in using for a given patient, or for a given, or several sessions, a frame of reference considered the most appropriate for each occasion. Thus there will be, for instance, "Freudian," "Kleinian," "Lacanian" patients or sessions. Even though it implies a progress with regard to the former ones, the eclectic position maintains a latent skeptical attitude, namely, in some way it gives up an attempt to make different views converge or integrate.

4. Blending of frames of reference. It consists in using theoretical concepts from different frames of reference and applying them to the understanding and description of clinical cases or psychopathological entities, either referring or not to their source. This is an *integrating position,* which means a real advance in relation to the previous ones. This

position is liable to be questioned for epistemological reasons, for instance the out of context nonvalid usage of certain concepts.

It is my view that psychoanalysts group themselves in decreasing numbers with regard to these positions. Faced with this situation, it is necessary, as I see it, that we take a stand on scientific discussion, research, and dialogue. We hope that this attitude of facing overtly the problem of "one psychoanalysis or many" may clear up the situation and prevent dispersal.

A scientific and rational attitude toward the problem of the psychoanalytic Babel implies that it is not possible to approach it from a partial standpoint—for instance only from the clinical level of our *common ground*. On the contrary, it seems not only indispensable but also inevitable to resort to theoretical levels and ideas. It has become highly necessary for us to study and state our agreements, both clinical and theoretical.

A CLINICAL-THEORETICAL EXAMPLE

As clinical illustration I shall go into what I think to be an issue upon which various authors, who are conspicuous representatives of different schools, converge. It is a concept both theoretical and clinical with which we could define (in a language that I claim to be "common") an aspect of the early mother–infant relationship where an interchange takes place that produces a structuring effect in the infant's psyche, an effect generically called *identification*.

This has been thus depicted by these authors.

When describing the "value of illusion," Winnicott

speaks of an infant with "the growing need that arises out of instinctual tension," in other words, the need for the breast in all its meaningful complexity. If the mother, at the right moment, comes near her baby and "gives her breast and her potential feeding urge," they meet halfway, so to speak, and an illusion arises in the infant's psyche: "the illusion that there is an external reality that corresponds to the infant's own capacity to create" and that "the infant takes from a breast that is part of the infant." When this complementary and convergent experience takes place over and over again, "a subjective phenomenon develops in the baby, which we call the mother's breast."

Mahler described a similar phenomenon from her own frame of reference when referring to the "mutual selection of cues" in the mother–infant relationship during the symbiotic phase. She states that the child presents a large variety of cues to express "needs, tension and pleasure." The mother responds selectively to some of these cues and thus conveys "a mirroring frame of reference," to which the child adjusts himself until he becomes "the child of his particular mother"—that is, the one whose character structure reflects that of his mother.

Within the Kleinian school, Bion has made valuable contributions concerning the object's role in the reintrojection of the infant's projective identifications. With regard to this subject, he says, for instance, when referring to the mother's "capacity for reverie," "normal development follows if the relationship between infant and breast permits the infant to project a feeling, say, that it is dying, into the mother, and to reintroject it after its sojourn in the breast has made it tolerable to the infant psyche. If the projection is not accepted by the mother the infant feels that its feeling that it is dying is stripped of such meaning as it has. It therefore reintrojects, not a fear of dying made tolerable, but a nameless dread.''

Lacan also refers to this phenomenon, I think, in his inaugural paper ''The Mirror Stage . . .'': ''We have only to understand the mirror stage *as an identification,* in the full sense that analysis gives to this term: namely, the transformation that takes place in the subject when he assumes an image. . . .'' This concept was later developed, especially when considering ''the Other's desire,'' as a structuring element for the subject.

Within Lacan's theory but at the same time drawing his own conclusions, Leclaire has postulated the ''primary narcissistic representative'' which would be the mother's (parents') desire embodied in the infant's psyche.

It is my view that these theoretical and clinical notions develop Freud's concept of primary identification as the ''earliest expression of an emotional tie with another person.''

These quotations, as I see them, represent a point of convergence of many different schools of psychoanalytic thought. In spite of the obvious differences in shades, I think that we have thus been able to rescue from the psychoanalytic Babel, a common concept, a *common ground.* Although it would be possible to make many interesting comments on this point, I will restrict myself to the main aim of this paper. I will then say that the various authors, while theorizing diversely, have used a common psychoanalytic method. This means, among other things, that the observations that have led to the formulation of the different theoretical models were made in the course of psychoanalytic processes, and that the events observed (1) have taken place when the patients were regressed, (2) were observable in the transference, and (3) were repetitions of the original event.

Thus the clinical event I am speaking about is not the same as that depicted by phenomenologists or classical psychiatrists. This is a *psychoanalytic clinical event*—that is, its observation and description as a singular entity presupposes (1) a technique and (2) a series of common theories, all this constituting *common ground*.

Every analyst, when faced with this phenomenon in the course of a psychoanalytic process, will psychoanalyze it. He will use the psychoanalytic technique, namely words, to deal with it. What will he be aiming at? If we wish to state it in such a way that this aim may be included within the *common ground*, we may say: to modify his patient's psyche. If we wish to be more specific, we shall have to give up the *common ground* and make use of a given frame of reference: "To produce a mutation in his persecutory internal objects," as a Kleinian might put it; "to unbind the subject," a follower of Lacan would say.

COMMON GROUND

As may be inferred from the previous section, the psychoanalytic method seems to be one of the most important elements of the *common ground* among analysts. In its more restricted sense, psychoanalytic technique constitutes the core of the psychoanalytic method. Freud's discoveries were made possible by his invention of a tool: technique—that is, free-floating attention and interpretation on the analyst's part, free association on the patient's part. These are invariants that have not changed since Freud invented them.

The use of the psychoanalytic technique has paved the

way for clinical and theoretical discoveries and the subsequent building up of a scientific corpus, first as Freud's works, which the different frames of reference later diversified. Thus, knowledge and understanding have widened and therefore the content of interpretation has varied, and the hard core, the technical invariant, has been enriched (that is, the use of transference and countertransference) to build up the psychoanalytic method. (The relationship between technique and method would compare with that between interpreting and psychoanalyzing.) So central this *common ground* seems to be that some authors (including Herrmann) think that it constitutes the possible basis for analysts' convergence.

I shall depict some of the theoretical aspects of the *common ground* involved in the aforementioned "clinical event." I am aware of the risk enumerations entail—that is, that they may consciously or unconsciously be considered as restrictive, or, even worse, as a superego imposition. Having made this clear, I shall postulate as *common theoretical ground:*

1. The existence of unconscious mental processes. This is the notion of an active, constant and timeless dynamic process with contents that are grouped as ideas, wishes, fantasies, needs, defenses; their continuous presence and influence being shown in dreams, parapraxes, symptoms, transferences, in the discourse and in behavior. Conflict, defense, and their manifestation as resistance are central concepts here. The analyst interprets all this to the patient in connection with every possible area: his present life, his transferences, with relation to his infantile-historic origin and as models of intrapsychic processes.

2. The assumption of a progression in the shaping and

structuring of the unconscious and conscious psyche. According to the frame of reference either a genetic or a historical viewpoint is preferred. This will determine respectively a more linear or a less linear concept of the process.

At this point we can add the idea of deficit or deprivation to that of conflict, both as key notions to explain each particular development.

3. The existence of crucial or nodal points in this progress or development. The successful passage through these landmarks bears a determining importance on the subject's psychic and psychopathological future. For the Freudian frame of reference the main nodal point is the Oedipus complex, the resolution of which implies the passage from the dyadic to the triadic relationship. This situation is replicated by different frames of reference—for instance, the passage from the paranoid-schizoid to the depressive position for the Kleinian school; and the passage from the imaginary to the symbolic register in the Lacanian frame of reference. Mobility, either forward or backward (i.e., progression or regression), is important (as is immobility, or fixation) with regard to this point.

A component element of the psychoanalytic common ground that I deem of considerable interest does not relate either to theory or to technique, but to psychoanalysts themselves. I believe analysts share a certain particular feature of their characterological structure that seems to be an effect of their peculiar training. This makes them different from other professionals who merely practice the profession they have been trained for. It is a subtle difference; however, it may be discerned clearly in the group of psychoanalysts as a mass. It is difficult to define: it mainly consists in an internal and permanent special attitude to take a certain stand on facing problems; it is neither a common ideology nor a Weltanschauung, even though it may share elements from both.

I cannot go any further here into either the description or the genesis of this characterological structure. I shall just say that I think that it is training psychoanalysis, with its special obligatory condition, that produces that feature. It is therefore a consequence of training; it does not constitute either a previous characteristic or a requirement.

BEYOND THE FRAMES OF REFERENCE?

The proliferation, extension, and vitality of the current frames of reference tell us of the existence of an erotic development—in the widest Freudian sense—but the ever-increasing remoteness between them warns us about the possibility of complications, disunity and misunderstandings. Is it possible to avoid a thanatic fate—in its Freudian sense, as well—of splitting, "cold war" atmosphere, or eclecticism? As I see it, the only way out of this situation would depend on putting into practice the tenets of pluralism and tolerance.

Pluralism with regard to frames of reference, schools, or ideological groups does not merely mean that they can all live together under the ceiling of one and the same Society. It is an attitude supported by the philosophical and scientific idea that there is not such a thing as a complete science, that there are no absolute truths and that, consequently, there are not any owners of *the* Truth. Pluralism is therefore necessary and it implies an active attitude, an attitude of seeking for the other, for his opinions, thoughts, and theories. Pluralism, therefore, is something that is neither graciously bestowed nor mercifully granted.

Tolerance as a principle does not simply refer to a type of living together that can be tolerated or tolerable. It holds as its central issue rational discussion and confrontation as a means of sorting out—or not—differences. This requires consensus, which is necessary as well with regard to "the rules of the game" of these situations. Again, this implies an active search for—and not passively making allowances for—confrontation and discussion.

The International Psychoanalytical Association is a pluralist scientific organization, and the subject that we are dealing with shows this type of agreement necessary for the scientific and open discussion of problems. If this attitude already exists or is liable to be created in the Component Societies, it may be assumed that there will be progress in the understanding and widening of our *common ground*.

As I see it, the future is uncertain with respect to *non-common ground*. I think that there is consensus among analysts, at least among the majority of them, in relation to not giving up metapsychology. There is also some skepticism with relation to the possibility of unifying in a more or less near future the various frames of reference under "an overarching consensually accepted general theoretical structure" (Wallerstein). Thus we would just be waiting for the difficult task of comparing, translating, and adjusting the theoretical terms from the different frames of reference to be carried out in the various sectors, should this task be possible.

However, there still exists another alternative which does not exclude the previous one. I have called it "beyond the frames of reference." This "beyond" would be a new product yielded by pluralist psychoanalytic societies. It would be the outcome of living together and being increasingly familiar with some other schools than one's own, and this latter fact would soften distrust, diminish fear of the unknown and appease the anxieties *vis-à-vis* change, and it would increase the conviction that the frames of reference are just models to think about the psyche and not revealed truths.

I think it would be feasible in this way to reach a new type of dialogue among analysts, *beyond and in spite of* different frames of reference: a dialogue without renunciations or exclusions, a dialogue equivalent to a renewed "psychic act."

6

A Shared View of the World

Arnold Goldberg, M.D.

The search for a common ground for analysts who work with differing viewpoints has its parallel in the search between analyst and patient for a similar unity of vision, a shared view of the world. No two people live in exactly identical worlds; we mainly manage to communicate with one another by varying degrees of sharing, negotiating, and ignoring. Every patient who comes to analysis struggles with a combination of wishes to be understood by the analyst along with hopes that certain aspects of his psyche remain opaque. And every analyst, in like fashion, wants to understand his patient yet also needs and hopes to move the segregated or split-off material into the open. My thesis here is that the analytic process is one that reverses this sequence of sharing, negotiating, and ignoring. It says that this is the essence of commonality both in the analytic relationship *per se* as well as in the larger world of analysis. Let us begin with the first of the trilogy.

SHARING

To some degree we all share a similar perspective with our patients in a wide number of ways. This similarity is what allows us to make a beginning with patients, and it extends from a common language to a familiarity of customs, to an overlapping of like experiences. This need to overlap in a significant segment of life is what is essential for any sort of treatment, and it is why it makes the truly alien person untreatable. Phrases such as *therapeutic* and *working alliance* may possibly point to this shared vision that unites people with a minimum of effort. Indeed, the achievement of sharing becomes the major work of analysis as we initially aim to see the world as the patient does and then subsequently to enable the patient to see the world as we do. The world we see is one defined and delineated by our theories, just as Freud could see things in his patients that he felt they should ultimately likewise be able to see. Freud asked his patients to look at things in a new and different way: his way. The method of doing this may vary depending upon technique, but the goal remains that of the achievement of a mutually agreed-upon view of the patient's life and history.

Some aspects of this effort of sharing are almost automatic, and some require the kinds of communication that all patients and analysts engage in. It is in the exercise of empathy that all people learn about others' inner lives; and this is true of each and every analyst no matter what particular theories he may employ. We aim to see the world as the patient does by a sustained effort of empathic linkage. Although analysts (like everyone else) pick and choose what to see and what to ignore, they must still employ this basic human device of empathy. In a reciprocal manner all patients struggle to understand their analysts and so to achieve this desired shared vision. The exercise of empathy does not differentiate analysts one from the other, but the utilized theories certainly do. Although we succeed in understanding one another, a shared state of understanding is short-lived.

NEGOTIATIONS

All analyses begin with enough shared understanding enjoyed by both participants, enough common ground to move on to the inevitable next phase: that of misunderstanding. From understanding—that is, a basic set of like-mindedness between persons—we move to misunderstanding—a breach of the unity. The ensuing work of achieving a new understanding from the misunderstood state is that of negotiation. The beginnings of all analytic treatment involve a minimum of negotiation in terms of fees, hours, rules, and vacations, the process of free association and a host of idiosyncratic (or personal) standards of conduct that every analyst presumes and assumes. But negotiation takes the dominant role in the entire analytic adventure, since analyst and patient are not of one mind, and each attempts to win over the other to his way of thinking—the one by interpretations that lead to insight, and the other usually by some form of special pleading. The patient in one way or another beseeches the analyst to join him in his view of reality, and the analyst exerts his effort to disabuse the patient of that set of supposed facts. It would seem that this is the arena where the patient is most disparate from the analyst, and thus the place where the technical interventions of the analyst become most meaningful. The patient who sees you as the parent feels it as real and does not yet see that this is an arguable perception. Interpretation or learning should allow him to see that as an error.

The fundamental stance of the analyst in his participation in the negotiating process is governed by his analytic theory. Here is where analyst differs from patient; a given phenomenon, such as a dream or an association, is necessarily seen in a different way, because all of our facts are soaked in our theory. We never see any part of the psyche without a theory of the psyche, and thus analytic theories, whether articulated or not, distinguish analysts from nonanalysts. They also differentiate one analyst from the next, and here again is where the commonality of analysts falters; and therefore, here is where the practice of negotiation between analysts becomes paramount.

I believe we agree that the major tool of our analytic interventions is the awareness and interpretation of transference. It would also seem to be the case that different analytic theories should and do primarily concern themselves with different comprehensions of transference. Psychoanalytic self-psychology, for example, has added to the list of the observable transferences those of self-object transferences—that is, the mirror, the twinship, and the idealizing. This is subject to the same sort of negotiating process between analysts as that between patient and analyst, albeit in a more cognitive sense. To not participate in this form of negotiation is not a scientific position but rather reflects a similar sort of insistence on seeing the world in a fixed fashion—an insistence that our analytic patients enjoy to their detriment.

The reciprocal part of negotiation between patient and analyst asks of us to change as well. Inasmuch as we allow every aspect of analytic practice to be subjected to scrutiny, no part of it can ever be immune from reappraisal and alteration. There are no absolute rules for the analytic process save that of freedom of inquiry. The patient's insistence on keeping the world as is, is attributed to transference and is altered by interpretation. The analyst's own insistence on having it his way is considered to be attributable to countertransference along with limitations in his theoretical knowledge—the latter due to ignorance or the limitations of the state of the theory, or both. Thus there is no bedrock of truths in psychoanalysis that allow us to know things for sure, since the essence of the negotiating process is a willingness on the part of both participants to move from their initial positions. Since psychoanalysis is not suggestion or indoctrination, it is either revelation or negotiation. It is tempting to believe that it is revelation, but each new finding in our science undoes that neat knot. Only in a closed system that is not science can one ever be allowed to practice the unearthing of revealed truths, but psychoanalysis can never be a finished product. New and unpredictable ideas come into the relationship between patient and analyst in a way different from other sorts of negotiations that begin with fixed ideas and positions.

The give and take of negotiating in psychoanalysis is made unique by the existence of the unknown that resides primarily but not exclusively in the patient. It is this awareness by the analyst that tilts the process in his favor, and it is the introduction of the unknown into the analytic process that makes for the issues that demand negotiation.

THE UNKNOWN

Repressed or disavowed mental contents become a part of the continual misunderstandings between patient and analyst. Because of the nature of the transference, there occur inevitable empathic disruptions or breaks in understanding. These are brought about because the achievement of a stable transference is never a static phenomenon, but rather one that continually makes demands, or has desires, or proceeds to develop. Since transference unfolds, it has changeable demands, and, since transference is repetitious, it has inevitable frustrations. The intrusion of unconscious contents, the existence of disavowed material, and the lack of the necessary structure to process this new set of relationships, all lead to misunderstandings. The reestablishing of understanding from misunderstanding by way of the negotiating process allows for the inclusion of the repressed and disavowed and the establishment of a suitable structure for its tolerance and expression. Thus the sequence of movement is from unknown or ignored material to inevitable misunderstanding, on to negotiation, and then to a shared set of perceptions that represent understanding—that is, the desired state of sharing. This is the reversed sequence of the trilogy.

Since the analyst knows about the existence of and the forms of repressed and disavowed material, his theory allows him a vision denied to the patient. And it goes without saying that the more one knows the better; and thus no one can ever dismiss Kleinian or Kohutian or Lacanian ideas out of hand, any more than one can do without any therapeutic tool. The potential variants of transference are additional tools to one's analytic and therapeutic armamentarium. The restriction of analytic knowledge to one or another form of theory reveals the same sort of opaqueness that we see in our patients. Analysts who have limited or closed concepts of transferences, who do not learn Kohut or Lacan, who insist that their vision of the world is correct, live analogous patterns to those patients who likewise keep their ignorance at bay.

Even more to the point of the expansion of analytic knowledge being reciprocal to that of the patient is that of the analyst's active participation in the creation of misunderstandings. No matter how inevitable an empathic break may be, it always asks of us that we examine what we did or did not do to cause it and what we learn from it as we negotiate our way to new understanding. This is the part of the equation that consists of the analyst's countertransference or ignorance that, in a hoped-for smaller amount, adds its input to misunderstanding. Thus the understanding that should follow from this temporary disruption should always include the possibility to the analyst of a level of comprehension that was not previously available to him. In the words of Gadamer, we strive to remake ourselves by way of these cycles of achieving a shared vision of the world. The goal of this process would then be an achievement of a mutually new reality for both patient and analyst. This is not to say that analysis cures the analyst as it does the patient, but rather that no one can emerge from an intense and prolonged analytic relationship in the same way that one enters it.

PSYCHOANALYTIC SELF PSYCHOLOGY AND THE COMMON GROUND

Since psychoanalytic self psychology sees itself in the mainstream of psychoanalysis in terms of the formation and resolution of transference, it can make a further contribution in its elucidation of this effort in all analysis. The three phases of sequential action: the activation and intrusion of

117

repressed and/or disavowed material, the misunderstandings, and the ensuing understanding are all conceptualized
by way of the self-concept. The formation of selfobject
transferences parallels the state of understanding which
results from empathic union. The breaks in empathy come
from disavowed and/or repressed material that expresses
and allows for the emergence of regressive forms of selfob-
jects. The repairs in empathy lead to a state of understanding that moves toward a firmer self structure. No
matter what theoretical stand an analyst may take, it would
seem that this sequence has a universal applicability. The
major point to be made is that content issues such as
castration anxiety or oedipal dynamics play a subsidiary role
to those of form and structure.

Such an overview of the work of all analysis is an
umbrella. It covers a variety of seemingly different and
sometimes contradictory ways of analyzing in the sense of
explaining why they all may seem at times to be effective. It
does not, however, say that all psychoanalytic theories are
basically alike or of equal value. Our theories are different,
and they cannot and should not be translated one into the
other. They compete in the marketplace of science, and it
behooves every analyst to be skillful enough and knowledgeable enough to make a decision for himself as to which
theory explains more and better.

CONCLUSION

Psychoanalysis has moved from revelation to negotiation,
from the image of a detached analyst enabling unconscious
material to emerge, to one of mutuality that demands a new
theory to explain how two people affect one another. Such
a theory cannot and should not be one that neglects our

capacity to see beyond explanations that keep the negotiation on a conscious level—that is, those of linguistics or sociology or game theory or whatever. Rather, we can use our analytic theories to explore the nature of change in terms of infantile demands, transference distortions, structure building, or similar forms of explanatory concepts. The same should apply to how we change in our scientific exchanges; and one could hardly hope for a better testing ground for our ideas than is found in our willingness to see how well we can listen to and learn from one another. It is the exercise of a willingness to move from certainty to skepticism and to a resultant posture of openness to new insights that is the mark of the analyst who joins hands with his colleagues in the search for common ground. Such willingness is what we ask of our patients. Can we ask less of ourselves?

7

Necessity and Risks of the Control of Regression

Claude Le Guen, M.D.

Of all the clinical experiences I have ever had, there is one that never ceases to surprise me; yet I have often had it and shall have it again. I am referring to my encounter with the effects of a different form of psychoanalytic practice.

Such encounters may arise when reading or listening to a colleague who practices by techniques other than those familiar to me, with different theoretical reference points and even perhaps claiming allegiance to a different school. However, the particular case I am thinking of is when I have on my couch a person who is entering upon a second analysis after having previously lain on a Kleinian or Lacanian couch. (I shall refer mainly to these two schools because, apart from my own approach—which I would describe broadly as "orthodox Freudian as practiced in France"—they are the ones I know best.) The final possibility that occurs to me is supervision of students whose approaches are molded by these other orientations.

This, then, is the sum total of my clinical experience of encounters with the practices of other schools. Apart from its effects on my moods and prejudices, it does not seem to be enough to give me a valid opinion of these other techniques. Intuition rather than rational argument suggests to me that how a treatment proceeds has much more to do with the "analytical qualities" of those involved than with the virtues of each school's specific techniques. It follows that, both in the process of treatment and in the observance of certain technical principles, there might be a dynamic determination that controls what takes place in this process, beyond all the technical variations (which would then be limited to understanding more or less well and taking account more or less relevantly of what is happening). We should also need to be able to specify these technical principles and possibly also these dynamic determinations.

If we could at the same time trust the therapeutic results, our judgments would become more reliable. But, as we know, first it does not seem possible to conduct a credible epidemiological survey in psychoanalysis, and second, while failure disqualifies, success too is no proof: a cure, and *a fortiori* the disappearance of a symptom, is not in itself sufficient evidence of the efficiency or validity of the technique used.

However, this reminds us that in the sciences theoretical models are meaningful only if they attempt to take account as efficiently as possible of the object of their study; the specificity of each science is a function of its objects only and by no means of its theoretical apprehension (unlike the situation in philosophy or religion). Consequently, the answer to Wallerstein's question "One or more analyses?" is self-evident: there can be only one psychoanalysis whose object is the unconscious working of the mind, regardless of the diversity of the theories that attempt to understand and explain it.

This, I believe, is a good criterion for validation of theories. For all that, their relation to practice generally remains extremely vague. For instance, there is no *a priori* reason in Lacanian theory why analysts of that persuasion should have short or very short sessions (ranging between 20 and 5 minutes); yet the vast majority of them do so, following the example of their master. In a different camp (if I may use the term, which is not intended to imply the slightest equivalence or symmetry between the two), it is noteworthy that the feeling of rejection often experienced by "orthodox" psychoanalysts on hearing of Kleinian interpretive practices is stronger the more they are interested in or even attracted by many of the theoretical approaches of the Kleinian school or its derivatives: here again, it is not obvious in what respect the theory necessarily entails the practice. Indeed, all kinds of permutations are conceivable: there is no apparent reason why a Lacanian should not practice by a Kleinian approach and vice versa.

In general, however, this does not occur. This may well indicate that the relations between theory and practice in our discipline are much closer, constraining and determining, than they are generally stated to be. The fact that these relations are so much more often implicit than explicit is equally unfortunate. This to my mind shows conclusively that it is in fact practice that can and must instruct us about theories.

I therefore believe I am justified in stating that the only demand that can and must be made on the various systems is that they should respect both the object on which they work and the production of its manifestations. So there would be no problem if psychoanalysis, in addition to being an "investigative procedure," were not also "a method of treatment."

Since it sets itself the aim of modifying or changing the object of its study, it runs the risk of possibly denaturing the manifestations of that object, even to the extent of obliterating it. This is why so much emphasis is placed on the neutrality of the analyst, as a necessary barrier against the temptation of manipulation—a temptation that is as constant as it is frequently forgotten. All these procedures together go to make up what we call our "technique." It is obviously at this level that variations are most strongly in evidence, extending even to the point where they need to be justified by an appropriate theory.

These principles being settled, it should be easy for us to agree on some others. I shall mention only a few that seem to me to be essential. I shall therefore begin by repeating what many others have said before me, that the facilitation of regression by the patient in the treatment is a means of ensuring, and a necessary condition for, its efficacy. Here again, however, matters are complicated by the fact that this regression must in all cases be controlled by the analyst. In using the word *control*, I am in no way calling into question the necessary neutrality of the analyst. In fact, I would say that this control is a fundamental condition for the observance of his neutrality, allowing both the fundamental rule and the rule of abstinence to be complied with.

It may seem logical to take the view that the more regression is facilitated, the more watchfully it must be controlled. For instance, not long ago a Kleinian colleague explained that he preferred to intervene relatively early in a session in order not to run the risk of finding himself swamped by the accumulation of material. This attitude could be contrasted with the almost absolute silence so often practiced by the Lacanians: Does this signify avoidance of regression, or insufficient control of it, or both? In this case, the only possible way left for control to be exercised would be by an early interruption of the session and/or by directive interventions (indeed, this is in practice what eventually happens in most cases). Clearly then, even more than the achievement of regression, it is the need for it to be controlled that organizes the therapeutic techniques used, presumably in accordance with the particular theory of regression underlying them.

Be that as it may, this implicit demand for control inevitably has some practical consequences; the more these touch upon the margin left for associative freedom and the conditions for listening to it, the less negligible these will be. Although ideally this freedom should be absolute, it is emphasized that it has to be sufficiently under control for the material thereby revealed to remain capable of being heard both by the analysand and by the analyst. However, this necessity entails the risk that the analyst's thought might be imposed on the patient, to such an extent that it might ultimately no longer be possible to recognize who really thought what. I shall probably never forget a comment once made to me by a female patient: "You ought not to have told me that I had thought that, because now I shall never know whether this thought is really mine and has always been there or whether it is you who suggested it to me now." Beyond her resistance to the transference, she was expressing an important truth that is still exercising me.

Freud, of course, felt that there was no danger in making suggestions of this kind—either they were wrong, in which case the patient would take no notice of them and they would have no effect, or they corresponded to some historical event, aroused some unconscious memories and were therefore perfectly relevant. Many psychoanalysts have placed their trust in this idea, since, at the risk of oversimplification, it might be said that the Kleinian technique of multiple and frequent interpretations (which is, incidentally, liable to encourage regression) is in fact based on this postulate. I personally am not fully convinced that it is correct; I feel in fact that nothing the analyst says can possibly be indifferent or have no effect. Admittedly, nothing is suggested that is not already implicit in the preconscious or unconscious of the suggestee. Nevertheless, the resulting associations do not then necessarily follow the paths most favorable to psychical transformation; indeed, everything we know about resistance militates in favor of the opposite view.

What is more, considering Freud's view (expressed in a long note in "Symptoms, Inhibitions, and Anxiety") that "it is not self-evident, perhaps not even usual, that those [repressed] impulses should remained unaltered and unalterable in this way," it may ultimately be felt that excessive intervention carries the risk of excessively influencing these repressed impulses. In other words, the danger is that the analyst may shift from a suggestion (which is implicit and inevitable, but controllable and perhaps beneficial) to a subjection (which is constraining, distorting, and necessarily harmful).

This is not the place to continue the discussion of this question of alteration of the repressed impulses, interesting as it is and whatever view may be taken of it. I raised it merely in order to stress again one of the major difficulties of analytical work: the analyst must at one and the same time remain neutral and intervene in order to change something in the patient. Indeed, there is no denying that this is one of the firmest foundations of psychoanalysis; but while it is a fundamental condition of its validity, this does not mean that it is always so easy to observe on that account and in all circumstances. The analyst constantly risks falling between the two stools of ineffectiveness due to excessive neutrality and conditioning due to abuse of intervention. But the dividing line between control and constraint may be very thin.

Everything I have just said shows that the use of the transference–countertransference is at the heart of our practice; it is both the crux of any psychoanalytic technique and the condition of its validity. All analysts would surely agree on this point. However, it is also probably the respect in which our technique and our understanding of our practice have developed most since Freud. He himself, of course, took a long time to move on from the idea of the transference as a particular case of displacement to its generalization as the organizing process of any treatment; it took him just as long to recognize it as a privileged instrument rather than a formidable obstacle. He then had to follow the same route with the countertransference. It was only when this was accomplished that psychoanalysis had finally broken with the reference to surgical asepsis as a therapeutic model.

I believe that at present the transference–countertransference relationship increasingly appears as an indissoluble one: the effect of change acts on the couple itself or, more correctly, on the relation between its two terms—and no longer on the transference alone. Nevertheless, the two processes cannot be equated with each other; they do not work in the same way, whatever the similarities in the forces underlying them (the treatment cannot possibly be reduced to an encounter between two transferences).

It seems to be self-evident that the transference, together with the countertransference that accompanies it (I personally would say, that makes it explicit), is organized by the

Oedipus complex. The latter thus assumes a new position as a basic reference of the treatment. However, this also tends to alter the meaning of the Oedipus complex, which is now not only the prime mover that structures the individual (this is significant enough in itself), but also the organizing process of exchange—an exchange which is asymmetrical. Indeed, all ideas since Winnicott that have stressed the part played by the mother in the development of the infant are based, I believe, on this finding. I would merely add that a third term needs to be introduced into this early relationship, as the condition for all possibilities of symbolization—that is, for all controls—but that is another matter.

Be that as it may, we are brought back to the question of regression and its control, the factors best suited to enlightening us about the relations between the transference and the countertransference. Oversimplifying somewhat, I would say that the transference is a pure product of regression, while the countertransference can be used only to the extent that it takes the form of an instrument in the service of the control of regression, while at the same time facilitating this regression and rendering it explicit. I believe this to be the case in all truly analytical treatments; indeed, this may perhaps be an excellent criterion for distinguishing between what is psychoanalysis and what is not.

The work on the patient's regression and its control is not the only foundation on which psychoanalysis rests, whatever the "schools" to which the practicing analysts may claim allegiance; yet, in a way, the others may be reduced to it (particularly if the analytical field is extended—perhaps rashly—to the psychoses). This foundation is one that is common to us all; it is therefore also the criterion of belonging to psychoanalysis.

At this point I must break with a certain ecumenicism.

The more clinical experience I accumulate of other forms of practice, the more convinced I become that we are not all psychoanalysts—at least, as understood by Freud. As regards the Kleinians and, of course, the so-called orthodox Freudians, I do not think this can be a problem: they all actually respect and facilitate regression, just as they all work on its control, whatever the technical variations introduced by particular groups.

Conversely, all my experience with analysands who have previously lain on the couches of Lacanians proves to me that the techniques of this school impede the development of free regression and exacerbate control to the point of making it "wild." In this way they eventually either abandon the patient or enslave him. In so doing, they depart from psychoanalysis.

I believe—indeed, I know—that some of them are becoming worried by this and are tending to return to a Freudian technique (as regards the duration and frequency of sessions and also the content of the analyst's interventions). I welcome this; but I believe that by so doing they are in danger of ceasing to be Lacanians. After all, the Lacanian theory contains its practice within itself; because of its *de facto* exclusion of repression and the Oedipus complex, as well as its failure to recognize the status of affects, it inevitably neglects both regression and its control in the treatment. If these are reintroduced in practice, albeit incognito, the theory is bound to be thereby changed.

Once again, therefore, it is found that whatever the speculative power of a theory, it is constrained and overdetermined by the practice it inspires, even as regards its objectives and methods.

8

Clinical Aims
and Process

Eustachio Portella Nunes, M.D.

Time past and time future
What might have been and what has been
Point to one end, which is always present
. . . In my beginning is my end.
                                        —T. S. Eliot

The notion of paradigm has an important role in the idea that we hold of the progress of science since Thomas Kuhn published his book *The Structure of Scientific Revolutions*. Kuhn shows that normal science, as we usually understand it, develops in a context that includes a whole constellation of beliefs, values, and techniques that function as models shared by researchers in their scientific practice, and oriented toward the refinement of this paradigm. Researchers tend to resolve the problems that appear, arranging them so as not to break the established norms. Difficulties arise when scientists discover new facts that do not fit into the accepted norms. The initial tendency is to reject them as not scientific or as metaphysical. However, when anomalies are important and new conceptions start to explain phenomena not understood until then, a crisis is generated. Scientific revolutions, following these postulations, would be preceded by periods of crisis in the sense that the present paradigm shows deficiencies in explaining new facts.

This occurred in psychiatry in the nineteenth century, which culminated in the Kraepelinian system. After having offered important services to a more rational psychiatric classification, it threatened to distort it with formal schemes and diagnostic preciseness in which there was no place for the whole reality of the patient.

Freud, from the very beginning, started to use the difficulties as challenges for new discoveries. His practice and theory broke off with the scientific dogmas of his time.

The discovery of the dynamic unconscious led to a necessary division in subjectivity. From then on, it is no more understood to be a unitary whole identified with consciousness under the mastery of reason but becomes a divided reality in two great systems: unconscious and preconscious/conscious, in a constant internal struggle in relation to which reason is a mere superficial aspect.

The theory of psychic trauma that had a profound repercussion on the initial discoveries of Breuer and Freud became, paradoxically, an obstacle for the development of analytic theory. The demand of a real traumatic event so that symptoms should appear, blocked the discovery of infantile sexuality and of the oedipal fantasies of all children. Freud was already aware that the dreams of neurotics did not differ from the dreams of normal people.

"The Project" was Freud's last try to conciliate what was revolutionary in his discoveries with the narrow frame of neuropsychiatry. Already in 1897 he had rejected the theory of early trauma according to his letters to Fliess. The publication of "The Interpretation of Dreams" represented an enormous step forward for psychoanalysis. There is a radical difference between the mode of exposition of "The Project" and Chapter VII of "The Interpretation." Instead of the energy postulated in "The Project" and the neurones that constitute its material support, in "The Interpretation of Dreams" he speaks of desire and of invested ideas. In Chapter VII, places are metaphorical and not anatomical.

The theory of resistance and repression, infantile sexuality, the method of interpretation of dreams, the psychopathology of everyday life constitute fundamental discoveries that offered a base for analytic theory. During the development of his work, Freud revised his own concepts and added new dimensions to technical procedures. There are phases that mark these changes.

Initially he exaggerated the importance of real traumatic events. With the rejection of this theory, he began to value, after 1897, the desires and urgencies of the internal world, of unconscious impulses and the way these impulses manifested themselves. At this time these unconscious desires were mainly of a sexual nature. In the twenties, with the introduction of the instincts of life and death, aggressive and sexual impulses were leveled in importance and with the structural conception that postulated the instances of id, ego, and superego, there is a return of external reality as one of the components of the superego. All these changes, made by Freud himself, gave the psychoanalytic paradigm an enormous opening where we can place the different "models": Kleinian, Lacanian, ego psychology, hermeneutic, classical Freudian, object relations, self psychology, or Kohutian. These are all models that try to fill the gaps left by Freud's paradigm. All are legitimate and even necessary because they stress certain aspects that in this way can be better studied.

It is possible to practice psychoanalysis following any of these models. What is there in common in any one of these trends that can characterize them as psychoanalysis?

Freud (1923) defined those who could count themselves psychoanalysts:

> The assumption that there are unconscious mental processes, the recognition of the theory of resistance and repression, the appreciation of the importance of sexuality and of the Oedipus complex—these constitute the principal subject-matter of psycho-analysis and the foundations of its theory. No one who cannot accept them all should count himself a psycho-analyst. [p. 247]

In "On the History of the Psycho-analytic Movement" Freud (1914a) stressed the recognition and management of resistance and transference:

> It may thus be said that the theory of psycho-analysis is an attempt to account for two striking and unexpected facts of observation which emerge whenever an attempt is made to trace the symptoms of a neurotic back to their sources in his past life: the facts of transference and of resistance. Any line of investigation which recognizes these two facts and takes them as the starting-point of its work has a right to call itself psycho-analysis, even though it arrives at results other than my own. [p. 16]

Considering this broad perspective, every dynamic psychotherapy would be psychoanalysis. Almost all analysts who also practice psychotherapy feel a different atmosphere compared with that of psychoanalysis. What is this difference? It would be extremely superficial to distinguish them only by the number of sessions per week. However, the smaller or longer interval between sessions is related to this difference. A long interval makes it easier for the patient to drown the session with external and defensive material. There are patients who do not enter into the atmosphere of analysis even with five sessions a week. With a few patients this is possible with three sessions. What is this atmosphere? It is characterized by the suspension of the privilege that we usually concede to the logic of secondary process. What characterizes an analytic session is the regression that permits analyst and patient to stand the confrontation between the secondary and the primary processes.

The analysand regresses by way of free association and talks about dreams, symptoms, *lapsus*—speaking of dead people as if they were alive, losing temporarily the dominance of secondary processes that normally is guided by the conventional and by what was learned.

Associations will be led by displacement or metonymy and by condensation or metaphor, with no respect for external reality. The analyst, in a state of free floating attention, takes that momentary "madness" seriously with the objective of permeating secondary process by primary process.

The instrument that he uses is interpretation. Through this he tries to translate the absurd narrative of the patient, transforming it into a more intelligible text. To understand is to make this substitution. What Freud wants is that the analysand, in possession of the meaning of that which was unknown, amplifies his field of consciousness and in this way, becomes more free. Spinoza teaches us the lesson: "We discover ourselves slaves, we understand our slavery.

We rediscover ourselves free in our understood need.'' This therapeutic regression leads to a movement of free affects that orient themselves to the person of the analyst, making the transference process easier. This climate is also difficult for the analyst, who can get involved in a countertransference movement.

It is important to be aware that during the whole analytic process there are resistances in the patient and in the analyst that oppose themselves to the climate of deeper truth in the relationship. In the measure in which the therapist's insecurity makes him need idealization, no interpretation can be made which would threaten this idealized image. In analysis, the permanent climate of idealization of the analyst indicates that important problems of the patient have not been touched.

Another resource of the patient consists in the constant and systematic degradation of the therapist, seeking to intimidate him and so paralyze the process of transformation that is the objective of any analytic process. These procedures work in relation to their needs that are often also those of the analyst. The negative therapeutic reaction is, very frequently, a *negative therapeutic relation*.

In many situations the interests of analysts block the appearance of truth in the relationship. Patients use their wish to escape from uncomfortable truths when they authorize analysts to use their own falsifications. To be true is for this reason, in our activity, not only an ethical duty, but also a technical imposition.

In psychoanalysis, the role of the analyst is to facilitate the upsurging of truth.

In ''Observations on Transference Love'' Freud (1915b) states:

My objection to this expedient is that psychoanalytic treatment is founded on truthfulness. In this fact lies a great part of its educative effect and its ethical value. It is dangerous to depart from this foundation. Anyone who has become saturated in the analytic technique will no longer be able to make use of the lies and pretences which a doctor normally finds unavoidable; and if, with the best intentions, he does attempt to do so, he is very likely to betray himself. Since we demand strict truthfulness from our patients, we jeopardize our whole authority if we let ourselves be caught out by them in a departure from the truth. [p. 164]

In Freud, truth and freedom are united in an irreversible way. The whole analytic method seeks to leave the patient free so that truth may appear.

In "The Ego and the Id," there is a footnote in which Freud (1923), mentioning the difficulties in dealing with the negative therapeutic reaction, states:

Perhaps it may depend, too, on whether the personality of the analyst allows of the patient's putting him in the place of his ego ideal, and this involves a temptation for the analyst to play the part of prophet, saviour and redeemer to the patient. Since the rules of analysis are diametrically opposed to the physician's making use of his personality in any such manner, it must be honestly confessed that here we have another limitation to the effectiveness of analysis; after all, analysis does not set out to make pathological reactions impossible, but to give the patient's ego *freedom* to decide one way or the other. [p. 50]

There is no unanimity as to the position the analyst should have in the context of treatment. The development of the work of Freud shows that the analyst cannot appear as a "real figure," precisely to allow the patient to grow progressively closer to him as a real person. The evolution of a true analysis is marked by an approximation that the patient makes to the real analyst.

When the analyst is a "real figure"—that is, someone who shows his own political, moral, or whatever tendencies to the analysand—these necessarily become dominant. This is a frequent cause of negative therapeutic reaction.

The analyst is more real to the patient, not when he tries to show himself as he really is, but when the patient is able to acquire a better capacity to see him. The technical attitude should not be that of showing oneself (blocking the projections of the patient) nor one of hiding oneself (blocking the development of a sense of reality). The analyst should only show an attitude of respect to the positions of the analysand (that does not mean approval or condemnation).

This attitude of suspension of the natural position that is adopted technically by the analyst is rather disquieting for the analysand because it makes it difficult for him to identify with this model.

For this reason, it assures great freedom to the patient; that is, it leads to greater truth in the relationship. Psychoanalysis, in its essence, is linked to this technique. This means that the analytic encounter is more free and allows greater truth precisely because it is not a spontaneous encounter. It is subjected to technical procedures that limit the dominating tendency of the analyst and the corresponding willingness of the patient to be dominated.

One of the important discoveries of Freud was to show the value of parapraxes. These errors that violate a conscious attitude, show the strength of the dynamic unconscious in determining human behavior. It is important to consider what one could call *continued parapraxes*. A whole action that reveals itself in disagreement with the conscious thought of the patient and that, in spite of this, controls his behavior for years, is shown in the following dialogue:

P—I have been in this marriage for nine years, having to stand this boring husband who devalues me. I was completely wrong when I married. I think I was taken in by my friends' good opinion of him. I believe he married me for my money.

A—It is possible that in this analytic marriage you feel you were cheated; you have already said that you looked me up because of my fame.

P—No, not with you. If I didn't like you I would go away. I don't have to stay with you.

A—But you feel you are obliged to stay with this husband?

P—I was wrong when I married. Doctor, so what am I going to do?

A—You did not marry; you are marrying. Every day you choose to be married.

P—But Doctor, marriage is not a game; I have two children.

A—During more than 3,000 days and two children you have been choosing to continue with this husband. Today you choose to go on with this marriage.

P—Do you think it's better for me to divorce?

A—With this question you show that you don't want the responsibility of another decision. I would have to decide for you. It's important that you assume the possibility of a separation even to be able better to evaluate your marriage. You are living your marriage as something that is imposed on you. You don't feel the responsibility of trying to make it better.

The discussion about the existence or not of the death instinct has been darkening a fundamental fact of the human being: *we are born to die*. Among those who either believe or do not in the death instinct there is a common denominator: we are all going to die. Each instant of life is a step toward death. Nevertheless, only intellectually do we admit the end. As Freud (1915c) says in "Thoughts on War and Death":

> To anyone who listened to us we were of course prepared to maintain that death was the necessary outcome of life, that everyone owes nature a death and must expect to pay the debt—in short, that death was natural, undeniable and unavoidable. In reality, however, we were accustomed to behave as if it were otherwise. We showed an unmistakable tendency to put death on one side, to eliminate it from life. [p. 289]

In analytic theory there is a clear distortion in relation to temporality. The origin of psychoanalysis was an effort to discover traumatic facts in very early childhood. Although Freud rejected this theory almost a century ago, an incessant and endless search goes on that prolongs analyses beyond any reasonable limit.

Rank, along this line, proposed the "birth trauma" as the first and never-overcome source of neurosis. Some professionals suggested the investigation of the intrauterine phase. Up to now, we have only considered one aspect of time: the relation of present to past. The dimension of the future is generally denied. This is strange because the theory of psychoanalysis is centered on desire, which also has an unequivocal link to the future. The reference to the future is sensed very precociously. One cannot even agree entirely with Freud when he speaks of the atemporality of the unconscious. In terms of physical time, the time of the scientific-technical project of man, this is true. In terms of a more primitive temporality, it is not. We all know that in dreams there is a sense of time that mixes past, present, and future that are superimposed, but not confounded. What doesn't exist in the unconscious is time in the sense given to it by physics.

We believe that the most important perspective opened by Freud, with the introduction of the death instinct, has been little used in clinical practice. We usually don't work on material about death that is brought to us daily. The real trauma of birth consists in throwing the human being to his death. Human anxiety is, fundamentally, an anticipation of this limit.

When we consider this, we can interpret clinical material linked to death in another horizon besides that of simple aggression:

P—Yesterday I dreamt that the airplane that you are going to travel in had an accident and no one survived.

A—The envy and jealousy that you have of my trip made you bring up the problem of our death.

P—Not our death; I wasn't on the plane.

A—You are on the airplane of life. Do you think one can only die on an airplane trip?

P—Are you angry with me? I am not guilty of my dreams.

A—Your dream pointed to one of the possibilities of my death. I might even die before I travel, or you might die before I go.

P—What's this talk about killing me? You are angry with me. I know I dreamt about the accident because you are going to travel with your wife and abandon me.

A—Yes, that seems to be the interpretation that you were waiting for. As it didn't come in this form, you are very upset.

P—I don't know why you are talking about death.

A—I wasn't the first one to speak of death. You spoke about the possibility of it.

P—These airplanes are very reliable. The other day I read an article that said that it's one of the safest means of transportation in the world.

A—You are trying to reassure us, saying that if we travel only on safe transportation we will never die.

P—I don't know what you are getting at. I don't want to kill you.

A—Our death doesn't depend on your wish. Even if you were against it, we are going to die one day. We are alive and so headed in the direction of this limit.

P—Do you know I'm afraid I am pregnant?

A—We shouldn't speak about death; let's deal with life.

The feeling that we are finite drives us away from our usual frivolity and throws us in to a life richer in meaning. In some people this happens almost by chance. After escaping from serious danger to their lives, these people change radically. They give life a new meaning.

The difficulty in accepting death has as a basic defense the fantasy of omnipotence and, in this way, there is a defense against accepting the daily pain of the limits of daily life. When the great limit is incorporated, we cannot allow the frequent postponements that lead us to make Methuselanic projects of life.

To incorporate this radical limit of the human being that he is born to die, although uncomfortable initially, makes it possible to live with greater vigor in the limited time we are given. To accept the end of all our possibilities makes us all more humble and responsible for our own lives and also more tolerant with other men, our mortal companions of imperfections.

As T. S. Eliot teaches us: "The only wisdom we can hope to acquire is the wisdom of humility: humility is endless. . . ."

In my end is my beginning.

9

An Analytic Break and Its Consequences

Max Hernández, M.D.

The aim of this chapter is to give an account of an analytical process that began just under two years ago and in which there was a five-month break at the end of the first year. The break had been arranged in advance, but its effect on the treatment was no less intense on that score. Perhaps because of this separation, the report falls into two parts, linked by some clinical reflections arising out of my thoughts around the time of the break in the treatment. To illustrate the course of the treatment, I give a narrative of the process, which includes some vignettes and two sessions, one before and the other after the break. The first part of the chapter discusses the sequence from evaluation to the break in the psychoanalysis, while the second reports on the initial period after its resumption. The process shows how the fear of accepting her womanhood and of embarking on motherhood, together with a feeling of abandonment, combined in a painful experience of physically felt exhaustion to constitute one of the fundamental aspects of the patient's analysis.

As Freud says in the "Studies on Hysteria" (Freud and

Breuer 1895), the clinical report is the appropriate form of communication for our scientific purposes. Merendino stresses the epistemological functions of clinical reports in making possible "the public communication of the research experience taking place within the analytic setting . . . [and allowing] . . . the formation and transmission of scientific (and therefore "public") knowledge about psychoanalysis" (Merendino 1985, p. 327). In this case we have a fragment of the early stages of a treatment. In my opinion, this illustrates certain aspects of the clinical work and can certainly be read from a variety of theoretical standpoints.

Mrs. L. telephoned me at the beginning of 1986. She wanted to embark on a psychoanalysis. I told her that I had no vacancies for the time being but that I could give her the name of a colleague. She replied that she had thought carefully about this and would rather wait. After a few months—a little sooner than the date I had given her—she rang again. She insisted that she wanted to have analysis with me. In retrospect, her insistence might have had something to do with the fact that I gave her an appointment. She came to the appointment dressed more correctly than smartly. She looked younger than her age (28). Although she was attractive, she did not give the impression that she knew it. She spoke deliberately and seriously, sometimes sadly, but was capable of smiling. She was successful in her work. She had married four years earlier, but this had not interfered with her activities; it seemed to me that she emphasized the word *activities*. Of course, she did not yet have children. She was more decided now. Perhaps she was afraid to have any.

She was the second of three children. Her childhood had not been happy but in fact sad. She had been born in a neighboring country, of which her father was a native and where he had worked. The family had moved to Lima when she was 3½ years old. Earlier, at the age of 2½, she had undergone surgery for a congenital heart malformation. She had been in hospital for two months. She felt that this had marked her for life. Physically, she had recovered. She was an excellent sportswoman. As a girl and in her teens, she had suffered many accidents, bumps, and falls. Some very sad things had happened to her during the course of her life, but she had learned to endure them. Her mother, with whom she had had a bad relationship, died when she was 19. After her mother's death, she went on living with her father. She had always felt abandoned and ill-treated, sometimes even furious. Her father had been affectionate but had often been away.

When, against all the odds, she had gone to university, she had felt very good. She had read economics. She had been a good student and taken part both in sports and in student politics. She had been involved in all the activities of the university. After graduating, she went abroad for a couple of years for a postgraduate course. Although she felt very homesick, the challenge of the studies had done her good. She got her degree and made valuable contacts. Her father remarried. On returning to Peru, she secured an interesting job, coordinating the reception and distribution of economic and material aid from abroad for the poor. She greatly enjoyed the work.

At a working meeting she met the man who was to become her husband. She fell in love although he had not yet formally separated from his wife. He was coming to the end of a relationship in which he had suffered. At first there had been complications, but love had proved stronger. Later they had been able to live together and finally to marry. At this point a certain tendency toward sadness and tears had intensified, or perhaps appeared for the first time. At any rate, she was happy. Her work was interesting but confronted her with difficult situations. She was indefatigable. Always alert, wherever she was needed she was there, especially when outside the office, she supervised the distribution of food in the poor districts. Her salary was very good; in addition, her work took her abroad at least once a year. For all these reasons, she felt herself privileged, but her contact with people from the needier population groups made her feel divided.

She referred once more to the difficulties with her mother and said how wounded, ill-treated, and misunderstood she felt. She repeated that she needed analysis. At the end of the interview, even before I had formed a diagnostic impression, I realized that Mrs. L. felt that the relationship with her mother had been disastrous and that her relations with her body were characterized by very great exigency that denied pain and suffering. I understood that she was suffering from very profound deprivations but nevertheless was acting as if she were surmounting them. Difficulties concerning her sexuality could be anticipated, although she had not made them explicit. The depressive tone was obvious.

I had no major reservations about her capacity for analysis. I told her that I could offer her an analysis of four sessions per week, but that in a year's time I would have to interrupt it for some months. She immediately accepted, saying that was all right. This was a clear example of her way of minimizing difficulties. I pointed this out to her, suggesting that she should think about it as it might be difficult for her. A few days later, she telephoned saying that she wished to begin.

In the first few sessions she referred constantly to her work. At this point I had a rather odd impression; I did not know whether it mattered to her that I should know how important her work was to her or whether she felt that it mattered to me that she should be efficient and productive. I decided to associate this point with her way of working in the analysis. Early on, in a session during the second week of treatment, Mrs. L. mentioned, as if by the way, that she had started smoking again after beginning her analysis. The wish to do so was particularly intense before the sessions.

For this reason she would arrive in her car a few minutes before the time of her appointment and light a cigarette. She knew that smoking was not doing her any good but could not help it. She even thought she could feel her heart palpitating.

In a session midway through the second month, she showed concern for my health and urged me to look after myself; nothing should happen to me. She could not stand it if I were to die. I pointed to her most vulnerable aspects, which made her attack when she felt herself to be in danger, thinking that she was doing so in her own defense. She told me that she did not dare to feel angry with me, that she did not notice that she felt annoyed; if such a feeling did exist, it must be very much inside and not conscious. In other words, she did not live (that is, experience) this feeling. Using her own words, I interpreted that she was not living it, but was killing it and killing me. That week there had been a holiday. She remembered that I had told her of the dates when I would be away and that she had accepted the arrangement. At the end of the session, she told me that when she had not seen my car parked in its usual place, she thought that I had left her in the lurch. At any rate, she rang the bell and when I opened the door she felt immense joy at the fact that I was there especially to look after her. I pointed out how she switched from fear at my disappearance to the astonished illusion of my presence, as if I had survived her unfelt violence.

After a few months of analysis, just before the long midyear holidays, she began a session by reporting that she had dreamed that I was dead. She had been in my consulting room with Elena, a friend of hers. She thought it would disturb me to find her there. Elena, who was working at my desk, told her that I had died of a heart attack. She was frightened. She was standing beside Elena and clasping her bag tightly. She remembered that Elena had taken part in a seminar with me and was now working abroad. Perhaps we wrote to each other. Her friend and I had something in common. That would make the separation more bearable. When I asked her what she associated with the heart attack, she told me that she knew that it was not definite that I had died. I referred to her jealousy. She remembered the nightmare her husband had had the previous night. She even listened to him talking in his sleep. He smoked a lot, and his parents both had heart complaints. Now that she smoked, she felt bad and got much more tired when doing gymnastics. He was on a strict diet, which she also followed because she felt like it.

She associated the bag with her work, when she left home with her case. She said that she had seen me with a case at that seminar and liked this image, but felt that papers and books might occupy a great deal of my time. She remembered that she had bought her case with her first salary; it was big, and even the computer would fit into it. As a friend had told her, she seemed to be a snail carrying its house on its back, in the case; she was like a nomad. I pointed out that, when she was confronted by her fears of abandonment and her aggression, she took her case and set about leaving covered with the shell of her work, taking her house on her back, feeling mistress of herself and capable of moving about wherever she wanted. After a short silence she told me that her father had bought each of her elder brothers a writing desk and that she had got hold of a little table only a third of the size of their desks. She now had a big, comfortable desk in her office. I pointed out the manic elements she was mobilizing as my absence approached: she had to carry her mind like a weight. I also told her that, fearing that I would throw her out, she was clinging to her defenses and to an inanimate, manageable object, as she imagined me to be clinging to my papers. I was afraid that I had not referred to her feeling of vulnerability or pointed out her most fragile and threatened aspects. I remained somewhat concerned.

After the holidays the patient was surprised that I had returned and had not abandoned her; the contrast between weekdays and the weekend showed how the accumulation of absences left a precipitate in the here and now. Her zeal for her work intensified as if she were driven by a systematic aggression turned against herself. The idea recurred in the analysis that she was a heavy burden on me: insistent, demanding, and tedious. I could not detect any of these feelings in the countertransference register. I could see that Mrs. L. thought I had accepted her as a patient in the same way as she committed herself to her work: as a moral obligation.

In one session she told me of her discovery of a novel dimension. She had never been able to imagine that she was not a burden on me, but this occasion had been different. On leaving the consulting room on the previous day, it seemed to her that I had smiled when I said goodbye. This had amazed her. She thought about it a lot and became sad when she had realized that in her most important relationships she had been a burden on all the people around her. The analytical relationship seemed different to her. She felt that, the previous weekend, she had been waiting calmly, without getting depressed or agitated. She felt that her depression had "lightened." Just after a one-week break in the analysis, when I made a comment that linked the current situation with something that had happened earlier in the analysis, she had again been surprised. It seemed incredible to her that I should remember what she had told me; she felt cared for. The changes reported by Mrs. L. were manifested in a modification of her attitudes; however, it was difficult for me to understand why they had occurred. At one point she mentioned an interpretation that had helped her to reduce her smoking by 90 percent. I could not precisely remember any interpretation to this effect. She also asserted that the analysis was for life; she felt that I was caring for her and that she was killing herself.

During a session shortly before the end of the year and the Christmas holidays, she said that it would not be long before the analysis was interrupted for several months and I went away. She had a present for me but did not dare to give it to me "so as not to be a burden on you." It was a very big diary she had received from Europe, which might be extremely useful to me; it was big and fine. Without any prompting from me, she said that the diary had to do with time, that perhaps she would like me to take it with me. I interpreted that she wanted to leave me a tangible sign that would remind me of her, like a diary, that would weigh me down slightly and remind me that she needed me. It was as if, after having made herself feel very light, she was resuming her weight as a patient. I did not make any connections between Christmas, birth, and the calendar.

With one month to go before the break in the analysis, she was very sad in a session after the weekend. The weekend or even a week without analysis was one thing, but several months was another. At that point the telephone rang. The patient began to cry. She said I would be going away very soon now. That month she felt depressed and occasionally had headaches. The craving to smoke was very intense, but she could control it. She felt that everything related to my imminent absence. Perhaps it would be worse than she had thought. She had a dream in which she was pregnant and asked the nurse at the clinic whether the amniotic fluid was all right. Earlier she had had a short menstrual period, lasting only a day. She thought she was in no state to stand a pregnancy. She was very turned in on herself. She felt it more and more urgent to come to her sessions.

The tree she could see through the window seemed to her to be smaller, just as it had appeared when she had seen it on coming into the building. She was afraid that the relationship would end. It was something very important that might go away. I commented that objects got smaller before the separation. She then remembered another fragment of the dream or perhaps of a different dream. She was beside the tree and I was going to take a photograph of her with my camera. She thought of her clothes. She did not have many dresses, particularly smart dresses, that she could wear to weddings or special occasions. She had also dreamed, a day earlier, that she was in a clothes shop at the Camino Real Shopping Centre. She was looking for some costumes (*conjuntos*), but the ones she liked were very expensive. I told her that it cost her a lot to form a *conjunto*.[1] The pain and sadness at the separation, the headache, the anxiety about pregnancy, and her wish to dress up as if to go to a wedding converged in this dream in which she appealed to the analyst out of her suffering, out of her feeling of impossibility and out of her wish to be attractive. She again thought about my health. The needier she felt, the more afraid she was about what her unconscious aggression might have brought about in me. Toward the end of the session she said she thought the only way to

---

[1]A play on words: *conjunto* can mean either "a costume" or "a whole."

be accepted was by not being a woman. Mrs. L. was stuck: it was very difficult for her to accept any kind aspect of her mother, as well as the sexual aspects of her father.

I shall now give a comprehensive account of the Friday session in the same week.

Mrs. L. arrived punctually. She lay down on the couch and began to speak:

P—I have been thinking about how hard it is for me to accept myself as a woman. . . .

I do not know what the associations with the tree mean. I have been looking at it from the waiting room and can now see it from here. Well, what I thought is that I can see a nest which I did not see yesterday. And it is quite a big nest. Either it wasn't there or I didn't see it. . . .

P—As you said, it is difficult for me . . . I remember the games I played with my brothers. They always laid down their conditions. I could never play at dolls or tea parties; it had to be wars or spaceships or soldiers. I have a photo of me in a go-cart; I could drive well. When I played with dolls I did so by myself; if they came, they would treat them badly. I had a little baby doll called Carlitos. He used to stretch out; he looked like a real little child. My brother J threw him out of a second-floor window. It was very sad for me. I have just remembered something else that hurts me. They called me Pecosa ["freckled"]. I wanted them to call me by my proper name. They used to call me Pecosa-Petosa, meaning *apestosa* [stinker]. How it annoyed me. My mother used to call me by the pet name of Peque or Pequitas. I also had another doll, Lili, which I still have today; they tied Lili up and put her in the shower. I had yet another one, a rag doll that I used to take everywhere. They also threw him out of the car window and I never saw him again. When I told my mother, she said why had I not told her when it happened; when we went back, he was no longer there. I was very upset.

160

A—Now that you have been able to see a nest, you are afraid that my trip will put you at risk and perhaps you feel that, like your brothers, I will interfere by my absence not only with the nest you might find here but also with the capacity for nesting that you can develop.

P—Hmmm . . . I had so many new toys . . . she kept them. What was she waiting for; did she want to keep them for her grandchildren? Once we were staying with my great-aunt. It was very nice, she was very good. We formed a club; they made a rule, "No women allowed," but I went in and played with them just the same. She sent me to the ballet and would not let me play "cops and robbers"[2] in the club any more, or swim; when I got home very tired and sweaty or perhaps with a bump, a scratch, or a wound, she would tell me off. Eventually I left the ballet, to oppose her or to assert myself. Now I like the ballet very much, it is very nice, there is so much grace in the movements. At the time this escaped me. I also escaped from school, from the "nun-mother" warden.[3] I always went back; I only pretended to escape. Once I heard that the nun was coming; to let my friends know, I pressed my forehead against the spikes on the barbed wire fence and dirtied my dress with drops of blood; I was afraid to go back.

A—Afraid of the "nun-warden"—who looks after you and also keeps watch.

P—A friend I had at the time loved to play men's games. She ended up mad. . . . I used to play with her. My mother said I had driven her mad by asking her for a rope and a gun.

A—Mad?

P—Nothing occurs to me. . . . Nothing comes into my mind.

Yesterday I was thinking that I had never made myself smart to attract anyone. I was thinking of my convenience, my

---

[2]In Spanish, *celador* means warden or one who is jealous.
[3]A play on words: *madre* can mean either *mother* or *nun*.

clipped-together jeans . . . That way it was easier to wash them. My clipped-together hem and my Andean bag . . . That way I was happy. Now I make myself more presentable, but I am afraid that the ladies in the food distribution section and my woman friends on the left criticize me.

A—Like the "nun-warden" mother?

P—. . . I'm not thinking anything. . . . Now I am ashamed. I have remembered what I feel when people say I am pretty. This always makes me feel very ashamed. Once at university, a super-rightist friend told me: "Little Inés, the communists have brain-washed you, you cannot go about like this and dress this way; you must make yourself presentable." I didn't realize. I thought I was proselytizing. He told me: "Remember that you are a woman" . . . I believe I did not notice.

A—That you were a woman.

P—Right. Now I dress differently. I feel that they criticize me . . . I have not changed my way of thinking. Two of my female colleagues at the office look at me very critically.

A—It is as if you were saying you have not changed your way of thinking, but only of dressing.

P—Yes . . . when I dress well . . . I feel so vulnerable . . . for my father, particularly, being a woman meant not to exist, being anonymous.

A—It is as if, when you realize that you are a woman and I am a man, you feel that I am going to plunge you into anonymity, especially now that the session is coming to an end. . . .

The separation anxiety, feeling of vulnerability, and fear of femininity appear clearly in this session. The interplay between the transference and the appeal to the analyst to intervene establishes a counterpoint between repetition and possible openness to change. This counterpoint constitutes the fundamental aspect of this stage in the treatment.

The sessions prior to the five-month separation reveal a material biased explicitly toward feelings of abandonment. The patient was writing a paper on the economic situation of the country, its impact on the poor sections of the population and the trends of political, social, and urban violence. I pointed out to her that it was as if she were afraid that the privation to which she felt exposed because of the analyst's absence and the lack of analysis might unleash enormous violence, which worried her and which she did not know how to express. She mentioned a fall she had had as a little girl, when somebody had pushed her. She had been greatly affected by a film about a boy lost in the jungle who had been rescued by a tribe of cannibals. She also referred to her consultations with the gynecologist and her irregular ovulation.

During this period I was acutely aware of the difficulties the patient might have during my absence. Mrs. L. experienced the separation not only as an abandonment but also as a violent push giving rise to a damaging and traumatic fall. This explained her tendency to have accidents, but I think that it was only then that I was able to become clearly conscious of her feeling of fragility and also of the violence with which her internal objects—if we may use the term—acted on her, giving rise to traumatic and painful feelings of helplessness. I often remembered her heart operation and thought of the effects it might have had on her, as if it had constituted an interruption in her very existence. In these circumstances, she was clearly not prepared to withstand a pregnancy. If the analyst was unable to act as a container and provide a holding for her, Mrs. L. had few resources that she could mobilize beyond a compensatory narcissistic cathexis.

The analysis resumed after five months. Early on the

Monday morning, she telephoned me to ask if I could change her time on Tuesday as she had swimming practice as the schedule for the week had been changed. I answered that I could not manage it, and she said she would come anyway.

The patient arrived, smiled, and gripped my hand tightly and warmly. She lay down on the couch and immediately began to speak.

P—When I came I thought how near the consulting room is to my house. Hmmm, I see you have new curtains. . . . In the waiting room I felt like crying . . . it was an intense feeling . . . very intense.

During these last few months I have cut off all my feelings . . . everything I felt in myself I had cut off . . . Like a parcel, I did not want to feel anything painful . . . As the date of your return approached, I began to feel something . . . Now everything is opening up and pouring out.

I do not want to feel such a need for you . . . I wanted to write to you . . . I actually did write to you . . . I even found out where I could send the letter . . . I didn't do so because I did not want to be a burdensome patient.

Now I am feeling a lot . . . I am reconnecting with my feelings . . . You travel a lot . . . too much . . . This has only just come up . . .

I have a magazine with a photograph of you . . . At first I looked at it . . . all the time . . . I decided not to do so any more . . . It didn't seem right to me. I don't want you to travel again . . . I want you not to go away for so long . . . Please . . . no . . .

I thought of not coming today . . . I wanted to "throw you a dead dog,"[4] but I could not, it was impossible . . . What am

---

[4]Literal translation of Spanish expression meaning "I wanted to stand you up."

I going to do . . . I feel that I am very fond of you.

At a meeting a couple of months ago I tried to sound out people who knew you . . . I wanted to find out some details of your whereabouts. They said you had a generous grant . . . one of those that lets you go about as you please . . . I said you were doing important things . . . writing.

A—As if you felt that this was more important than you are. You make out that I am somebody important while you are left behind as a suffering, heavy parcel which I would like to cut myself off from and from which you cut yourself off so as to be able to bear the separation.

P—I heard them say . . . that you prefer to do research . . . to write . . . I heard you were leaving the country . . . to teach. This made me very afraid.

A—That is why you are afraid to express your grief and pain to me.

P—It is what I need . . . it is very important for me.

A—I have the impression that the break has made you feel that all this is so precarious that you cannot allow yourself to feel anger . . . You cannot return the dead dog you are carrying around to me without mourning for it. The dead dog you feel they threw away, with which you have identified.

P—(Weeping bitterly) . . . That's right . . . I feel like a dead dog . . . This is obliterating me, killing my capabilities . . . my desire to live. These last few days I thought I wanted to do things . . . I deploy incredible tenacity, will power, and effort, but everything is exhausted.

A—As if the effort you deployed while I was away had exhausted you . . . As if the process begun in the analysis had been overwhelmed by the weight of my absence . . . As if some early experience that demanded all your strength had been repeated.

P—I am afraid . . . I feel that I am opening up the hatches . . . if you go away again, I shall sink . . . I must have firm ground under my feet. I have just finished drawing up a project with which I hope to get some funding. I did not think

I had succeeded. I discussed it with an economist who was my teacher. He told me it was fragmented and lacked unity. That is how I feel, living in parcels. Of course, the project was approved right away, but my teacher, is right . . . I do not know what fear I have to integrate.

A—To integrate?

P—Yes . . . I cannot process the whole thing. When the time comes for me to begin the work, I find an excuse, I stop and go away. It isn't laziness. It is obviously a problem. But it is not like that in my practical work. There I am efficient and I tackle the urgent problems. We have set up an organization but it is still fragile. When I am away and not supervising activities, they get held up. Sometimes I even feel that what we have built up might collapse. It is impossible to resolve in just a few months a situation of endemic privation and poverty . . . for people who are only just surviving.

A—It is impossible to do a thorough job in just a few months, to process the whole thing.

P—Phew . . . you are telling me it is as if I were referring to the analysis . . . I don't know . . . I feel ashamed . . .

One of the important agreements runs out at the end of the year and there is no certainty that we can refinance it . . . If we do not succeed, it will be difficult . . . very difficult (changing her affective tone), but perhaps we shall be able to do enough.

A—At the cost of a tremendous effort to survive.

P—I also thought that the money I get paid to administer this project represents an important part of my income . . . it would affect me . . . I thought I might not be able to pay for my analysis . . . that would screw me up . . .

A—It is as if you were telling me that you have the will and the desire to be analyzed but you feel that you might lack the objective conditions . . .

P—I hope it will not be like that . . . You know . . . my aunt told me that they put my mother to sleep after she gave birth to me . . . and she didn't breast feed me . . . You know, I will not do that to my children . . . it would be unfair.

166

A—You must feel that you had only just begun your analysis when I went away and deprived you of all sustenance.

P—But I value what you have given me . . . I have been able to work during these months . . . I also thought . . . of myself . . . of my childhood . . . of you . . . I asked my father and my aunt how things were when I was small . . . I asked about the operation . . . we were living in the provinces and their diagnosis of me was wrong . . . my father did not accept it . . . he brought me to the capital . . . there they diagnosed me correctly and I was operated on by Dr. P., a very good specialist . . . before I had the operation I used to get very tired; he then recommended me to swim . . . that is why I learned at such an early age . . . Today I am swimming as I did when I was a little girl.

A—You told me that you gave up your swimming lesson to come here today.

P—Swimming, that does not matter to me . . . This is more important than swimming . . . in the swimming pool I feel good . . . it was a long time since I had last done it, but I have started doing things again that I have not done for a long time. Today I came on my bicycle . . . I cycle to lots of places . . . In this terrible country it is nice to do that . . . the way here is very beautiful . . . On the way I met a girl who was my private student when she was preparing to go to university. She called out to me . . . she looked very well . . . we spoke for a few minutes and she told me that she remembered me fondly, that she had managed to get into the university and that I had taught her a lot, not only academically but also about life . . .

At this point the session ended.

At the end of the session I noticed that I had been pleased to see her and that, when she had mentioned the provincial doctor's incorrect diagnosis, I had felt put on the spot. I also thought that I had intervened actively—perhaps excessively so. Nevertheless, toward the end of the session

I felt calm and thought that there was in Mrs. L. a capacity to regain contact with her good experiences; in spite of the difficulties of the separation there seemed to be an ability to maintain the continuity of the relationship.

The next sessions contained references to gratifying meetings. For instance, she mentioned that she had met the person who made her up on her wedding day, with whom she later became friends. She taught her to use makeup, which she had never used before. In another session, she said that she had rung the consulting room during the weekend because she was feeling very sad and depressed. She had seen an old, very sweet and tender boyfriend who read poems to her. Her period was late; she thought she might be pregnant and was very frightened. She had begun to have doubts about her partner, and when her period came she felt relieved but at the same time dried up and empty. She began to talk about her sexual difficulties. At present, the fear of pregnancy is reappearing powerfully.

CONCLUSION

This is a clinical report of an analytic process which began under two years ago and in which there was a five-month break at the end of the first year. The break had been discussed in advance, but its effect on the treatment was no less intense on that score. The separation was experienced through feelings of pain with a heavy bodily quality, by which the patient evoked the somatic memories of a heart operation she had when she was a baby. The analytic process seems to be allowing her to symbolize her painful experiences of separation and loss as well as the traumatic effects of her heart surgery.

10

The Centrality of the Oedipus Complex

Michael Feldman, M.D.

INTRODUCTION

In 1920 Freud wrote: "It has justly been said that the Oedipus complex is the nuclear complex of the neuroses, and constitutes the essential part of their content . . . With the progress of psycho-analytic studies the importance of the Oedipus complex has become more and more clearly evident . . ." (Freud 1905, p. 226).[1] We have indeed come to share an understanding that the pattern of introjections and identifications based on oedipal fantasies constitutes a crucial element in the development of the personality and in the manifestations of pathology.

In our analytic work we have learned to focus on the way in which the conscious and unconscious elements of the Oedipus complex are lived out in the transference. We are familiar with the oedipal fantasies that involve representations of the patient's primary objects that are clearly differentiated from one another, relating to each other and

---

[1]Three essays on the theory of sexuality. *S.E.* 7 (footnote added in 1920).

to the patient himself in ways that involve conflict, jealousy, and guilt. Many analysts have, in addition, come to recognize the presence of earlier, more primitive versions of the oedipal fantasies, and here the primary objects are often represented in a damaged state, not always differentiated from one another, and often felt to be very threatening.

The way in which fantasies, conflicts, and anxieties, particularly those connected with primitive versions of the Oedipus complex are worked through in the transference affects the patient's tendency to move toward, or away from, greater psychic integration. This will be reflected in many ways, including his capacity to recognize and tolerate his own impulses and needs, and the pain and conflict to which these give rise. It will also be manifested in the extent to which he is able to use his mind for understanding and for creative thinking.

In this chapter I will present material that emerged six months before the end of a long analysis of a single woman in her mid-forties, tracing how the patient's conscious perceptions of her parents and her unconscious fantasies about them influenced what was experienced and enacted in the transference. When it was possible to tolerate and interpret the expression of primitive and disturbing versions of the oedipal configuration in the session, the patient's longings, jealousy, and sexual wishes indicative of a more mature Oedipus complex became more readily available, this change being manifested in a different quality to the transference and in the way in which the patient was able to integrate and use her own intellectual and emotional resources.

The clinical themes addressed in this chapter had, of course, been worked on in many different ways during the course of the analysis. Any movement forward was usually followed by long periods of silence, immobility, or destructive attacks on my work and her own understanding. In the recent months she had seemed more available and more communicative, and in the sessions I am going to describe, I was allowed a much clearer picture of the anxieties, conflicts, and pain that beset her.

To some extent, the slowness and difficulty in this analysis could be understood as resulting from the patient's internalization of, and identification with, primitive and damaged versions of her parents individually and as a couple. In particular, she conveyed the experience of them as both damaged and hostile toward any form of vitality and creativity. She defended herself against the persecutory anxieties arising from these fantasies either by identifying with such figures or by splitting off and disowning the qualities that they embodied.

Both types of defense gave rise to a serious impoverishment in the quality of her thinking and her emotional life. In the analytic situation this led to serious anxieties connected both with the experience and expression of her thoughts and feelings, and with her fears about the consequences of any kind of interaction with her analyst. The partial elucidation and working through of these fantasies and anxieties, and the way in which they were mobilized in the transference, enabled the patient to move toward a greater degree of psychic integration. In the period of the analysis that I will describe, this was reflected in the way she was, at times, able to be more open to the analytic work, and could allow herself to experience the analyst more directly as a helpful figure, whom she would miss. There seemed to be a greater capacity for thinking and understanding, and she seemed able to give more space in her mind to hopes and desires, even though these were accompanied by intense pain and regret.

HISTORY AND BACKGROUND

The patient is the younger daughter of hard-working professional parents. Her mother has emerged as an anxious, defensive woman who manages to cope by imposing a harsh and rigid control on herself and others. The patient was regarded as a very "good" child, which meant, for example, that as an infant she could be left in a room and would not have moved when mother returned. In the course of the analysis it became clear to her how much this must have been an expression of her anxious concern not to challenge or disrupt her mother's precarious equilibrium.

Her sister, three years older, seems to have been a more difficult and troublesome child. She is married and has three children, but her relationship with her parents is not a good one, and she sounds like a troubled person. Within the family, special criticism has always been reserved for the patient's cousin Janet, who lived with them when she was 3 or 4, while her own mother was ill. The complaint was that she was so lively and messy, always moving about, looking in cupboards, and creating disorder. The family broke off contact with Janet's family, as they had done with other relatives or acquaintances, when they had been hurt or offended by some slight or an unfavorable comment. The notion that there could be a discussion or reconciliation was inconceivable.

The patient shared some interests with her father, and there were occasionally hints of an alliance between them, but any contact was more likely to lead to a furious argument, or long, injured, and resentful silence. The atmosphere within the family seems to have been bleak and cold, with little sympathy, affection, or understanding. The patient was, however, close to her grandmother, to whom she could tentatively turn for support, although she was always very aware that her mother felt threatened by their relationship. Grandmother died when the patient was 8, and she was sent off to boarding school very soon afterward. She functioned well academically, and in some ways I believe she felt relieved to be away from home, although she was very lonely.

She is highly intelligent, with a sharp perceptiveness and wit, which she can use in a very cutting way. She is successful at her work, which demands technical knowledge and skill, and she has, during the period of her analysis, risen in her field and now earns a high salary.

She came into analysis when she encountered recurrent difficulties in her relationships, especially with men, where she would easily become upset, angry, and frightened, particularly when there was a threat of intimacy. This gave rise to frigidity, an intense feeling of panic, and the need to get away. There was an almost delusional terror of becoming pregnant. There were a variety of other claustrophobic and agoraphobic symptoms and psychosomatic problems.

In the course of the analysis there have been important changes. The agoraphobic and psychosomatic problems have become much less troublesome or disappeared completely, and she has been able to develop relationships with men that have been satisfactory from the sexual point of view, but she has, until fairly recently, felt the need to protect herself against the development of too great intimacy or dependency by restricting the contact. There has been a marked lessening in the panic associated with the thought of pregnancy, and she no longer reacts to the idea with the conviction that she would immediately and un-questioningly abort any fetus. She has more frequently found herself encountering painful feelings of longing and regret about not having found a partner and not having had children.

Her behavior in the analysis has followed a very stereo-typed pattern, and has changed only very slowly. For long periods she would arrive late, by a fixed amount, not wishing to appear too eager or too needy, and regarded any patient she saw hurrying to his or her session with scorn and contempt. On the other hand, she does not wish to frustrate or provoke me too far, and she monitored my reaction to her lateness very carefully. She avoids any greeting or eye contact, while remaining acutely sensitive to any changes in the analytic setting or in the condition of her analyst.

The analysis has been characterized by her silence and her need to defend herself, both against the analyst and the analytic process and against her own dreams, thoughts, and feelings. In an early session she had a terrifying dream of a monstrous figure breaking through the hedge in their garden at home. It became clear from her associations that this figure was linked with her mother, and I came to understand this as representing a very primitive fear of invasion which her anxious rigidity attempted to defend her against.

She was sometimes completely silent for several days, and when she did eventually speak it often had a defensive tortuosity that required very close attention but actually gave me little direct access to anything real and alive. She would give very little response to my interpretations, except when she felt I had misunderstood something or had gotten something wrong. Then she showed no difficulty in engaging me in an argument in which she might become quite excited, but which usually felt sterile.

When she did bring material that felt more alive, she relied on me to listen carefully, think about it, and say something to her that indicated that I had done so. She hardly ever seemed willing to think about the issues herself, and the two of us rarely seemed able to look at anything together. Most commonly, once she felt she had got something across to me, and somehow made it my responsibility, she would withdraw into silence. It was made clear to me over and over again with this patient that the straightforward interpretation of the material that she brought, its links with her history and its symbolic content, was unlikely to lead anywhere. It was only when I tried to address as closely as I could her experience in the transference, and put into words what I thought was being enacted between us, that any movement occurred. These issues have, of course, been repeatedly addressed in the analysis, and there has been slow but significant progress. She is more often able to engage in the analytic work, and less prone to attack my efforts or turn a cruel destructiveness on herself and her own capacities. However, any progress was very often followed by long periods of withdrawal and the undermining of what had been achieved. It had been immensely important to her that I had not given up, but the question of the amount of further progress it was reasonable to expect arose in both our minds and began to be discussed.

Six months prior to the period under discussion I decided to set a termination date, a year ahead. The patient's reaction was very complex but contained a great deal of relief. She did not seem to feel this was primarily an aggressive or a despairing reaction on my part. On the contrary, she felt relieved that I had been able to think it through with her, make the decision, and give her adequate warning, rather than either feeling trapped and paralyzed in an endless analysis or making a precipitate move to escape. For the first few months, however, she seemed to become more silent and unresponsive, but then slowly softened, strengthened, and became more available, appearing willing to risk greater contact with her internal world and with her analyst.

CLINICAL MATERIAL

In the first session after a holiday she arrived a few minutes late, and began speaking in a way that sounded dramatic and prepared. "I dreamt that you had murdered some-one," she said. She continued, "At first it was very vague, just that someone had been murdered, but I had the idea that there might be a connection with you." She said there was some evidence, such as the fact that I was knitting, and there was some way in which this confirmed that it had been me. She explained that she felt uncomfortable while still dreaming because she knew it would be difficult to return to the analysis and face me, and tell me that she knew.

"Then we were in my parents' house. You were there, and the police were there, investigating the murder. I took the senior policeman aside and said in a rather urgent way, 'I have documentary proof upstairs,' and went to fetch it. However, I realized that you would have witnessed me talking to the policeman, you would know that I had proof, and this would make you want to get rid of me—murder me, or poison me.''

The patient went on to describe an event that had occurred while her elderly parents had been staying with her over the holidays. Her sister Angela had come over one day with her son Roger. "Father had a bath, and then couldn't get out of the bath. Part of the tap broke off, so he had nothing to pull himself up with. Mother couldn't manage to help him out. Luckily Roger was there, because if it had just been myself and Angela, he would have waited hours and hours before he would have let us help him.''

She went on: "Angela recalled something she remembered vividly from when she was a child. Father was in the bath and called mother to come and talk to him about something. She came in, and Angela wandered in with mother. Father wasn't aware she was there at first, and went on talking, but when he realized she was there, he shouted 'Get out!' in a very angry, nasty way.'' The patient then emphasized her reaction to the picture her sister had painted by saying, "I didn't want to know about that, I wished she hadn't told me.'' The patient was then silent and expectant.

I interpreted that although it had been vague in the dream, I had become identified as the murderer. This conveyed something of her experience of being expelled during the holiday, and shortly, from the analysis. I added that by contrast once she was back in the session with me, she seemed to use me more as the policeman, trying to bring the situation to my attention, offering to produce evidence from upstairs. It seemed important that I should be experienced as an ally, in order to fend off any attack which might be provoked by her accusations arising out of her knowledge of the bad and neglectful aspects of myself (which were closely linked to things she found so difficult in her mother and father).

I should like to interrupt the narrative of the session at this point, to consider more closely the issues that had been raised. I believe we have, in this material, different versions of the patient's relationship to the oedipal situation, both past and present, that derive from different levels of psychic organization. The holiday break, particularly coming as it did not long before the end of the analysis, had evidently revived the experience of being excluded and abandoned by the oedipal couple.

The scene between her parents in the bathroom, into which their elder daughter (with whom the patient is identified) wanders, can of course be regarded as a representation of the primal scene from which the patient is excluded both by her actual parents and by her analyst during his holiday. The dream, and the rest of the material produced in this session, gives us information about the underlying fantasies that reflect the nature of her primary objects, and the nature of the intercourse between them.

The experience of exclusion was not only a source of intense pain, but provoked the patient's hatred and murderousness toward the couple. The defensive projection of this into her objects was partly responsible for the production of the fearful situation represented in her dream.

Her opening remark drew attention to the existence of a murderer. At first I seemed connected with this figure, although my identity in the dream was complex and ambiguous, being linked with her mother (who used to knit) as well as her father. However, while there evidently were times during the holiday break when I had been experienced as a murderer, the rather prepared way in which she referred to this at the start of the session, and the atmosphere that subsequently prevailed, suggested that the view of her analyst as hostile or dangerous was split off and not available to her at this point. On the contrary, during this session she did not seem so frightened of describing her observations to me, and was able both to experience and to use me more as the policeman in the dream to whom she turned, and who was expected to help her to deal with the frightening fantasies connected with the actual parental couple, and those fantasies relating to the analyst that were projected into it.

It seemed important in my interpretations to be guided mainly by what I felt to be the predominant quality of the patient's current experience in the transference. I had little doubt that there would be times when the more frightening, violent, and disturbing aspects of the transference were much more available.

The material suggested that the patient experienced the danger arising not only from the representation of her primary objects as powerful and threatening, but the more serious and worrying threat derived from her perception of them as damaged, like the disabled and helpless father who was prepared to suffer for hours rather than let himself be helped by his daughters, who might directly observe his nakedness and vulnerability. It is as if there is something about her objects and their relationship that they cannot bear to have discovered and are willing to go to any lengths—even murder—to protect.

I am suggesting that when we extend the concept of the Oedipus complex to include the expression of early and primitive fantasies about the nature and interaction of the parental couple, we encounter features of these objects— including their vulnerable and damaged state—that are more frightening and more damaging than fantasies of apparently powerful, successful parental sexuality, and these consequently constitute a more serious threat to the discovery of psychic truth.

On the one hand, my patient identifies herself with these figures, in her fear and hatred of knowledge (as when she said, with force, that she wished her sister had not told her about the incident with the parents). On the other hand, she brings into the analysis an urge to discover the truth about the nature of her internal (and external) objects, and her relationship to them, however frightening and disturbing such as exploration might be. In the next part of the session it became increasingly clear that the patient was using me as a policeman to whom she turned in the hope of getting help to discover and face very difficult issues.

Following the interpretation I had made about her need to experience and use me as the policeman to whom she could turn for support, to fend off the consequences of her discovery of aspects of her analyst, or her parents, which she found so threatening, the patient paused for a while and then said that a couple of hours before her parents had left, her mother was writing a check to repay my patient for some expenses during their visit. Mother had asked, "Shall I write 'F' or 'F.I.N'?" (the patient's initials). Father overheard and said, jokingly, "The end of the Bs" (their surname). The patient commented bitterly that it had taken him a long time to make the connection with her initials; she herself had made it many years ago. Her father then turned to mother and asked, "Have you told her about Janet?" (As I have mentioned before in her history, Janet was a cousin who had lived with the family for a year, before the patient was born, while her own mother was ill. She had always been criticized by the patient's mother for being lively and adventurous, and adversely compared with the patient, who had fit in so well.)

Mother then told her that Janet had died. The contact with Janet and her side of the family had been severed for a number of years, and they had only read about her death in the local paper. The notice in the paper hadn't mentioned the cause of death, but had referred to a husband and child, which she hadn't known about.

Her parents felt that they couldn't contact Janet's family; they didn't feel it was appropriate. It would have been hypocritical, since they had not been in touch for years. My patient had only recently understood that her parents had fallen out with Janet's mother when they discovered that she had criticized their treatment of Janet, behind their backs.

I interpreted that she seemed to be recognizing more clearly how vulnerable her parents were, unable to face difficult issues, and how strongly they reacted to anyone else discovering or saying anything about them. While there were ways in which she also felt very threatened by any knowledge, she also communicated a desire for help in discovering the truth, even though this felt like a dangerous exposure and betrayal of her parents and some aspects of herself.

The patient remained silent and still for the remaining 15 minutes of the session.

The fearful and disturbing fantasies connected with the parental couple, which had been provoked by the experience of exclusion and abandonment (both by her analyst and her parents) and which were reflected in the content of her dream, were then reinforced not only by the analyst's long absence, but also by what she encountered in relation to her parents—in her sister's vivid description of them, and more alarmingly in what she saw in their relationship to Janet and her death. This seemed to confirm a view of them as turning on Janet (representing a more healthy, lively, and creative side of herself) in a murderous fashion.

What I am suggesting, in other words, is that although the damaged and vengeful qualities of the oedipal figures in these fantasies may primarily reflect the patient's jealous and envious attacks on the creative couple, and the projection of her own envy and hatred into them, they may be reinforced by her actual experiences and perceptions of her parents, or, at times, of her analyst.

Her panic at facing her own psychic reality, which has been such a feature of the analysis, is partly based on her identification with such vulnerable parental objects, partly on the intolerable guilt and fear associated with their condition, and partly on the belief that what she encounters in reality is likely to reinforce, rather than disconfirm, her beliefs about the nature of her objects.

I believe that during her childhood the patient had attempted to cope with the anxieties associated with such fantasies by fitting in, being the very still child who showed no sign of curiosity. By this means she hoped both to protect their vulnerability and to avoid provoking the vengeful and castrating couple. By contrast, her cousin Janet had not been willing to fit in; she was lively and adventurous, constituting a threat to the precarious equilibrium within the family. The way in which the reference to Janet's death emerged, immediately following her father's comment about the last of the Bs, seemed to confirm her belief that any manifestation of sexuality and creativity (the reference to Janet's husband and child) was linked with exclusion and death.

These fantasies have been powerfully present in the

analysis, influencing her experience of the analyst, the way she has been able to use interpretations, and her own capacity for thinking and understanding. While she has become more able to use the analysis to help her face the truth of her external and internal world, this is always a difficult and dangerous process. There remains a strong pull by something very deadly and deadening in the patient herself, which reinforces her identification with a parental object that hates and fears knowledge and understanding, and she is then driven to attack both her own thinking and mine.

I think both these aspects were manifested in the following sessions, when she became almost totally silent. She seemed to have been relieved at having been able to reestablish contact with me after the break, and to communicate how difficult the experience had been. I think she also felt anxious and guilty, both about betraying her parents (behind their backs, like Janet's mother), and frightened of a violent retaliation, for example, if she spoke to the policeman. Her method of coping was to attack the link that had been established with me, as well as her own capacity for understanding, forming a defensive identification with her parents, both as vulnerable figures willing to suffer for hours rather than summon help, and as capable of a murderous attack on anything that threatened them.

She either made no response at all to my interpretations, or after a very long pause spoke of a sense of hopelessness. There was no point in trying to work out what this was about; she just gave up. She also referred vaguely to there being a violent quality to her thoughts.

Toward the end of the week there was a slight shift; after a long silence she spoke in a slow, puzzled, and rather hopeless way. She said she waited to say something but felt herself caught up in a process she couldn't understand, which made her feel hopeless. She found thoughts connected with violence and death coming up in her mind, including thoughts about her own death. She had considered mentioning some of these things to me during the silence, but couldn't go any further with them, and suspected that whatever I said would leave her cold and would lead nowhere.

This withdrawal into a world of silence and hopelessness had been a marked feature of the analysis over the years. Any belief that things might improve, any attempt to talk, to work out what this was all about, seemed to arouse something violent within her that insisted that everything was hopeless, and nothing could change.

I thought the cold, deadly response to most of my interpretations during this period was the expression of the patient's own hatred of anything vital or creative, as well as her identification with the representation of the vulnerable and destructive parents.

She felt driven to project into me, as the analyst, the more healthy infantile aspects of herself that were capable of moving and of showing interest and liveliness, and that she probably had tried to get through to her parents. It seemed essential for me to repeatedly endure the painful experience of being in the presence of a cruel, almost impenetrable object, which evoked the response of wishing either to attack it desperately or to submit in a hopeless fashion. It was partly because at these times I became so identified with this more healthy infantile aspect of herself and responsible for sustaining it that the issue of my capacity to survive was crucially important to her. She was acutely sensitive to my state of mind, my mood, and my response to the difficulties in the analysis, and would sometimes become quite desperate and hopeless if she detected any sign that I might not survive.

At other times, as we have seen, the patient herself was more evidently identified with the child (represented by her sister coming into the bathroom, or her cousin Janet), who could be curious and adventurous.

I believe that one of the important reasons for the defensive projection of vital elements of her own personality, particularly the more healthy ones, was to avoid the disastrous possibility of the powerful destructive aspects of herself being concurrently present and interacting with more normal infantile elements. Before the emergence of true integration, this is conceived of as a catastrophic situation, which would inevitably result in the destruction of the more healthy infantile side of herself, if not her total destruction.

Although these sessions were difficult and discouraging, it was also clear that the patient had not abandoned herself to an identification with these damaged and destructive figures as completely as she had done in the past. When it became clear that I had been able to survive the frustration and the attacks, there emerged a sense of puzzlement, of conflict, a wish to say something, and the observation that she was caught up in a process she couldn't understand. This seemed to represent a movement toward greater integration, the patient's assumption of some ego functions that she had, at the start of the week, almost totally disowned. I believe this shift could take place only with a lessening of her paranoid anxiety and with the partial internalization and identification with a figure who is not too vulnerable nor too damaged, and not too threatened by the prospect of discovering something about either psychic reality or external reality.

In the following week, there seemed to be evidence of further integration in her mode of functioning. Unlike the response she had had to the long holiday, which had a primitive, frightening, and persecutory quality to it, she spoke about the pain and loneliness of the weekend in a more direct and touching fashion. She seemed to feel more secure in the analysis, as if I had been able to tolerate what she had exposed me to without either becoming too damaged or too filled with violent hatred for her.

On the Tuesday, she went on to speak about the relationship with her boyfriend Peter and about how she had been feeling rather isolated. She and Peter had been getting on better recently, and had enjoyed being together on the weekend. Last night, however, he had come back early, and let himself into her flat, and when she arrived he was there, watching an old film. She prepared supper, and he suggested it would be nice to have a fire, which she proceeded to light. He remained absorbed in the film, not taking much notice of her and what she was doing for him. After the film, they went to bed and that was all right, but he didn't seem very interested in sex.

"Ostensibly everything is all right—I suppose I feel cross—wouldn't it be nice if someone said 'Thank you for cooking the supper and making the fire.' I don't usually mind, but I felt I wasn't getting enough attention; Peter doesn't provide me with support, or nourishment, he's no use in that way." She was silent for a while, and then said: "I feel I've got to manage by myself, without any help from anybody. I could tell myself it's up to me and I will manage, but it doesn't feel like that at all—I feel hopelessly isolated. There's nobody to turn to!" At that point she became very upset.

After a while she said she was very aware of the limitations of the help she got from her friends, and the limitations of her family suddenly seemed very threatening. She anticipated feeling very isolated, with no one to turn to when she stopped coming to her analysis.

The patient now seemed very much in touch with the anxieties and pain connected with being left alone and not properly cared for, and she linked this with the prospect of losing the analysis. She was able to turn to me in an unusually direct and open way, recognizing how much she depended on the help and support she did get, which she could not find anywhere else, and which she would be losing. She emerged in the session not only as someone in pain, but as someone capable of reflection, capable of desiring and enjoying intimacy and sexuality.

It was therefore not entirely unexpected that she found herself in the next session "caught up in another silence," as she described it, very powerful and difficult to fight. She said she was surprised, although perhaps she should have expected it; she recognized something quite uncompromising, even aggressive about it.

I commented that when she was better able to communicate with herself, and with me, this seemed to provoke a very powerful, uncompromising attack on the contact between us. She could feel safe and protected only if she remained silent and immobile, as if capitulating to the hostile force. She said, "I was thinking about my cats, and about them dying—especially one of them. Then I thought of having them put down, if I wanted to do myself in. Then I thought of them being hit by a car, attacked by a dog— thought of burying them—the one that was dying is the more adventurous one."

There was something quite chilling about the way she spoke. I did not think this was simply a manifestation of a defensive withdrawal, but rather the expression of something deadly in her that became allied to the destructive aspects of her parents or her analyst. She seemed to confirm the fact that it was especially the more lively, adventurous aspect of herself that became the victim of this deadly attack. Instead of being able to tolerate the conflict and anxiety that this aroused, she seemed to ally herself with the cruel and sadistic agency that attacked her, her adventurous cat, and any progress in the analysis.

She began the next session with another long silence. I said that I thought we had seen how she turned to a world of suicide and violent death to avoid the pain of being left out, wanting things and minding about what was happening, and the fears that were aroused when her adventurousness, hopes, and wishes might be discovered. I seemed to have to bear the frustration, pain, and disappointment instead.

She said she had been thinking about the fact that Peter was shortly going abroad for a while. She was surprised it had come into her mind, and surprised that it seemed to matter: she couldn't simply take it in her stride. She added it was all very vague, and she didn't want to think about it.

I said it did seem to surprise her when she recognized how much someone mattered to her, since she often had to hide or to disown such knowledge, even though in some ways this increased her worry about being left, as the other person carried these functions for her. She was then faced with having to either bear some painful awareness herself or attack her own mind so that everything became vague.

The patient said that she had recalled the fact that Peter's sister had been expecting a baby, and yesterday Peter heard it had been born. It was a bit early, but everything was all right. They were calling it Peter, and he was very pleased.

She said she found herself saying, "Why don't they give it its own name?" and then felt a bit guilty—she should have been more generous, kept the thought to herself, and not been a dampener on his pleasure.

When I had been able to tolerate her silence, and then addressed the destructive processes in which I thought she split off and/or attacked her own mental functions, there was a shift. She not only raised the difficult and painful issue of Peter's sister's baby and his evident pleasure and excitement, but also the uneasiness and guilt she felt about her lack of generosity and her inclination to dampen his pleasure. Although she herself did not relate this to the analysis, there was a link to the way, in the previous session, something alive and adventurous had provoked a violent attack, which I thought was continued into the beginning of this session. However, in the course of the session she had moved from this position to one in which she became identified with a more integrated, more alive object, able to look at things with less fear and hatred. The quality of the attack is much milder and is accompanied by affection, guilt, and concern.

At the start of the following week she was again silent and withdrawn. When I commented on this she remained silent for a long time and then said that when she was not here there didn't seem to be any problem about talking, it seemed straightforward and quite clear to her what she should do. When she came into the room with me, however, she got into a muddle of some kind that she could not understand. I said I thought that when she encountered me she became muddled about what kind of person I was for her—whether I was cold, hostile, or preoccupied in the way she often experienced her mother, or someone who did attend to her, understood and cared for her.

After this interpretation she visibly relaxed and began to speak in a different way. She referred to something I had said the previous week, which had had an impact on her, although she hadn't been able to say anything about it, or do anything with it. "You said if I behave like this, don't talk, don't cooperate, I feel that I must be hated, or some word like that. It was much stronger than you usually say or I expect; there must have been something there that I recognized."

I said she tried to find an explanation for why she felt she was hated, and told herself it was because of the way she behaved. What I had actually addressed in the earlier session was the pain and distress associated with the belief that she was hated anyway, without being able to understand why. She sometimes got into a muddle because when she came she wasn't sure if it was also true in her analysis or not, and couldn't sort it out.

I felt the patient to be very well in contact with me, and what I was saying. She became visibly upset, cried for a while in a way that was moving, and then lay quietly.

I thought the experience of the weekend had reinforced an experience of a cold, hostile, and rejecting parental figure or couple, which was palpably present in the early part of the session. It seemed, however, to have less grip on her, and after my intervention she was able to describe, in a thoughtful and puzzled way, the pressure and muddle she experienced when she encountered me.

The issue of feeling herself hated—by her primary objects and at times by her analyst—was clearly important, as her response to my earlier interpretation indicated. The patient had told herself that she was hated because of the way she behaved, and I thought it had been important to make the distinction between this explanation and the much more painful belief that had been emerging—namely, that she was unwanted, and often hated, in a silent and cold way, without being able to find any explanation.

This enabled her to differentiate between the object that she felt hated her and the analyst in the room with her, who at that moment she did not feel hated by, and who was able to face painful aspects of her psychic reality with her. This seemed to indicate the existence of a space within her for thinking and reflecting, and a growing capacity to stand the truth about her inner world, and led in turn to a greater sense of psychic integration.

In the following session she began by saying that she felt very preoccupied with the question of what made her acceptable or not acceptable. A way of behaving that was acceptable at home might not be right elsewhere; indeed it might actually be quite wrong, as she has gradually discovered. She paused and said, "And then I dream that I'm going to have a baby. At least it was one of those confused dreams, it was sometimes me and sometimes someone else. Someone I was at school with, I think. Now I remember it must have been me, because I thought, "Oh, I have been drinking earlier on, before I realized there was any pregnancy. Oh, dear, has this caused any damage?"

The patient recalled that a few days previously she had been at a lunch in connection with her work, and there had been a woman there who was pregnant. "It wasn't obvious, her clothes disguised it, and she drank—not excessively, just three glasses of wine. I thought that it was a bit excessive, even for lunch. She is in her late thirties and is living with someone."

She went on to tell me that she had been monitoring the amount she herself was drinking, adding, "When I woke up from the dream, I thought, that's very odd, I couldn't see any connection between my behavior and my desperate search to be acceptable, and babies. Perhaps they aren't connected, but I felt they were, somehow."

I said that she felt her desperate need to be acceptable, especially at home, had not allowed the possibility of babies, and for a long time she had accepted this herself, and disguised or got rid of her own desires in a way that she now thought might have been wrong for her. When we had been able to recognize and speak about the difficult and painful issues the previous day, she seemed to have felt sufficiently accepted and supported here, which enabled her to dream about something alive and valuable inside her, like a baby, which she was concerned to protect from damage.

I thought that what had emerged was the link between her oedipal wishes and preoccupations—the jealousy, long-ing, and feeling deprived of a baby of her own, and questions about *why* it had felt so unacceptable for her to manifest any liveliness, sexuality, or creativity. She was allowing herself to struggle with very difficult questions about her parents—their relationship to her and the nature of their sexuality.

Behind the painful questions about why her father or her analyst had not given *her* a baby, preferring sexual intimacy with another woman, there lay a much more disturbing sense of being hated and never wanted as a baby (by her parents, or her analyst) and thus never allowed to be creative. It had been important to her that I had been able to think and speak about this, as my doing so provided some reassurance against a fantasy of me as a damaged and fragile parental figure unable to face or talk about such issues, and liable to take violent revenge on her if she dared to acquire anything valuable and alive. Such reassurance was particularly important when she felt her silence, her lack of appreciation, or more open attacks had injured me and reinforced the feelings of hatred.

I believe that the experience and internalization of a figure that, by addressing these feelings, made her feel accepted, enabled the patient to take greater responsibility for her own destructiveness and capacity for spoiling, and to tolerate guilt without feeling overwhelmingly persecuted by it. A more integrated and creative aspect of her could then emerge, heralded by a dream in which she was able to feel protective toward an infant inside her.

DISCUSSION

I have attempted, in this chapter, to illustrate the interaction between the patient's primitive oedipal fantasies and the perception of her actual parents, and the way in which these fantasies, originally reflected in the symptoms that brought her into analysis, were subsequently lived out in the transference. I have indicated how the patient was at times identified with the frightened, isolated, and helpless child (with little hope of support from a protective grandmother), while at other times her identification was with the damaged, murderous figures that felt threatened by any movement or creativity.

The mutual reinforcement that exists between these primitive fantasies and the impulses that they embodied and the patient's actual experiences of her parents contributed to the slow and difficult course of this analysis, as she had little hope that what she discovered about the nature of any object would reassure her.

I also suggested that these fantasies of the oedipal couple were closely related to the way in which the patient has been able to use her mind, to create links between her thoughts and feelings, and to tolerate anxieties that result from such links. Any communication, thinking, and the possession of knowledge was confused in the patient's mind with a disturbed and frightening version of the parental intercourse. This made it very difficult to use her own mind properly, because of both the anxiety that resulted from thoughts and ideas coming together and the threat and betrayal this was felt to represent to the parental couple.

The origins of such primitive oedipal fantasies are inevitably complex, and our view of the relative contribution of different factors shifts as the analytic work progresses.

There is, for example, the fantasy that the violence of the patient's sexual jealousy has brought about irreparable damage in the oedipal couple. The guilt that this brings is unbearable, and their hatred of her understandable. All she can do is to try to avert a murderous revenge by abandoning or concealing her own sexuality.

The other, more difficult and disturbing fantasy is of a vulnerable and damaged oedipal couple, full of hatred and violence of an incomprehensible nature, for which she does not feel responsible. It was particularly when this latter fantasy was addressed in the analysis that an important shift could take place.

By a long process of testing and exploration in the analysis, the patient seems to have been able to move toward the discovery (or rediscovery) of an object able to survive the difficulties and attacks, and on which she could depend. This experience gave rise gradually and intermittently to evidence of a greater degree of integration in the patient's psychic apparatus. I believe this greater integration is based on the introjection and identification with an object and/or a couple that is not threatened by the knowledge, observation, or the prospect of two things coming together—whether it is two thoughts or two people coming together sexually. It also implies the belief in the existence of an object that is able to protect itself and what it has inside and to survive without irreparable damage, whether the attacks are felt to come from inside or out. The consequences of this identification are considerable and are manifested both in her capacity for reflective thought, which is no longer felt to be so dangerous, and in the appearance of the capacity for concern with something alive and valuable inside her, rather than feeling driven quickly to attack and abort it.

She is, however, confronted with painful and insoluble difficulties concerning aspects of her life that, because of her age, she feels it may be too late to change. There are intense feelings of loss about the analysis ending, with regrets about the long periods during which progress was so slow and difficult. This process of mourning not only for the loss of the analysis and all it represents for her, but also for the approaching loss of her capacity to have a baby of her own feels very different however from the situation in which such feelings had to be quickly and violently projected, when her safety lay in an identification with a murderous parental figure who did not have to tolerate pain, guilt, or conflict.

CONCLUSION

An attempt is made to relate the severe restriction in the patient's life and in her mode of functioning within a long and difficult analysis to the internalization of, and partial identification with, primitive and damaged versions of the parental couple, which she experienced as threatened by and hostile toward any form of vitality or creativity.

When the expression of these more disturbing versions of the oedipal configuration could be recognized, tolerated, and interpreted within the sessions, the patient's longings, jealousy, and sexual wishes indicative of a more mature Oedipus complex became more readily available. This change was manifested in a different quality to the transference and in the way the patient became better able to integrate and use her own intellectual and emotional resources.

Part III

SHARED UNDER-STANDING

11

Psychoanalysis: The Common Ground

Robert S. Wallerstein, M.D.

At the 1987 International Psychoanalytical Association (IPA) Congress in Montreal, I gave an opening day plenary address under the title "One Psychoanalysis or Many?" The topic, which I felt to be of central importance to the worldwide psychoanalytic community, both scientifically and organizationally, was that of our increasing psychoanalytic diversity, or pluralism as we have come to call it, which I called then "a pluralism of theoretical perspectives, of linguistic and thought conventions, of distinctive regional, cultural, and language emphases" (see Chapter 2).

The task I posed in that address was to delineate what it was that still holds us together as common adherents of a shared psychoanalytic science and profession, and this task I set in terms of two main questions. The first question was, what do these diverse theoretical systems, diverse philosophy of science perspectives on the nature of psychoanalysis as a discipline, and diverse regional and cultural and language emphases, nonetheless still have in common so that they are all recognizably psychoanalysis in terms of fundamentally shared assumptions about the human mind and the way we understand its functioning? The second question, perhaps the other side of the same coin, was, what differentiates them, all together, from all the other, nonpsychoanalytic theories of mental life, for surely, to quote, "not every psychology of human behavior is psychoanalytic, and there is only intellectual destructiveness in a posture that 'anything goes' or that anything, anything mental that is, can somehow be construed as psychoanalytic."

In that address in Montreal, I considered these questions in the context of a historical review of the evolution of our current posture of worldwide diversity and pluralism despite Freud's own strenuous efforts throughout his lifetime of work to maintain the unity of *his* psychoanalysis, the psychoanalysis that he had singlehandedly created, to maintain it as a unified "movement" through attempting to define the official parameters of this new science of the mind and to fiercely protect its unity against both destructive or diluting pressures or seductions from without and also against fractious human divisiveness from within. But powerful as Freud's influence was during his lifetime, it is now approximately a century since his earliest psychoanalytic writings and a half century since his death. The structure of psychoanalysis has by far burst the thought boundaries set for it by Freud, boundaries that he had intended to be enduringly maintained by the famous committee he created, of the seven ring holders.

Yet within the widely diversified theoretical structure that has so incontrovertibly evolved so that we are now identified by ourselves and by each other as Kleinian analysts or ego-psychological analysts or object-relations analysts or whatever, with all the presumed implications that these labels carry for our clinical technique as well as for our (theoretical) explanatory frameworks, within this diversity we also live with our everyday commonplace feeling that somehow all of us, adherents of whatever theoretical position within psychoanalysis, seem to do reasonably comparable clinical work and bring about reasonably comparable changes in the comparable enough patients with whom we deal. I proposed in my paper that the resolution of this apparent paradox and the answer to the questions that my Montreal address posed lay in the shift of our focus from the diversity of our general theory (Klein 1976), or, more familiarly, our varying explanatory metapsychologies, to the commonality of the clinical observational data of our consulting rooms and the low-level, experience-near *clinical* theory (Klein 1976), the theory, that is, of transference and resistance, of conflict and compromise, actually of course the original fundamental elements of Freud's famous 1914 definition of psychoanalysis that "Any line of investigation which recognizes these two facts [transference and resistance] and takes them as the starting point of its work has a right to call itself psycho-analysis . . ." (p. 16). In my paper I proposed, even more sweepingly, that, at the present stage of our development as a science and a profession, all our various theoretical perspectives, our general theories, or our various metapsychologies are but our chosen explanatory *metaphors*, heuristically exceedingly useful to us, in terms of our varying intellectual value commitments in explaining the primary clinical data of our consulting rooms, but effectively, at least at this point, beyond the reach of the scientific enterprise in the sense of not being amenable to comparative and incremental scientific testing. By contrast, I proposed that our far more experience-near clinical theories, anchored quite directly in observables, in the data of our consulting rooms, were indeed amenable to all the processes of hypothesis formation, testing, and validation just as in any other scientific enterprise, albeit by methods adapted to the peculiar subjectivistic nature of the essential data from the psychoanalytic situation. On this, of course, our whole claim to be a discipline of the mind that is also a science of the mind can and does rest. In that sense, I stated positively my conviction that we indeed represent a science of the mind dealing in common with the shared phenomena of our consulting rooms, employing interactional techniques built around the dynamic of the transference and the countertransference, as we try empathically to relate to the psychic pressures that disturb our patients' lives and bring them to us. And in that sense, I declared that there is but one discipline of psychoanalysis.

I can remember no other paper of mine that provoked more immediate or intense response, and of course not all of it in agreement. Letters to the editor appeared in the *International Journal* taking exception to aspects of my historical interpretation (Plaut 1988, Samuels 1988). And an article has been published in the *Psychoanalytic Quarterly*, on the future of psychoanalysis, in which a significant segment of the argument has been a specific response to the main thesis of my Montreal address, an article written specifically from the ego psychological/structural theory point of view (Rangell 1988). To this I will later return. At the same time, others have reacted very affirmatively. Two statements of the impact of my message on our conceptual perspectives and our clinical strategies were put in similar and actually quite related ways. Southwood (1988), both in correspondence and in print in the *Adelaide Review of Psychoanalysis*, saw it as a shift in our central analytic focus from theory to clinical interactions, to wit, "the elevation of clinical experience to *primacy* over the traditional idea that our clinical work is the mere practice of what our "scientific" theorizing has taught us should surely lead to an enormous change in the way that we understand what we do" (p. 3, my italics). Weinshel put it as a shift in focus from our usual concern with our various psychoanalytic *differences*—and our Congresses over the years have amply attested to that focus—to a concern with what we have analytically in common, what unites us. It is indeed this latter consideration that led the program committee for the thirty-sixth IPA Congress in Rome to choose that shifted focus to the *common ground* of psychoanalysis as its theme, in effect to use this Congress to explore both the heuristic and the scientific implications of this perspective, of seeking out the conceptual common ground for our psychoanalytic clinical and theoretical understandings.

It was this decision that led me in turn to choose as the subject of my presidential address—this time placed at the end of the Congress week—the further development, from two perspectives, of the ideas I presented in Montreal. The one perspective is the further consideration, or rather the reconsideration, of those ideas in the light of the specific responses to them, including the six pre-published (see Chapters 3–8) statements for this Congress. The other perspective is the application of those ideas and their testing, within the limitations of my own capacities and biases, in my own comparative assessment of the three plenary clinical presentations of this week, by Max Hernández, a Latin American, trained by the middle group, or the so-called object-relations group at the British Institute, by Michael Feldman, a British Kleinian, and by Tony Kris, a representative of what can be called the post ego-psychological or contemporary American perspective. I will also take the opportunity to try to correct some misconceptions of my position to which my remarks in Montreal may have inadvertently lent themselves.

Perhaps I should start this exegesis with a further clarification of my perspective on our *theories,* the overarching general theories that identify us, that differentiate us, within whose frameworks we have been trained and practice, and in accordance with which we declare our psychoanalytic intellectual allegiances—and pursue this clarification in regard to the purposes and uses of our theories, their adequacy to those purposes, and finally their ontological status. Actually, a major part of my Montreal paper (Chapter 2) addresses these issues, and in considerable detail, and I will not repeat any of that here. A major point there was that each of these explanatory frameworks—the ego-psychological or now the contemporary or post–ego-psychological, the object-relational, the Kleinian, the Bionian, the self-psychological, the Lacanian, and so on—each purports to explain comprehensively the entire range of clinical phenomena that confront us in our consulting rooms, and most of us, brought up psychoanalytically within, and committed ideologically to, one of these, feel that our theoretical perspective of choice is both heuristically more useful and effective, and intellectually more satisfying and elegant, than the others we have not chosen.

This is, however, *not* to say that all these theoretical perspectives are truly equal in ultimate explanatory power and in their capacity to evolve beyond the metaphoric, and therefore scientifically untestable, status that I think more or less characterizes each of them at this stage in our historical development; to evolve beyond that in the direction of greater correspondences between the constructs of the theory and the relationships between the observables in our consulting rooms that would ultimately grant those constructs a truer ontological status as reflections of real relationships between real phenomena in nature. It is to say that none of these theories is there yet, none has evolved yet to that degree. Although I have my own prejudices in terms of the American ego-psychological theoretical framework within which I have been raised analytically and to which I have made my commitments, I also feel that we have no demonstrable basis at this point to assert the ultimate superiority in the sense of greater or "truer" explanatory power of any one of these theoretical perspectives over the others.

And here I want to make a specific correction. My Montreal paper could perhaps be read as a statement of the present (and also forever) *equal* status of all our overarching general theoretical perspectives in their metaphoric and therefore ultimately unscientific character, an opening for the intellectual acceptance of the hermeneutic view of psychoanalysis. Briefly, this is the argument that psychoanalysis is in no way in the natural science world of causes, but resides rather only in the humanistic world of reasons and meanings, where the criteria of evidence and proof are not those of scientific method and testing but rather are only the so-called hermeneutic criteria of coherence, of inner consistency, and of narrative intelligibility, so that ultimately psychoanalysis becomes but a matter of stories about lives, with the psychoanalytic reconstruction of a life only the construction of the best possible—that is, most persuasive or aesthetically most satisfying—story, without any necessary correspondence to historical truth. The full equality of each explanatory theory would follow as long as each could create a congenial and satisfying story line or accounting of the clinical interactions of the consulting room (at least for its adherents). None would be burdened with the task of endeavoring to evolve toward an approximation of the relationships in nature, of the facts of development and the historical truths of a life.

This extrapolation is clearly not what I intended in my Montreal address and my detailed consideration of the hermeneutic argument and why I feel it to be ultimately invalid and a cul-de-sac that would take us away from the proper, i.e., the scientific, development of our discipline I have spelled out at length elsewhere (1986a). I did intend though in my paper in Montreal to state my conviction that at least at this stage of our evolution as a discipline and a science, we have no empirical or logical warrant for asserting the greater validity or usefulness of any of our major theoretical systems over the others, except via the beliefs and predilections and biases—evolved through and based upon our personally agreeable and persuasive clinical trainings and practices—that each of us has come to live by, professionally and intellectually.

This position that I have thus presented is, however, by no means a consensus within our psychoanalytic ranks. A notable dissent has been vigorously expressed by Rangell (1988) from within what he calls the (American) mainstream of "traditional" or "Freudian" analysis, which he fears is in danger of becoming a minority position, no longer "main." Rangell builds his case for the gradual growth and development of this mainstream by accretion in a direct line from Freud through the most notable and significant names associated with the flowering of the ego-psychological metapsychology paradigm on to what he calls "total composite psychoanalytic theory" (p. 316). He sees this as *the* comprehensive psychoanalytic theory, stating, "I have pointed out repeatedly that self, object, interpersonal, preoedipal, all elements which have served as nodal points of alternative theories, are included in this total unitary theory, whereas the converse is not true: that other theories, of self, or object, or the Kleinian view, eliminate variable essentials of the developed, cumulative, psychoanalytic theory" (p. 317).

This is made even more specific further along: "For Wallerstein, the alternative to one unitary theory was not two or three but many theories, Kleinian, Bionian, self psychology, object relations theory, were all considered on a par, with clinical theory bridging them all. It is not what any of the new alternative theories adds which creates a problem, but what each of them, without exception, eliminates" (p. 326)—and he goes on to give examples of what he feels each of these other psychoanalytic theories discards from the central Freudian corpus. And in summation, further on the same page, he says, "All of Rapaport and, in more recent years, the theories of Hartmann have been rejected and shunted aside, together with the second half of Freud's contributions from which their work stemmed. I am speaking of monumental, not trivial, lifetime works, second only to the legacy of Freud. First, it was predominantly in Europe where these works were discarded, now in America as well" (p. 326).

This position by one of the major psychoanalytic contributors of our time is certainly representative of a significant and serious body of opinion within our ranks. It is, in fact, implicitly supported, at least to some extent, in Abrams's Chapter 3. Abrams seeks the common ground in the explication of the clinical process and in reducing the ambiguities that he feels beset it, to tolerable, or, better yet, to optimal levels. He talks of an interactive clinical process in which suitable amenable patients and (of course to be taken for granted) suitable amenable analysts come together and interact around what he calls hierarchies of resistances, of character, of transference, of recall and of reconstruction of central childhood experiences—and Abrams finds therein our (clinical) common ground. Explicit in his paper is that oedipal conflicts provide the specific thrust to the shaping of the tripartite mind and *pari passu* play the central role in those neurotic deformations that are properly amenable to psychoanalysis. It is when one can distinguish the obstacles to healthy functioning that arise from faulty ego equipment or limited developmental progression from those defenses and resistances originating in the dynamic unconscious, that one can have a differentiated perspective on analysis and on analyzability, of sufficiently reduced ambiguity. In other words, the ego-psychological perspective provides the encompassing framework for proper analytic work that will be stripped of its obstacles, if its ambiguities—that is, the emphases offered by the other theoretical perspectives in analysis—can be removed or at least sufficiently reduced. But of course, this again, as with Rangell I think, takes for granted what is at issue in this theoretical debate through trying to draw the common ground too narrowly around one major theoretical perspective in psychoanalysis, in this instance the ego-psychology paradigm.

To turn to the other five of the pre-published statements coming from all of our major regions and each from a different country, I would say overall that they all, in contrast to Rangell and Abrams, substantially agree with my proposition of the historical and contemporary true diversity and multiplicity of our theory formations, with our common ground to be found, if at all, in our clinical enterprise, but they differ among themselves, and in various ways each differs from me, in how they assess this state of affairs and in the implications for how we should or can proceed from here to our betterment in our theoretical understanding and in our clinical functioning.

Both Aslan and Portella Nunes laud the theoretical diversity as an expression of our richness and our vitality as a discipline, and actually repeatedly during the course of my visits with most of the Latin American psychoanalytic societies just a short time ago, I was informed by colleagues there that they attributed the recent explosive growth of psychoanalytic interest, training, and practice in their continent to their open receptivity to the confrontation and clash of every psychoanalytic theoretical perspective, originating from wherever around the world, all hungrily imported and debated in their psychoanalytic discourse. In little more than a decade the Latin American presence within the IPA has grown from that of a distant third party to that of a co-equal partner fully warranting equality of vice-presidencies and of rotation through the presidency. The problem that I see with this course is that this debate—in terms of general theoretical perspectives—may be chimerical, irresolvable, and therefore ultimately sterile.

All of the five, though agreeing that our common ground should be searched for in the clinical enterprise, differ nonetheless about its defining parameters, about how secure or even real it is, and the extent to which it can be broadened and extended toward the arena of the overarching theoretical frameworks. For example, Goldberg (see Chapter 6) sees it in the shared awareness and interpretation of the transference, which I feel is too narrow a focus unless we take the transference (and of course the countertransference) in an expanded way to represent and encompass the totality of the interactions in the analytic process, which to me would stretch the conception of the transference to the point that all precision and specificity in its meaning would be lost, and its usefulness as a central pillar of our psychoanalytic clinical understandings be sharply diminished. Similarly, Le Guen in Chapter 7 sees the common ground in the properly managed and controlled regression of the analytic process, with the analyst oscillating between the dangers of ineffectiveness due to an excessive and passive neutrality on the one hand, and of coercive conditioning due to an abuse of his intervention power on the other. This dividing line between proper restraint and proper control he feels to be indeed a thin one. Again, I feel this to be too narrow a reading of our common clinical ground especially with the various reconsiderations going on in the analytic world about the concept of regression altogether, as a necessary or even as a useful aspect of the unfolded analytic transferences (or transference neurosis) and also about the possibility of truly "controlling" in any meaningful sense any regressive process that does eventuate in the course of the analytic work. (See Gill 1984 in this connection.)

Goldberg goes on to posit that the inevitable misunderstandings among us of our common clinical ground or within our common ground, misunderstandings that can derive from the coloring of our clinical perceptions by our different theoretical preconceptions, can be systematically addressed and overcome through processes that he calls "sharing" and "negotiating," completely akin to the manner in which analysts have to negotiate endlessly with their patients within the frame of the transference–counter-transference interplay in order to arrive at a shared vision of the patient's psychological reality. Goldberg in his paper holds out the hope that his own, self-psychological, or Kohutian perspective will have more to contribute to that negotiating process and its outcome, than do its other theoretical rivals—but who among us does not hope the same for our own perspectival predilections?

Appy, although he, too, agrees (see Chapter 4) that the common ground begins with the shared concentrations on the clinical interactions in the consulting room (and like myself, in the broadest sense) at the same time doubts that that common clinical ground can ever be consensually achieved and consolidated. He in fact goes on to state that the clinical interactions of the consulting room is where these conceptions of the common ground also "end and dissociate." And he further talks of the "serious and potentially irreconcilable controversies" that arise in discussion of clinical technique and clinical theory. I will develop my own conceptions of how to cope with and transcend this thorny and complex problem further on. Oppositely to Appy, Aslan not only fully supports the conception of consensually accepted clinical common ground but also tries to show that it can—and should—be extended toward the arena of explanatory theoretical frameworks. He takes the important conception of identification and tries to illustrate a convergence of understandings of this concept across widely divergent theoretical perspectives by showing the comparability of underlying ideas about the understanding of the meaning and the place in our work of the concept of identification, stated in very different explanatory languages by Winnicott, Mahler, Bion, and Lacan. One can indeed agree with Aslan in this statement of a convergence of meaning—despite such different languages— and yet remind oneself that this is still after all at the level of clinical understanding and clinical theory—for the concept of identification is certainly closely anchored in clinical observables—and not yet at the level of our general theories or metapsychologies. And I don't see how Aslan's strategy of "progression upwards" will get us there just because of the, to me, wide ontological gap between the nature of our clinical theories and the nature of our general theories (Klein 1976), granted that some of our constructs, and identification may be one of them, can take their place within the one context (the clinical theory) and also within the other (the general theory), albeit with different meanings and different referents in each context.

This represents what I hope is a fair summary overview of the range of viewpoints on the issues of the nature of the common ground in analysis expressed prior to, and in preparation for, this Congress. Before turning to examine the observational data offered to us in the major clinical presentations of each of the preceding days of this Congress, I next want to pose two other questions. The first is: what have been our understandings, in our accumulated psycho-analytic experiences, of the range of differences in our clinical work and clinical technique, whether felt to be theory-related or not? The second is: what is the relationship of theory to technique anyway, and how tightly or loosely are they linked? You will, of course, recognize both these questions as foci of long-standing and still inconclusive discussions within our discipline.

With regard to the first question of the existing literature on variations or differences in clinical technique, the first who undertook a serious and systematic study of this issue was Edward Glover (1955), with his detailed questionnaire sent in 1938 to 29 members of the British Society, of whom 24 responded. Glover's findings are well known. Central was that "on only six of the sixty-three points raised [for response in the questionnaire] was there complete agreement. Only one of these points could be regarded as fundamental, viz. the necessity of analyzing the transference" (p. 374). He found that "the technique of interpretation is a much more individual matter than has previously been assumed . . . [and that] there is also a marked disagreement on questions of etiology, nature of anxiety, significance of aggressive impulses, termination, technique in psychoses, etc." (p. 348). This led him to disagree sharply with the "sedulously cultivated assumptions that participants in . . . [our] discussions hold roughly the same views, speak the same technical language, follow identical systems of diagnosis, prognosis, and selection of cases, practice approximately the same technical procedures and obtain much the same results, which incidentally are, by common hearsay, held to be satisfactory. [In fact] *Not one of these assumptions will bear close investigation*" (pp. 375–376).

Glover by no means looked unhappily at these questionnaire findings. He spoke, to be sure, of the importance of preserving the basic principles of psychoanalysis but hopefully without any sacrifice of "elasticity" in their application (p. 349), and he stated that the young analyst should "adopt such methods of procedure as are consonant with his own personal character and abilities. [For] Transference traditions may sit well or ill upon their wearers, but the most serviceable techniques are probably those molded to the measure of those who use them" (p. 264). What is curious in retrospect about all of this is that Glover ascribed this whole range of discerned differences in clinical technique and understanding to individual differences in personal character and abilities. He in no way invoked adherence to different theoretical frameworks in psychoanalysis despite the fact that the British Society at the time already contained active and very partisan protagonists in the crystallizing positions of the Freudian, the Kleinian, and the in-between middle or independent group.

Glover's perspective was pursued further and from a very similar vantage point in another well-known contribution: Anna Freud's (1954) discussion response to the American conference on the so-called "widening scope" of psychoanalysis. Her lengthy statement on this issue deserves quotation *in extenso* because of its range of implications for our theme today:

> Years ago, in Vienna, we instituted an experimental technical seminar among colleagues of equal seniority, and equal theoretical background, treating cases with similar diagnoses and, therefore, supposedly similar structure. We compared techniques and found in discussion . . . not only . . that no two analysts would ever give precisely the same interpretations throughout an analysis . . . but more surprisingly still, that . . . uniformity of procedure was never kept up for more than a few days in the beginning of an analysis. After that, the handling of the material would cease to run parallel, each analyst giving precedence for interpretation to another piece or even layer. These differences in timing would influence the emergence of the next material and this, in turn, influence the trends of interpretation. Even though the final results might be the same, the roads leading there were widely divergent. So far as I know, no one has succeeded yet in investigating and finding the causes of these particular variations. They are determined, of course, not by the material, but by the trends of interest, intentions, shades of evaluation which are peculiar to every individual analyst. I do not suggest that they should be looked for among the phenomena of countertransference. . . .

Just as "no two analysts would ever give precisely the same interepretations," we find on closer examination that no two of a given analyst's patients are handled by him ever in precisely the same manner. With some patients we remain deadly serious, with others humor, or even jokes, may play a part; with some the terms in which interpretations are couched have to be literal ones, others find it easier to accept the same content when given in the form of similes and analogies; there are differences in the ways in which we receive and send off patients, and in the degree to which we permit a real relationship to the patient to coexist with the transferred, fantasied one; there is, even within the strictness of the analytic setting, a varying amount of ease felt by analyst and patient. These wholly unintended and unplanned variations in our responses are imposed on us, I believe, not so much by the patients' neuroses but by the individual nuances of their personalities which may escape unobserved otherwise. If we become aware of these often minute variations in our own behavior and reactions, and cease to treat them as unimportant chance occurrences, their observation and scrutiny leads us directly to important findings. [pp. 608–610]

I wish to use this detailed quotation from Anna Freud in two ways. First, I just want to remark on how surely we must all have resonated with her description of these individual differences that mark all our distinctnesses as unique personalities, each of us clearly recognizable to our friends and colleagues by our own character constellation, including therefore all the individual differences in propensity and approach that we will inevitably bring to our professional work as analysts as well. All of this I think is clearly self-evident; and we can take for granted that these characterological differences among us inevitably impinge upon—albeit perhaps in somewhat muted form—the way we interact and display ourselves analytically. These are often talked about among us as differences in style, and they do weigh with us when we make referrals and try to match prospective patients with analysts whom we deem appropriate or suitable particularly *to them*. But my other point concerning these remarks of Anna Freud is that these are not the kinds of differences that are determinative of different conceptions of the analytic process or of substantively different ways of relating to it and to the analytic work. They are differences of style, of form, and are wholly compatible with a common and shared conception of and approach to the fundamental analytic task.

Others, more currently, have tried to demonstrate a more clear-cut relatedness of theoretical persuasion to technique, and of theory differences to discerned differences in clinical practice. A particular interesting research study to that effect is that of Fine and Fine (1988). They presented a brief history of a patient together with a detailed account of a single session to fourteen analyst participants, four designated American ego psychologists, four Kleinian, three self-psychological or Kohutian, and three advocates of Kernberg's modified and amalgamated ego-psychological/object-relational approach. When the case material was presented to the fourteen participating analysts for review, the treating analyst's interpretive comments were withheld, and the fourteen subjects were directed to formulate the kinds of interpretations that they would make and where in the hour they would make them.

The Fines's project did not purport to try to test the differential efficacy of work within these various theoretical frameworks, but only to determine whether systematic and significant variations could be found in the nature of the therapeutic interventions and therefore presumably the clinical interactions that would reflect the theoretical differences among the analysts. A positive outcome of the study could presumably be used as evidence of some determinative impact of one's theoretical position upon one's clinical analytic work, a presumptive argument that is against the conception that I, in accord now with many others who I have indicated are in agreement with my main outlines, have been proposing. And indeed, the Fines's results were largely positive. Independent analyst judges, themselves drawn from the same range of theoretical perspectives, did identify the theoretical positions of the analysts participating in the research at a significantly better than chance level according to at least one, and in some cases according to most, of six factors or variables: (1) the manner in which defenses and resistances were interpreted, (2) the manner in which transference was interpreted, (3) the degree of focus on the patient's vulnerability, (4) the degree of focus on the patient's archaic impulses, (5) the degree of focus on the patient's hostility and aggression, and (6) the use of theory-specific characteristic catch words and phrases. Lack of space prevents my giving some of their specific findings, which document how readily adherents of the four theoretical perspectives under study could in most instances be identified through characteristic and expectably phrased interventions.

The question is, for me, what difference do these kinds of differences make for our clinical understanding, clinical method, and clinical work? In Chapter 2, I drew on a clinical vignette cited by Kohut (1984). Kohut there described a patient troubled by a suddenly announced cancellation of a session in the near future. The patient reacted to this announcement with an immediate silent withdrawal from the analytic work. Three alternative therapeutic responses were presented, each couched in a clearly identifiably different theoretic language, a Kleinian, an ego-psychological, and a self-psychological. The point I drew from this description even more strongly than Kohut did was that each analyst, in an identifiably different language (which the study by the Fines confirms is readily possible), could, nonetheless, be seen as responding equally and understandably to the patient's distress and in such a way that the momentarily disrupted communicative link between patient and analyst was restored and the analytic dialogue could proceed. At least with Kohut's example, I think that I was able to demonstrate in detail that an analytic process could be clinically understood and reacted to in comparably empathically understanding ways despite the clearly differing theory-impregnated languages in which the interventions were couched.

Some have, however, taken the thesis implicit in the study by the Fines and have argued not only that differing theoretical perspectives lead to substantively differing intervention techniques, but also that these differing technical modes then elicit actually different observational data. For example, Arlow and Brenner (1988) have recently stated that

> All who consider themselves psychoanalysts use what they call the psychoanalytic method in order to gather the data on which psychoanalytic theories are based. Yet it is obvious that the conclusions they reach and the theories they propose differ from one another in many respects. Recent years have witnessed the development of many new theories in psychoanalysis. . . . How can one explain the differences among theories presumably based on the same data of observation? It has been suggested more than once that the

differences among all these theories, so apparent to every observer, may stem from the fact that the data of observation are not, in truth, the same. In fact, they are often very different. Perhaps all analysts do not use the same technique, even though all call the technique they use by the same name. This raises a serious problem, since it is obvious that differences in the method employed in studying any set of phenomena will produce very different sorts of data. The data and the theories based upon them become relevant in terms of the suitability of the method of observation. . . . Method, thus, is clearly important and one must ask whether there are indeed significant differences among the observational methods used by the adherents of the different psychoanalytic theories . . . [pp. 9–10]

If I understand this passage clearly, Arlow and Brenner argue that our different general theories determine different kinds of technical interventions, different not only in form and language but also in their substantive nature and in their impact on the analytic process so that different data of observation actually emerge from the analytic interaction. In this view there would be no real common ground, theoretical or clinical, and Aslan's Tower of Babel analogy would surely aptly describe the psychoanalytic enterprise however much we tried to disguise that by using some common words and deluding ourselves that we invest them with shared meanings. I feel, to the contrary, that there is no theoretical warrant or established clinical evidence for asserting that our theory determines or truly constrains our practice. In fact, I take the opposite position—that our clinical interventions (apart from differences of style and of theory-drenched languages) reflect a shared clinical analytic method, rest on a shared clinical theory of defense and anxiety, of conflict and compromise, of transference and countertransference, and evoke comparable data of observation, despite our avowed wide theoretical differences.

The central problem as I see it is that these comparable observational data get "explained" by us ultimately through widely differing theoretical explanatory frameworks, and that this is possible just because these overarching theoretical systems (that I have called our encompassing metaphoric systems) do *not* depend upon—that is, are not tightly linked to—our data. And this is the last point I wish to develop before turning to the clinical material for the study of the central thesis that I am proposing.

Stemming from Freud's original conceptualization of the threefold unity of psychoanalysis as a general *theory* of the mind, and also a *method* for investigating the processes of the mind and unravelling its nature, and also a *treatment* devoted to ameliorating the ailments of the mind, psychoanalysts have lived comfortably with the assumption that theory is thus necessarily closely linked to technique, and consequently that change in theoretical conceptions driven by new data or derived from fresh looks at old data, will of course be translated directly into appropriately altered method and technique. We take pride in the fact that uniquely in our field the road to understanding and the road to cure are presumed to be one and the same, and when understanding and cure are not achieved simultaneously, we assume that something untidy has taken place in the analytic implementation that more or better analytic attention would resolve.

And yet we also know that this coupling between theory and derived technique is often in practice far looser than we ideally conceive it to be. For example, so many practicing analysts, perhaps even a majority, clearly, if even somewhat self-deprecatingly, disclaim any special knowledge of theory. "I'm not a theoretician; I'm just a practicing clinician," they say, and they feel that they can do this comfortably, and reasonably confidently—that is, can carry on clinical psychoanalytic treatment employing techniques bequeathed to them by their analytic teachers without explicit recourse to intimate knowledge of theory, or to changed or changing theory. And in fact, many analysts, even those who follow the literature carefully, or themselves contribute to it, and feel reasonably *au courant* on the development and evolution of theory in our field, would be hard put to specify the ways in which their own technique, their own detailed way of working with their patients, has altered over their years of practice in the specific light of the theoretical alterations that they have incorporated into their understandings of the structure of psychoanalytic knowledge.

It is these reconsiderations of the once taken-for-granted assumption of a necessary and consequential relationship between theory and technique that is today finding more widespread echo in our ranks. Kris (1983) in an article on what he called the analyst's "conceptual freedom," decried the trend for theory to "co-opt the method of psychoanalytic observation and deprive it of its independence" (p. 408). He called rather for the "use of a method [of free association] that is described and defined in terms that are independent of the theory" (p. 408), and for a scientific conceptual progression from method to theory, not the other way around. Le Guen in Chapter 7 states that "it is not obvious in what respect the theory necessarily entails the practice" and puts it, via an extreme example, as follows, "For instance, there is no *a priori* reason in Lacanian theory why analysts of that persuasion should

225

have short or very short sessions (ranging between 20 and 5 minutes), yet the majority of them do, following the example of their master'' (p. 125).

These reconsiderations of the nature of the fit between theory and practice can indeed be looked at as but specific applications of the broader view advanced by Sandler (1983) that so many, if not all, of our psychoanalytic conceptions are by their nature elastic and become stretched to encompass new ideas and new insights, so that meanings inevitably change and enlarge over time and with accumulating experience, and that without our full and self-conscious awareness, familiar and fundamental concepts come to take on multiple meanings varying according to the context, old or new, in which the concept is being employed. This is an ''elasticity'' of our concepts, to use Sandler's word (p. 35), that is at least the analogue if not the underpinning of what I have called the loose coupling between theory and practice, *contra* to those who claim that theory constrains and determines practice, and very much the basis for my claim that our overall and overarching general theoretical diversity and pluralism can be fully consonant with the shared clinical theory, basic clinical method, and common observational data that I trust I can demonstrate to be our psychoanalytic common ground, that unites all the diversity that we collectively represent.

To turn now to that clinical demonstration: I want to make clear at this point before I begin that comparison, that my intent is just that, clinical comparison, and it is neither second-guessing the treating analyst (which is usually so easy with the advantages of hindsight and from a more objective position removed from the immediacy and intensity of the transference–countertransference interplay) nor an effort at gratuitous supervision of the work of eminent colleagues. I should also, of course, make clear that I undertake this task of clinical comparison from within the framework of my own theoretical perspectives in psychoanalysis, which are, of course, American ego-psychological and most similar to those of Kris, but I would submit that the conclusions reached should be (would be) essentially the same in substance, if not in language, if this clinical comparison were being undertaken by another writer, trained and practicing within a different psychoanalytic theoretical tradition.

The three patients described had, by chance, very much in common when they came to treatment. All were women between the ages of 28 and the mid-forties. Two were married but childless, and all three came with major issues around their interpersonal and sexual relationships, and the wish/fear dilemma around pregnancy and motherhood. Hernandez's patient was frightened of becoming pregnant, relieved when her periods came, and yet at the same time would feel dried up and empty; Feldman's patient was almost delusionally terrified of becoming pregnant, frigid, fearful of men and of intimacy, and constantly panicky; Kris's patient was purportedly trying to get pregnant, but this was beset by sexual difficulties on both sides in the marriage and a variety of conflicts over the baby-or-career dilemma. All three were overtly sad and chronically depressive; Feldman's was additionally severely phobic and suffering psychosomatic problems, and two of them, Feldman's and Kris's, had treatment courses described as slow, stubbornly silent, and anxiously rigid (Feldman's) and strongly silent, inhibited, and restricted (Kris's). Feldman's patient often came late, would be scornful of those who appeared too eager or needy in their analyses, and when she would reluctantly yield aspects of her inner life, would tend to withdraw into her silences, making the material that had been brought up somehow the analyst's, not her own, responsibility. Kris's patient took over three years of constricted interactions before she could reveal that her former therapist had made sexual advances to her at the termination of the treatment, which then could be linked associatively to her stepfather who, in a drunken state, had tried to seduce her when she was 18, as well as to her own father, who was finally lost to her consequent to his progressive alcoholism.

The childhoods of these three women were also similar. Hernández's patient described a sad childhood, a constantly bad relationship with her mother, with an affectionate father but one who was often away so that she felt regularly abandoned and/or mistreated, which was accentuated by a pending five-month analytic separation imposed by the analyst's own life plans. Feldman's patient described a bleak and cold upbringing, a need always to be a good, compliant girl lest she disrupt the precarious psychological climate at home, and great loneliness after being sent off to boarding school when she was 8. Kris's patient described a similar climate of a deteriorating relationship with her mother, whom she dared not offend and with whom it was best to maintain silence, and a father with constant psychological and real absences including wartime military service and his post-war progressive alcoholism.

All three of these women were deemed by their analysts to be within the neurotic character range with degrees of depressive, phobic, and constricted hysterical features and felt to be amenable to a full psychoanalytic treatment approach, although with Kris's patient, it took him over three years to bring about a true psychoanalytic situation. In one respect there is a divergence in these three presentations; both Feldman's and Kris's detailed clinical material has been drawn from close to the end of reasonably long analyses; Hernández's is drawn from the sessions before and after the five month interruption, which took place much earlier, in the second year of analytic work. Yet I do think we can agree that, given the uniqueness of each of our individual life histories, these three patients are probably as comparable as can be gathered from such widely disparate cultural and intellectual traditions, and are as suitable for our comparative evaluative purposes as we could ever reasonably hope to find.

To turn now to the detailed clinical presentations, first that of Hernández. The opening sessions in this analysis were occupied with the patient's need to establish with her analyst how important her work was to her. She wanted it to matter to him that she should be efficient and productive at it. She was also concerned for the analyst's health, that he should look after himself lest anything should happen to him, since she could not stand it if he were to die. In three variations over the course of a session, the analyst interpreted the impulses behind this defensive reaction formation. He indicated that when she felt in danger, she defended herself by attacking—killing—the analyst. When she responded that she had not seen his car in its usual parking place, and then was so relieved and joyful to find that he was nonetheless awaiting her at the hour and was there especially to look after her, he pointed to her pleasure that he had indeed survived her violent impulses—again, the hidden aggression, the fearfulness over it, and the relief that the danger had not materialized.

The next sequence described had to do with a dream in which a friend had informed the patient of the analyst's probable death and in which the patient remembered very tightly clutching her capacious briefcase—which reminded her of the analyst's briefcase. Here the interpretive response went further, the analyst pointing out that if he were to die and abandon her, the patient could take her briefcase, which a friend had likened to the house that a snail carries on its back—that is, the patient's own house, which she could protectively carry with her. And when she, in response to this, kept enlarging her own little table of her childhood to her present large desk, the analyst pointed to this "manicky" enlargement, a kind of transference warning that the adaptive defences could get out of control.

When the patient was surprised that the analyst returned after a holiday and did not abandon her, she confessed how much she always saw herself as a burden and a moral obligation to him. She was amazed once when he smiled at her and surprised when he remembered earlier material and referred back to it and took these as signs that perhaps he really cared and would take care of her. Here, without specific interpretation, there were importantly *supportive* meanings conveyed within the analytic relationship of the kind I have written about in great detail elsewhere (1986b, 1988b). The next significant event noted was the patient's gift of a bulky diary to the analyst, which would serve as a daily time reminder to the analyst during the coming five-month separation. Here the double-edged interpreta-tion focused on the complexly ambivalent meaning of the gift, the offering and the tangible reminder, but also something that would weigh him down, and remind him of her needful "weight as a patient." There was indeed open sadness that the long break was coming, and then a report of a sequence of three dreams in which the patient was first pregnant but anxiously unprepared, and then the analyst, camera in hand, was taking her picture, and then she was shopping, looking for an attractive costume. The interpretation of these dreams focused, in the transference, on the patient's multiple appeals to the analyst, and she in turn followed with her continuing concerns for his health and over her unconscious aggressions just as in the sequences from the very first hours.

Then comes a single session reported in much fuller detail. The patient associated to a tree that she could see outside the window and a nest in it that she had never observed before, and then to a childhood memory of her brothers, who were playfully quite mean to her and threw her dolls from an upper-story window and out the window of a moving car. Here the analyst took this directly into the transference, pointing out that the patient had built her analytic nest and now feared that by his absence the analyst would endanger her psychic security just as her brothers had. When there was a sequence of associations by the patient about the casual or careless way she dressed and the comments of friends who pressed her to be more present-able and feminine, followed by her own sense of vulnera-bility, and how, for her father, being a feminine woman meant not to exist, to be anonymous, the analyst again interpreted within the transference that she feared he would respond in the same way, alongside the wish that it be otherwise. Here the session ended, and the remainder of the material reported up to the planned analytic break had to do with a paper the patient was writing about the difficult economic situation of the country and the trends toward political and social upheaval and violence. The analyst was talking, during this period, of the patient's concerns with traumata, her own feelings of fragility, and her experience of the coming separation as an abandon-ment.

At the end of the five-month absence, the patient came

back warmly, expressing gratitude amid her tearfulness. She had functioned well, but at the price of blocking her feelings, and now she could begin to reconnect with her feelings. She had written a letter to the analyst during his absence but had not sent it, not wishing to be a burden to him. She was very fond of him and didn't want him to go away again. She had thought of being angry over this possibility but just couldn't be. She had discovered that, after all, he was doing very important things. The interpretive response to all this was directly in terms of transference wishes and fears. It was as if the analyst was so much more important than the patient, and he could readily go off to do important things and leave her behind to suffer.

The patient said that she was indeed afraid that he might go off again to do research and write, and he responded that this made her afraid to express her grief and pain and then with the colloquial Spanish expression of the "dead dog," meaning the patient's impulse to retaliate and stand him up, the analyst in turn interpreted her feeling precarious, at risk if she should express any of her anger. The patient talked about how all this had depleted her during the long separation, and the analyst, acknowledging how these efforts had exhausted the patient, tried to open the way from present to past by stating that it was as if some early experiences that had demanded all the patient's strength were being repeated.

For the rest of the hour the patient reiterated the feeling that she would sink if the analyst were to go away again and then dwelt on a work project for which she was seeking funding and that she felt she would get, although she thought that the project itself was still too fragmented and inadequately developed. But, after all, one couldn't resolve all the bad social conditions in the entire country in just a few months. When the analyst simply reiterated that it was impossible to do a thorough job in a few months, the patient immediately gathered that he was saying this as if she had been referring to the analysis, and this first hour after the long hiatus ended with the analyst again interpreting how great an effort the patient had made to survive, for, after all, the analysis had barely begun when he went away and had deprived her of sustenance. This was followed by brief statements of further material in which the patient recounted good experiences, such as that with a surgeon who had successfully diagnosed and surgically cured her congenital heart affliction in childhood, and her own adult experiences, in turn, of being helpful to her own friends and students who were so very appreciative in response. The patient had indeed reestablished the capacity to regain good experiences.

Here, then, is a review of the work of a Latin American psychoanalyst trained within the British independent group or object-relational school. The interpretive work reported focused on the immediacy of the transference, on resistances and defenses, on all the phenomena that I have called, following the terminology introduced by the Sandlers (1984), the domain of the "present unconscious." What is, of course, notably absent is any theory-based jargon or identifying terminology and I think one would be hard put to distinguish this specimen of clinical work from that of those trained within other theoretical, cultural, or linguistic perspectives. Let us now see how it does compare with the work of Feldman, a British Kleinian. The clinical material here, as I have already indicated, was drawn from the terminal phase of an analysis marked by long, painful silences and sullen immobility, alternating with destructive attacks on the analytic work and on the patient's own capacity for hope and understanding. The analyst felt the central analytic dynamic to consist of the patient's internalization of, and identification with, primitive and frightening visions of her parents experienced as vulnerable and damaged, and at the same time, as devastatingly hostile to any form of vitality or creativity; she would defend against the persecutory anxieties arising from these imagos by resort to projective mechanisms. The analyst felt that only through analysis of the immediacy of the transference could the fantasies, conflicts, and anxieties of this oedipal dynamic be successfully reached.

The clinical presentation opens with dream material expressing the fear that the analyst might be a murderer, trying to destroy her; then the picture of her elderly father, who was currently visiting her, unable to lift himself from the bathtub, and allowing neither the patient nor her sister but only the sister's son to come to his aid and help him out, and then a childhood story of a sister, who had once followed behind mother into the father's bathroom, from which she was angrily expelled when father realized that she was there. The portrayal is of the now-disabled and helpless father, prepared to suffer in the tub for hours rather than let himself be helped by his daughters, who might directly observe his nakedness and vulnerability. The analyst's interpretation of this material started with the analyst vaguely identified as the "murderer" who had expelled the patient during the holiday which had immediately preceded this hour and would soon be expelling her from the analysis altogether. The analyst followed with the further statement that this focus on the bad analyst also defensively protected the patient against the frightening view of her aging parents as damaged and vulnerable. Thus, current transference, the transformation of fearsome childhood parental imagos into weakened present-day imagos, projected aggressive impulses, and defensive displacement were all woven together into a transference context. The patient responded with further associations to the father's informing her that a once-favorite cousin who as a child had lived in the patient's home with her for a period, but who had become estranged from the patient's parents, had died recently. There had been a notice in the local paper, but the parents still couldn't bring themselves to contact the cousin's family; it would be too awkward. And here the analyst interpreted how vulnerable the patient's parents were, how unable they were to face emotionally painful issues. Implicitly he was at the same time actively supporting and commending the patient's desire to disidentify from her parents in this regard, and to search out her own psychic truths, however painful. Again, this is the kind of intervention that I have described elsewhere as truly supportive in the most psychoanalytically appropriate sense (1986b, 1988b).

This material was then followed by a regression into a sequence of hours in which the patient was mostly silent or spoke in a slow, puzzled, and rather hopeless way. She confessed to violent thoughts, including those of her own death. This was experienced as a particularly disappointing regression by the analyst, who described himself as having been buoyed up by the hope that the patient from now on would be able to communicate more directly and affirmatively. He, at the same time, could focus on the struggle within the patient, the simultaneous importance to her that he be able to tolerate these continuing attacks on his capacity to help, and that he preserve his belief in his own and the patient's survival and their joint working through toward the patient's inner capacity to become truly alive and vital, extricated from her identifications with the damaged and destructive figures from her past.

I hope it is clear by now that although the language and imagery that I have abstracted from Feldman's material in order to represent his thinking faithfully have a decidedly Kleinian cast, the clinical focus is uncompromisingly on the self-same elements of ambivalence and conflict and compromise as they play out in the transference–countertransference domain (and, to be sure, in the patient's extra-transference world as well) just as was the case with Hernández's presentation within an object-relational framework (if that is an appropriate designation) and just as I hope to show to be equally true with Kris's presentation within an American contemporary ego-psychological framework. Each, to the extent that they are on target, are touching equally, and illuminating equally, the contents of their patients' "present unconscious."

I would like to add a final comment. In a later sequence of interactions and interpretations in the material presented, the patient and the analyst had been talking of the patient's oedipal wishes and preoccupations—the jealousy, longing, and feeling of being deprived of a baby of her own, and why she felt it had been so unacceptable for her ever to manifest any liveliness or sexuality or creativity. The analyst then interpreted to the patient how important it had been to her that he could think and speak about all this with her, as his doing so had provided a reassurance to the patient that he was not a damaged and fragile parental figure unable to face these issues, or someone who would take violent revenge on the patient if she sought out a lively or sexual existence on her own. Feldman explicitly pointed out here how important this *reassuring* interpretation was to the patient at this particular juncture, again in a way no differently than a sensitively attuned analyst working within any other theoretical framework would, and far from the stereotype of the Kleinians as interested *only* in giving a running commentary on the patient's most archaic and most unconscious fantasy systems.

Next we will turn to Kris's presentation. As with Feldman's, this material is from the terminal period of a moderately long analysis that had long been beset by difficult silences, marked inhibition, and severe self-criticism. It took some three years before a fully psychoanalytic situation could be established. The material focused on for us was in the context of the patient's attempts to become pregnant, with both hope and disappointment running high, and was meant to illustrate particularly the analysis of the patient's self-critical trends. The patient had her period and simultaneously suffered another severe disappointment in her schoolwork. She brought another in a series of dreams of a hemorrhaging menstrual flow which in actuality was not the case. This led to memories of her unwanted brother's birth and her one clear memory of his tiny fingernails—this in the context of so much else being vague to memory. The analyst's interpretive focus here was on the patient's character defense, the continuing persistent block (over so many years) to so much visual memory with reference however to the single exception of the brother's perfect fingernails, an allusion to his little penis, a linkage that had been made in connection with an earlier dream. The patient's confirming response was reference to her childhood murderous intentions and how it had always bothered her that her mother had never noticed. This then led to the elaboration of material about her throttled childhood hostility toward her mother and her guilty

feelings over that. The analyst in turn interpretively suggested that the patient's self-criticisms had grown more
rapidly than her ability to express her feelings at that time of
her life—an interpretation geared again to the patient's
adaptive *and* maladaptive developing defensive and coping
strategies.

The next material focused on, two months later, was
centered on disappointments in lovemaking due to the
husband's failures and muted criticism of the husband's
seeming inability to tolerate a more intensive psychotherapy
than that which he was in. In this context the patient for
the first time was able to recognize and tolerate her
resentment at the role she had undertaken of being her
husband's "protecting angel." She saw this too as a
repetition of her childhood concerns for mother's sensitivity and well-being and the need to mute her own feelings
and be silent with mother. From this, over a sequence of
sessions, described in detail, the patient was able to express
real anger over grievances with the analyst beginning when
he made no time allowance for her unavoidable lateness of
40 minutes when another doctor (a radiologist) with whom
she had had a just-prior appointment had scheduled multiple patients simultaneously and then had kept her waiting
and taken her last. It was all so unfair. And the analyst was
just not sympathetic to her plight. Nor was her husband.
The patient ended what had almost become a tirade by
stating "that's all I have to say on the subject," to which
the analyst responded that it was a great deal more than she
had ever permitted herself to say in the past—again, an
interpretive comment in a supportive mode, indirectly but
clearly commending the patient and buttressing her ego-
coping capacities.

I will skip now to the end of Kris's presentation, to the

description of an hour in which the patient reported a dream in which she rejected a female friend's homosexual overtures. Her associations ran to a variety of difficult choices, homosexual or heterosexual, her husband as her vacation partner or her analyst, the analyst as mother or as father, and so forth. Whichever choice she made—male or female object choice, for example—she felt she would be misunderstood and rejected from one side or from the other. She thought of two operations, her tonsillectomy in childhood, which had been followed by severe bleeding, and the myomectomy that was being recommended now for fibroid tumors, also associated with bleeding. The analyst's interpretation was set in the framework of the patient's dualistic and dichotomized either–or thinking. He wondered if one meaning was to be found in the opposite purposes that she saw in her two operations, the childhood tonsillectomy as a punishment for masturbation along with her intense self-criticism for her forbidden wish to be a boy, and the pending adult myomectomy in order, oppositely, to become a woman who can accept her femininity and have a baby. Thus past, present, and also a new future could be optimistically linked together interpretively. The patient was both surprised and pleased. She associated to childhood sexual play with a boy cousin and then to a childhood friend who she understood was now bisexual. At this point the analyst interpreted the patient's growing understanding and acceptance of her own unconscious bisexuality which at the same time reassured her against her fear that a hidden homosexuality would turn out to be her total psychic truth. The analyst said that he would be available if needed at the time of the surgery, which would be in the midst of their summer vacation period, but he emphasized as well that she was no longer the helpless child caught up in uncontrolled sexual impulses, but rather an adult woman who could understand herself and her own strivings to have a baby of her own. The patient felt good when they parted for the summer.

I have tried here—I hope convincingly—to demonstrate my own conviction that three representative and respected colleagues, representing the three major regions of world-wide psychoanalytic activity, and trained within three of the major theoretical perspectives within psychoanalysis, have all approached, dealt with, and interpreted the clinical material of three surprisingly similar and quite comparable analytic patients in a clearly identifiable, and contrary perhaps to our preconceptions, surprisingly comparable way. They have each addressed in quite comparable fashion the phenomena of conflict and compromise, of impulse and defense, of inner and outer object world, of reality and fantasy, of uncovering interpretation and of necessary supportive intervention—that is, all the interactions within the transference–countertransference matrix that occupy the domain designated by the Sandlers as the "present unconscious."

This is, of course, not to say that individual differences of style, of temperament, of how the essentials of tact and timing, and of choice and selection, are experienced and expressed, are not present and visible in these three representative analysts. It is part of our common-sense knowledge of the bewildering diversity and range of human nature, as much as of psychoanalytic experience as expressed in the writings of Glover and Anna Freud that I have quoted, that such individual differences do exist, and I am reasonably sure that they can be discerned in the three specimen analyses and analysts studied here. Nor is it to say that theory-based differences in our analytic approaches, in choice of interventions, and in the style and language of our interventions don't exist. Clearly they do, and often in readily identifiable ways, as the research study of the Fines, from which I have quoted clearly attests, and I have in my own review of our three samples remarked on the Kleinian explanatory language discernable in Feldman's clinical exposition.

Rather, it is to say that I feel that the commonality of our clinical approach to the phenomena of the "present unconscious" (Sandler and Sandler 1984) within the framework of our shared "clinical theory" (Klein 1976) transcends both our individual differences as unique people and the conceptual differences of our theoretical explanatory frameworks, and brings us together as identifiably all psychoanalysts doing the common work of psychoanalysis. In this regard, I have personally had the opportunity to share clinical experiences with colleagues of other psychoanalytic theoretical persuasions and often in other regions of the world, of participating in clinical seminars and case discussions—in my case I am thinking of an entire week of living and presenting and discussing clinical cases in a strict Kleinian Institute in Latin America, where one could readily feel oneself into the clinical context and identify as quickly and as clearly as those native to that culture and that theoretical framework the interactions and interventions that were appropriate and well placed and advanced the psychoanalytic understanding, and those that did not. This is actually an everyday experience in such settings as the British Psycho-Analytical Society, where three separate theory streams live and work side by side, each very distinct, but at the same time in constant interaction with the others both in teaching and in scientific discussion.

However, I want to end this chapter, perhaps surprisingly, on a more personal note, one that is at the same time a promissory note, a statement of return to the ultimate place of overall theory in our psychoanalytic scheme of things. I have tried to persuade that we do have a common psychoanalytic ground in our shared clinical enterprise to which we react with common clinical purpose and understanding. I have concomitantly tried to persuade that our overarching theoretical structure or diversity of structures (as at present) is not yet adequate either to those common clinical understandings or to our deep needs as a discipline and as a science of the mind.

But if we are to become both the kind of discipline and the kind of science that we desire to be, we do truly need the kind of coherent and unifying overall theoretical structure that Freud tried so brilliantly to create, a theoretical structure that would properly match the soaring intellectual vision that his monumental labors bequeathed to us and upon which we will be able to build an ever-enlarging understanding of the human mind and heart. This is my personal testament and the article of faith that has guided me on this privileged platform that organized psychoanalysis has accorded me—that by cohering around our common clinical ground and by building our clinical theorizing incrementally upon that, we will have, we do have, the firm base upon which we can painstakingly fashion a truly scientific theoretical structure that can take its place properly and proudly as a full partner within the array of human sciences. We can, I am convinced, ultimately fulfill Freud's dream and enlarge it with our own dream for the theoretical structure of the discipline and the science of psychoanalysis.

12

The Search for Common Ground

Arnold D. Richards, M.D.

As we enter the centenary decade of the science of psychoanalysis, it is worth recalling that the birth of our discipline cannot be separated from the theoretical models—and especially the theory of mind—that underlay Freud's discoveries. Indeed, the psychoanalytic method *was* the operational correlate of the theory of mind that Freud brought to the treatment situation. From the outset, Freud's theory of mind informed both his data of observation and his theory of therapeutic action (Richards 1990). How striking, then, that psychoanalysis has in recent decades become a field of rival theories. This trend, which Michels (1988) has termed theoretical pluralism in psychoanalytic dialogue, shows no signs of abating. We are, for better and worse, a profession consisting of ego psychological analysts, object relations analysts, relational analysts, interpersonal analysts, self psychologists, Kleinian analysts, and Lacanian analysts, to name only the most important schools of thought.

This theoretical ferment, well-attested to by the lively dialogue at our meetings and in the pages of our journals, is constructive; the vitality of any science is a function of the vigor with which substantive issues are debated. The downside of theoretical pluralism is the organizational developments that so often accompany the growth of rival theories. Groups tend to form around a new theory and take as their *raison d'être* its promulgation and continued development. Hand in hand with the productive exchanges promoted by emerging theories, then, comes a push toward factionalism. The tendency toward institutional autonomy by proponents of particular theories is likely to promote isolation and an absence of intertheoretical dialogue.

Robert Wallerstein's espousal of common ground—a unity of clinical purpose and clinical understanding that subsumes theoretical diversity—is one of the most significant responses to the problems and promise of theoretical pluralism. According to Wallerstein, the shared definitional boundaries of psychoanalysis involve the facts of transference and resistance, understood from the point of view of conflict (Kris 1947). Drawing on Joseph and Anne-Marie Sandler's (1983) distinction between the past unconscious and the present unconscious, he argues that the clinical theory bearing on the present unconscious and guiding day-to-day therapeutic work encapsulates the unity among analysts. On the other hand, general theoretical perspectives that address the past unconscious, aiming at a more "causally developmental account of mental life from its earliest fathomable origins," account for the diversity among analysts. For Wallerstein, overarching theoretical perspectives (such as Kleinianism, object-relations theory, self psychology) "are metaphors—albeit scientifically necessary metaphors— that we have created in order to satisfy our variously conditioned needs for closure and coherence and overall theoretical understanding." It is owing to the difference between clinical theory addressing the present unconscious and general theory attempting to reconstruct the past unconscious that contemporary analysis can combine "diversity of theoretical viewpoints and unity of clinical purpose and healing endeavor."

Wallerstein's position is appealing. He believes that theoretical differences, while unresolvable, need not be organizationally divisive, given that "truth" resides in clinical theory and not in general theoretical perspectives. The latter are tantamount to heuristically useful metaphors that enable different analysts to organize the data of observation according to their respective sensibilities. To evaluate this call for a common ground, it is first necessary to "unpack" (Spence 1982) the philosophical assumptions that underlie it. Hanly's recent paper, "The Concept of Truth in Psychoanalysis" (1990), provides us with conceptual tools that are essential to the enterprise.

Hanly begins by outlining the two philosophical theories of truth: correspondence and coherence. The correspondence theory states that truth consists of the correspondence between an object and its description. Philosophically, this school of thought is equated with realism. The correspondence theory falls back on two premises, an epistemological premise that objects are able to cause our senses to form more or less correct observations of them as they actually are, and an ontological premise that a person's thoughts and actions are caused. According to this viewpoint, theories can be objectively tested, and minds are part of nature. Scientists from Galileo to Newton, Darwin, Einstein, and Freud have worked with a correspondence theory of truth. Freud's adoption of Charcot's credo,

"Theory is fine, but it does not change the facts," bespeaks his advocacy of critical realism, a position considered naive by its critics.

Proponents of a coherence theory of truth maintain that objects in the world make sense only within a theory of description. To quote Hanly, "Truth is some sort of idealized rational acceptability, some sort of ideal coherence of beliefs with each other and with our experiences, as those experiences are themselves represented in our belief system and not corresponding with mind-independent or discourse-independent states of affairs." The coherence theory of truth falls back on two premises, an epistemological premise that our ways of thinking and perceiving unavoidably condition what we observe (that is, facts are theory-bound, never theory-independent; context alone makes observations understandable) and an ontological premise that human beings are unique in nature on account of a consciousness that supports actions motivated by reasons rather than causes.

Advocates of the coherence point of view believe that there may be more than one true description of the world. Within philosophy the coherence theory of truth is equated with idealism; among its proponents are Kuhn (1962), Feyerabend (1981), Putnam (1965), Ricoeur (1970), and Merleau-Ponty (1965). Within psychoanalysis, the coherence theory of truth is represented by a hermeneutic position that replaces psychic determinism with uncaused choice. Hanly observes that the coherence theory of truth is used by Goldberg (see Chapter 6) to defend the theory of self psychology against its critics. The coherence theory of truth allows for more than one true theory about the same thing because observations are believed to be determined by the theories that order them. According to Hanly, Goldberg maintains that self psychology should be accepted because it can claim to be a coherent theory, subtended by observations that cannot be falsified by classical analysis. Paul Ornstein (1978), in his writings on self psychology, takes a similar position when he refers to different paradigms in psychoanalysis, an ego-psychological paradigm, a drive paradigm, and a self-psychological paradigm, and invites us to "get inside the particular paradigm in order to discover its usefulness." Hanly, however, shrewdly points out that this approach is a "double-edged sword because it implies that the observations of self psychology cannot falsify classical analysis or any other theory." A coherence theory of truth takes the position that theories are not falsifiable in principle.

Hanly feels that the use of coherence theory "results in theoretical solipsism and truth by conversion." Goldberg invites us to test his theory by making a commitment to it over a period of time. What he seems to be saying is that if we are unable to verify his propositions, it is because we have failed to make the requisite commitment. This line of reasoning, of course, probably requires a more scientifically investigative psychoanalyst than is humanly possible. The philosopher of science, Laudan, would maintain, I think, that the very request for such a "commitment" by one school implies a view of itself as a separate research tradition, one that stands apart from the traditional psychoanalytic research tradition.

Does Wallerstein, in his acceptance of theoretical diversity, also accept the notion that different psychoanalytic points of view indeed represent different scientific research traditions rather than different metaphors? Is there a psychoanalytic research tradition that includes ego-psychological psychoanalysis, Kleinianism, and object-relations theory, but excludes the theories of Adler and Jung? I think the answer is affirmative. But would such a tradition also include self psychology? The answer to this question seems less clear. Are we dealing then with a spectrum, a continuum of variation that at some point leaps out of the research tradition like a quantum to the next energy state? Is it significant that the Program Committee of the thirty-sixth congress of the International Psycho-Analytical Association, which took Wallerstein's common ground position as its organizing theme, included an ego-psychological analyst, a middle-group object-relations theorist, and a Kleinian in the cast of clinical presenters, but not a self psychologist? Could clinical common ground be demonstrated only by excluding presenters representing extreme theoretical perspectives, such as self psychologists, Lacanians, or Bionians?

Hanly acknowledged that there is much in current psychoanalytic practice that argues for a coherence theory of truth. The multiplicity of variables, the complexity of the data, the difficulty in distinguishing between fantasy and reality, past and present, the "complex, shifting nature of transference" all argue against a philosophical position of objectivity, as does the lack of a unified theory of psychoanalysis. And yet Hanly ultimately argues against a coherence point of view, averring that truth can emerge from the analytic situation. He believes, with Freud, that there is an operative unconscious with a definite nature of its own. For Hanly, the vagueness and uncertainty inhering in the analytic situation are themselves "determinate states of affairs that have an explanation; they are not characteristic qualities of mental contents and states as such." Hanly thus believes that there are intrinsic forces at work in psychic life that will allow for the emergence and delineation of fantasies, of memories, of pattern-finding rather than pattern-making. These forces are the drives. A commitment to a theory of drives, then, represents another shibboleth, a distinguishing characteristic of psychoanalytic theories. Theories that reject the primacy of the drives thus appear to differ from drive-based theories in more than metaphorical ways. As Hanly observes, "Psychoanalytic theories that repudiate the drives are also likely to employ coherence as a concept of truth."

A consideration of the self psychologist Anna Ornstein's discussion of the Kleinian Michael Feldman's presentation is illuminating of these issues, and especially of the problem of finding common ground with a psychoanalytic theory anchored in a coherence theory of truth. Ornstein followed Goldberg in averring that, in discussing Feldman's presentation, she would "remain within Dr. Feldman's own theoretical orientation." She contended that, unlike self psychology, ego psychology and object-relations theory do not "accommodate the importance of early psychic development in the psychopathology of analysable conditions." Rather, the latter two theories attempt to conceptualize these phenomena in terms of "the vicissitudes of the Oedipus complex." For Ornstein, then, the Oedipus complex in Freud's sense becomes a shibboleth. Her remarks explicitly put ego psychology, object-relations theory, and Kleinianism in one camp and self psychology in another.

Is the Oedipus complex, as Ornstein uses the term, a theoretical metaphor or a clinical observable and, hence, part of our observational common ground? Wallerstein states that what analysts have in common is the use of concepts like transference and resistance and acceptance of the centrality of psychic conflict. But what about the nature of conflict? What do we make of different theories of pathogenesis? I think Ornstein picks up on this quandary when she appeals to a comfortable common ground in relation to "transference and interpretation of the transference," but then goes on to accuse non–self psychologists of "stretch[ing the] Oedipus complex into the earliest phases of development." With respect to Feldman's case, she is unequivocal in stating that "It was not the patient's rage for not having been chosen as her father's sexual partner, but rather that she experienced herself as a hated and unwanted child."

According to Ornstein, the answer to theoretical differences lies in the transference, but Ornstein's own allegiance to self psychology leads her invariably to see in the transference issues transferred from pre-oedipal phases rather than oedipal issues proper. One could make a case that what should be common ground among analysts is an open-minded use of the transference as an investigative tool in which the chips fall where they may. But Ornstein's remarks on Feldman's presentation highlight the problem with this perspective: that the concept of transference is itself theory-bound and, in addition, is too general a concept to serve as a platform for all analysts to stand on, particularly when it is linked to radically different concepts of pathogenesis, development, conflict, and theories of therapeutic action.

Apropos Ornstein's remarks, I return to Hanly's point that self psychologists espouse a coherence theory of truth, which includes a coherence premise of indeterminacy. Kohut's idea that the empathic-introspective mode is central to psychoanalytic knowing is consistent with the epistemological view of the relationship between knower and known that typifies coherence theories in general. To quote Hanly, "Kohut's concept of empathy disallows the degree of epistemic independence of subject and object required by correspondence." And yet both Wallerstein and Hanly end their presentations by avowing that psychoanalytic science will eventually meet the requirements of a correspondence theory of truth. The point to be made here in relation to Wallerstein's belief in a common ground is as follows: if self psychology and other psychoanalytic theories espouse diametrically opposite views of the truth, then their theoretical differences appear to be more than metaphors.

Schwaber (1990), in her discussion of Hernández's clinical paper, was more sanguine than Goldberg about the possibility of clinical consensus. She noted that "While we might at first blush expect that our theory would determine our technique, it may rather be, as Wallerstein pointed out, that theoretical preferences effect primarily the language we choose for interpretations, and that our shared interest in such experience-near matters as transference, resistance, conflict, and defence transcend our different metapsychologies. Though we might agree that even these seemingly self-evident terms are also variably defined."

Schwaber espoused a correspondence theory of truth in observing that "our models and our conceptualizations originate as derivatives from empirical findings." In line with her antitheoretical predilections, she implied that all too often a commitment to theoretical truth leads the analyst away from the patient's truth. Her emphasis on listening derives, again, from a correspondence theory of truth: there is knowledge about the patient to be obtained only if we refine our listening instrument as fully as possible. Schwaber's critique of Hernández's presentation correspondingly focused on what she considered to be flaws in his listening instrument—that is, his leaps of inference. Schwaber is alert to instances where the analyst is imposing his point of view on the patient and where, in turn, the patient agrees with the analyst out of compliance rather than conviction.

For Schwaber, psychic reality can be determined through corroboration "affectively and verbally" by the patient. I believe that Schwaber places too great a burden on the patient with respect to mental processes that are beyond consciousness. The question is: How does the analyst help the patient know something that he or she couldn't know without analytic help? The problem of the unconscious complicates the data-gathering process as well as the problem of psychoanalytic knowledge. Unfortunately, Schwaber makes matters too simple in asking who is to be the arbiter—patient or analyst. She proffers too sharp a dichotomy between knower and known, without allowing for learning on each side. Analytic knowledge and its transmission are too complex to be adequately characterized in terms of simple dichotomies, patient versus analyst, psychic reality versus external reality, and so on. And Schwaber seems to realize as much when she says, "Our pathway to what is unconscious is more likely to be reached when it is jointly discovered rather than unilaterally inferred, and the yield will be more empirically derived data." Unilateral reference certainly will get us into trouble, but blind acceptance of the patient as arbiter may also lead to impasse and sterility. The patient's vantage point, it should be remembered, incorporates the capacity for self-deception.

In her final remarks, Schwaber urges us to wait and be prepared to be guided to unanticipated vistas. She makes a plea for psychoanalysis as an investigative tool and offers this position as common ground. And this is a position around which we can achieve a great deal of consensus, although analysts of all theoretical persuasions will often honor it in the breach as we look for our own favorite scenarios and narratives in our patients' productions. Object-relations theorists look for internalized object-relation scenarios; self psychologists for empathic failures and self-esteem problems; ego psychologists for ambivalence conflicts, sexual and aggressive. Schwaber's comments align her with the correspondence camp.

What Schwaber's discussion points to, interestingly, is the connection between a correspondence theory of truth and an open-minded, investigative, methodological commitment. It should be noted that Schwaber says very little about her own theoretical commitments. She presents herself as an analyst trying to distance herself from all manner of constraining theoretical baggage. Can one have a strong theoretical commitment and retain an open-minded investigative approach? Is it the case that when we have a strong theoretical commitment we must necessarily defend it against attack and look for confirmation of its precepts, to the detriment of an attitude of open-minded exploration? Another question: Are all theoretical positions equally anti-investigative? Are there differences among Wallerstein's theoretical "metaphors" in this regard? When asked the question, each analyst will probably offer his or her own theoretical commitment as being more open and less dogmatic than the theoretical commitments of others.

But such personal responses gloss over the basic epistemological issue implicit in the common ground position. In Hanly's (1990) words, the problem is "whether or not the process of free association is able to provide us with knowledge about the patient that is independent of the analyst's own theoretical orientation." Hanly continued that "The foundation of commonality consists of at least two elementary epistemological assumptions. One, that analysts of whatever theoretical persuasion have a common integral object to investigate the unconscious working of a person's mind which is what constitutes a human nature; and two, that there is a common method of investigation that is, at the same time, a therapy." Hanly, in line with his advocacy of a correspondence theory of truth, maintained that, at least in theory, through this process, "The unconscious functioning of the patient's mind should be able to communicate itself to the analyst and to third-party observers independently of the theories they hold.

"Without this common ground," he continued, "theoretical pluralism loses its potential to advance knowledge; without it, pluralism inevitably slides into idiosyncracy and solipsism."

Wallerstein, in his plenary address at the thirty-sixth IPA Congress (see Chapter 11), implicitly recognized the fundamental disagreement among analysts about the nature of psychoanalytic truth in observing that there are "diverse philosophy of science perspectives on the nature of psychoanalysis." But he reiterated his belief in a unity able to subsume such diversity: "Within this diversity we also live with our everyday commonplace feeling that somehow all of us, adherents of whatever theoretical position within psychoanalysis, all seem to do reasonably comparable clinical work and bring about reasonably comparable changes in the comparable enough patients that we deal with.

"At the present stage of our development as a science and as a profession," Wallerstein observed, "all our various theoretical perspectives, our various metapsychologies are but explanatory metaphors heuristically exceedingly useful to us in terms of our varying intellectual commitments in making sense of the primary clinical data of our consulting rooms, but effectively at least at this point beyond the reach of the scientific enterprise in the sense of not being amenable to comparative and incremental scientific testing.'' In suggesting that a correspondence view of truth is not possible ''at the present stage of our development as science,'' Wallerstein implied, of course, that it might become possible at some future stage, when our scientific enterprise would indeed be ''amenable to comparative and incremental scientific testing.'' But for the time being our theories are metaphors, or putting it more pointedly, ''heuristically useful,'' which, of course fits in with a coherence theory of truth. And yet Wallerstein maintains that ''Our formal experience-near clinical theories anchored quite directly in observables in the data of our consulting rooms are indeed amenable to all the process of hypothesis formation, testing, and validation, just as in any other scientific enterprise.''

As one reads Wallerstein, one discerns the tension within him, a personal commitment to science, ''a science of the mind,'' tempered by recognition of the problems analysts have. He concludes that there is one discipline of psychoanalysis. He does not say whether there is one science of the mind called psychoanalysis. Wallerstein's awareness of the tension between coherence and correspondence is evident when he discusses the different theoretical perspectives, each of which, predictably, is viewed as being more intellectually satisfying and eloquent to its own adherents than to others. But then Wallerstein speaks of the capacity of these perspectives ''to evolve beyond the metaphoric'' and therefore scientifically untestable status that now characterizes them, moving in the direction of greater correspondences with the truth. Such an evolution would ultimately grant these constructs a truer ontological status as reflections of real relationships between real phenomena in nature.

Wallerstein makes his commitment to a correspondence theory of truth clear in dissociating himself from the hermeneutic view of psychoanalysis. He characterizes the hermeneutic stance as not burdening theories "with the task of endeavoring to evolve toward an approximation of the relationships of nature, of the facts of development, and the historical truths of a life." Here he is clearly in sharp disagreement with philosophers such as Habermas (1972) and Ricoeur (1970), and with psychoanalysts such as Spence (1982), Schafer (1983), and Goldberg (1988). Wallerstein also considers the positions of Rangell (1988) and Abrams (see Chapter 3), who argue against too ready an acceptance of diversity. Abrams refers to ambiguity in excess, whereas Rangell talks about the need to accept what he calls "total composite psychoanalytic theory," which, predictably, is *his* theory of psychoanalysis. Wallerstein responds to Abrams and Rangell by observing that their structures work well enough when one is dealing with neurotic patients in whom "oedipal conflicts provide the specific thrust to the shaping of the tripartite mind." But one gets into difficulty when dealing with patients with "faulty ego equipment or limited developmental progression." And it is just these latter clinical situations that require the development of alternative theoretical viewpoints.

The clinical theory–general theory distinction, be it noted, has an important antecedent in the work of George Klein (1976), and in some ways, is cut from the same cloth as the work of the anti-metapsychology students of Rapaport: Schafer (1983), Gill (1976), Holt (1976), Klein (1976), and others. The distinction, which is carried over in Wallerstein's position of clinical common ground, is tested somewhat by two studies that Wallerstein himself cites, one by Glover and one by Anna Freud. Glover, in 1938, undertook a study of variations in clinical technique and found, among the members of the British Society, complete agreement on only six of sixty-three points. Anna Freud, several years later, undertook a study comparing the technique of comparable psychoanalysts and found that "no two analysts would ever give precisely the same interpretations throughout an analysis."

Wallerstein uses these findings, not to point out the problems in a unifying view of our clinical enterprise, but to stress that clinical differences are matters of character and style rather than being "determinative of different conceptions of the analytic process or of substantively different ways of relating to it and to the analytic work." This, of course, remains a troubling point, particularly in view of certain theoretical variants that Wallerstein would presumably have us include under his unifying clinical umbrella: self psychology, Lacan, Bion, and perhaps "radical" Kleinianism.

Another study Wallerstein cites, by Fine and Fine of Los Angeles, also seems to argue against his position, although he takes it otherwise. They studied a group of American ego psychologists, Kleinians, self psychologists, and Kernbergians, and found that independent analyst judges could identify the theoretical position of the analysts participating in the research at a significantly better-than-chance level when presented with process material that demonstrated variations in analytic technique. Wallerstein uses this study to indicate that there are differences, but asks, "What differences do these kinds of differences make for our clinical understanding, clinical method, and clinical work?" To which we might add: What differences do they make in regard to clinical outcome? To me that is the ultimate question for us as practitioners, as providers of mental health care.

Wallerstein believes that observational data do not entail theory, a position I have argued against in a review of Berger's *Psychoanalytic Theory and Clinical Relevance* (1988). Wallerstein believes that the rank-and-file analyst does not find a close coupling between theory and technique. A dissenting point of view would be offered by analysts such as Brenner, who has maintained that theoretical conceptions about defense, depressive affect, compromise formation, and the development of the concept of psychic conflict do indeed have a profound effect on technique. In fact, Brenner (1976, 1979), and analysts like Arlow (1981, 1986) and Gray (1973, 1982) as well, often frame their presentations in a way that focuses sharply on the technical consequences of their theoretical point of view. Finally— and Arlow (1981, 1986) has made this point in an important paper—one's theory of pathogenesis is crucial to technique. The notion that radically different theories of pathogenesis will not affect the way in which an analyst works is unconventional and counterintuitive, given that the goal of analysis is to understand pathogenic processes.

An interesting counterpoise to Wallerstein's common ground position is found in the contrasting papers of Schafer (1990) and Lussier (1991). Schafer began by directly taking up the difficulty of discussing common ground without first taking up basic linguistic, methodological, and ideological issues. Linguistically, he pointed out how *transference, analyze, resistance,* and *regression,* key words in any discussion, are "treacherous because analysts of the same and different persuasions use them in association with too many different conceptions of childhood development, of psychopathology, of repetition and its basis, functions, and modes, of the uses of countertransference in defining transference, of the so-called real relationship with the analyst, of appropriate kinds and degrees of analytic activity, and so on.''

For Schafer, words take on meanings through the contexts in which they are used. If we cannot agree on the context, then we have no consensus on the meaning of terms. On the basis of this critical stance, Schafer proceeded to question Wallerstein's basic conclusion about the three clinical presentations. Schafer was not convinced that there was common ground with regard to the concept of transference, because such a claim could be made only by "overlooking marked variations in clinical procedures and phenomena." Specifically, he felt that there were marked variations with respect to the extent to which the three presenters "stuck to interpretations of here and now transference." Schafer focused on the differences, whereas Wallerstein focused on the similarities. And Schafer posed an ever sharper question to Wallerstein that challenged his entire enterprise: "Furthermore, after claiming common ground in the analysis of transference, what could one go on to say? To what use could one put that claim? With so much overlooked, the claim could not guide our clinical work, nor would it stimulate us intellectually." Schafer was clearly implying that the yield of Wallerstein's effort was political rather than scientific.

Schafer went on to define what he believed to be our methodological common ground: he defined the analytic process or method as "the making, breaking, and remaking of contexts." This view of analysis as an understanding of narratives is something analysis shares with disciplines such as literature. Schafer's viewpoint clearly aligns him with proponents of a coherence theory of truth. In his words, "We must regard analytic understanding as the outcome of a dialogue between analyst and analysand, rather than the rapport of a detached, uninfluential, and uninfluenced observer." For Schafer, then, this hermeneutic view of psychoanalysis constitutes our common ground, a position that Hanly, Edelson (1988), and Wallerstein would all contest.

In a third section on ideological considerations, Schafer came down hard against the very search for common ground. For him, the search implies "a generally conservative value system. It turns us away from the creative and progressive aspects of the struggles between different systems of thought and practice." Schafer opposed our aiming for "a single master text for psychoanalysis," asking us, instead, to accept "the sense that our differences show us all the things that psychoanalysis can be, even though it cannot be all things at one time or for any one person." Keeping to his coherence theory of truth, he submitted that each school of thought had something to offer in helping us to understand our patients analytically.

André Lussier takes equal exception to Wallerstein's verdict, albeit from a different perspective. Whereas for Schafer common ground leads to excessive conformity, for Lussier common ground meant excessive pluralism. Lussier pointed out the problem with Wallerstein's position by turning, as I have earlier, to self psychology. He wondered whether Kohut would have agreed that a common view of conflict and compromise, impulse and defense, binds all psychoanalysts.

Lussier was dissatisfied with a common ground defined in terms of clinical work; he referred to the latter disparagingly as "raw material." He pointed out, as I noted earlier, that this criterion would qualify as psychoanalytic "any school of dynamic psychotherapy." For his part, Lussier thinks that analytic common ground presupposes an agreement on basic theoretical assumptions. For Lussier, contra Wallerstein, theoretical predilections are not mere metaphors, but determinative of the meaning of clinical concepts and the status of these concepts in clinical work.

As if to take up this challenge, Lussier offered his own credo, the basic psychoanalytic principles on which he stands and which, in his view, constitute the basis for common ground among analysts. These principles are (1) the aim of psychoanalysis as uncovering the unconscious factors in psychic functioning; (2) the centrality of the Oedipus complex as the source of conflict; (3) the centrality of the transference neurosis in the analytic process; (4) the centrality of the intrapsychic compared to the interpersonal and transactional; (5) the importance of the intersubjective dimension in regard to transference/countertransference; (6) the importance of defenses in psychological development and of defense analysis in psychoanalytic treatment; (7) the requirement of frequent sessions (no less than three times a week over a period of years); (8) the need for an economic point of view, focusing on drives, to account for central aspects of human motivation.

The contrast between coherence and correspondence theories of truth could not be more boldly stated than in the contrasting positions of Schafer and Lussier. And, in fact, the thirty-sixth IPA Congress, at which Schafer's and Lussier's papers were first presented, was a forum of starkly dichotomous viewpoints, of participants who believed that analysts must have a great deal in common, and participants who believed that analysts need have very little if anything in common. In reflecting on the Congress, we would do well to consider whether we must really choose between the incompatible positions of Schafer and Lussier, whether, that is, the analytic enterprise must be comprehended in terms of the coherence *or* correspondence theories of truth propounded by Hanly.

In supporting his commitment to a correspondence viewpoint, Hanly adduced an argument from mathematics. Euclidean geometry is complete and coherent, he observed, yet, owing to its inapplicability to extreme dimensions, fails to describe the space of the universe. This is all well and good, but it underscores my problem with Hanly's "either/or" premise. While Euclidean geometry may not work in outer space and at the level of quantum particles, it characterizes quite nicely the ordinary course of events; with it, we can build fine bridges and tunnels. This fact suggests that there may be a third philosophical option, that of the pragmatic, of what works. Berger (1985), in his recent book on the clinical consequentuality of psychoanalytic theory, *Psychoanalytic Theory and Clinical Relevance,* ably develops a pragmatic philosophical approach. The role of pragmatism in the psychoanalytic endeavor should not be downplayed. We are, after all, engaged in an activity for which there is a willing consumer. Unsatisfied consumers will, over time, exert a strong voice in directing us to certain theoretical positions over and against others. If our theories guide us to interventions that are not therapeutically efficacious, we will necessarily question our beliefs—unless we are willing to spend a good portion of the day in the office by ourselves.

The fact that we are ultimately dependent on the feedback of patients who will appraise their analytic experiences as either satisfactory or unsatisfactory serves as a kind of built-in corrective to the analytic process. (Such a corrective is not, I realize, without its own problems: some patients will accept an otherwise unsatisfactory situation in order to avoid new knowledge that will jeopardize their existing psychic status quo.) Hanly seemed to be saying the same thing when he referred to a self-critical capacity "which can facilitate our search after an understanding of our patients in their terms rather than our own." When Hanly spoke of a common human nature, of the analysand's struggle for self-honesty, and of the analyst's struggle for countertransferential self-awareness, he seemed to be pointing to a pragmatically qualified commitment to a correspondence theory of truth.

So what are we left with? Lussier quotes Robert Gardner, "Analysts help people to wonder." Gardner (1983) has written about psychoanalysis as a process of self-inquiry. Perhaps a parallel should be drawn between the analytic process as a vehicle of self-inquiry and the dialogue that has followed Wallerstein's call for a clinical common ground. In this regard, Wallerstein has provided a truly analytic service for the profession, directing our attention to what we do and how we think about what we do. We are left with the continuing task of examining our similarities and differences, the nature of our intraprofessional conflicts, and the underlying issues around which these conflicts are organized.

13

Psychoanalytic Pluralism: The Resolution of the Issue?

Robert S. Wallerstein, M.D.

Clearly, the issues of the nature and meaning of our increasing psychoanalytic pluralism, highlighted and bracketed by my plenary addresses to the IPA Congresses, in Montreal in 1987 (Chapter 2) and in Rome in 1989 (Chapter 11) have been brought to explicit and self-conscious focus in the contributions brought together in this book, but—as is amply evident throughout—far from brought to consensus. The present verdict is perhaps best expressed in the editorial (Tuckett and Hayley 1990) that opened the first issue of the *International Journal of Psycho-Analysis* in 1990, the issue that carried my presidential address to the Rome Congress (Chapter 11), as well as two of the three plenary clinical presentations on the designated theme of the common ground of psychoanalysis (Chapters 9 and 10 by Hernández and Feldman) as well as some commentaries on these presentations (Schafer 1990, Schwaber 1990). The editorial put it as follows: ''To many of those who attended the Rome meeting it was apparent that there is still very much room for further discussion of what, if indeed anything at all, does constitute the common ground of psychoanalytic work, especially if the exact meaning attached to particular psychoanalytic ideas and practices is to be explicated and exemplified'' (p. 1). The call in the editorial was for clinical papers that will ''present some examples of the way psychoanalysts do currently work'' (p. 2), in order ''To facilitate a greater degree of shared understanding of both psychoanalytic controversy and our common ground.''

The first issue of the *International Journal* in 1991 carried further commentaries on the main Rome Congress presentations, by Tyson (1991) and Lussier (1991), as well as an extended essay by Richards (Chapter 12) reviewing the totality of the Rome Congress presentations on the theme of the common ground. Richards's final paragraph echoes these questions of Tuckett and Hayley, ''So what are we left with, and what did the Congress achieve? . . . The Congress certainly helped us all to wonder about our theory and its relation to our clinical work. . . . Wallerstein and the programme organizers . . . have served as the profession's analysts, directing our attention to what we do and how we think about what we do. We are left with the continuing task of examining our similarities and differences . . .'' (see Chapter 12).

In parallel pursuit of this continuing goal set in the Tuckett and Hayley editorial and the Richards essay, I will in this chapter pursue these same issues further along combined theoretical and clinical grounds. I will organize this presentation in accord with the perspectives that have been raised by one or another of the central protagonists in the scientific discussions on these issues that I am reviewing. (1) Is it desirable to pursue this issue of the search for a psychoanalytic common ground?—a question of scientific values and ideology. (2) If so, at least to enough of us, is it possible to pursue it, in terms of the conceptual constraints purportedly posed—according to some—by the nature of psychoanalysis as a theory? (3) If enough of us can agree that it is possible, what are the specific directions in which this has either been attempted, or is being advocated, or is held out as inherent, if only implicitly, in current conceptualizations of the nature of psychoanalysis as science?—and this will involve consideration of the assumptive philosophical base of psychoanalysis as a general psychology of human functioning. (4) And finally, drawing upon the juxtaposition of clinical case material from two major theoretical perspectives, the contemporary Kleinian and the contemporary Freudian (American ego psychological), I will indicate the direction in which I feel that technical convergence of clinical approaches, originating within grossly differing theoretical traditions, is already happening and in keeping with the overall theses of my presentations (see Chapters 2 and 11).[1]

---

[1]This chapter was formulated, and mostly written, when I received the first issue of 1991 of *The International Journal of Psycho-Analysis,* which contained in sequence three additional articles from the discussions of the Rome Congress on the "common ground." The most comprehensive of the three articles, that by Richards, reviewed the totality of the Rome Congress presentations on the theme of the common ground. It appears, somewhat edited and shortened, here as Chapter 12 in this book and I discuss my areas of agreement and disagreement with it further on in this chapter in relation to an extended discussion of Richards's views on these issues. In this footnote I will comment, in briefest essence, on the other two articles.

Robert Tyson (1991) comments on Feldman's paper (Chapter 10) and agrees that the common ground could be best sought in "the realm of clinical theory and technique" (p. 39), but then goes on to demonstrate nuances of difference in clinical interpretation (in the relative emphasis on pre-eodipal as against oedipal manifestations) between himself and Feldman. To me this is simply the expectable degree of individual clinical difference within the frame of the consen-

First to the issue then of the *desirability* of this endeavor. This was raised directly by Schafer's (1990) response to my address to the Rome Congress (see Chapter 11). "A search for common ground should be based on a shared understanding of why it is a good thing to do, why it should be a rewarding thing to do, and how to go about it in a sound way. . . . Because in my view the ground for discussion has not been adequately prepared, I shall be devoting my opening commentary to a review, necessarily brief and incomplete, of the thorny, if not impossible, way to useful discussion of common ground" (p. 49). And he went on to develop three sets of considerations, linguistic, methodological, and ideological, that in combination he felt make the quest for common ground, both pragmatically beyond our capability (or, at least, easy capability) and also misguided, even mischievous, in the sense of being counter to the best development of psychoanalysis as an intellectual endeavor.

Under linguistic considerations, Schafer adduced the wide diversity of usage of our most significant conceptual and technical terms. "In the clinical setting we must not be beguiled by manifest content . . . (T)o agree that we [all]

---

sual clinical common ground, and in fact depends on the acceptance of that common ground as the operating framework within which to explore similarities and differences of clinical interpretation.

Lussier (1991) in his more theoretical presentation, raises the issue of how I could fit Kohut's self psychology, with its central and overriding focus on deficit rather than conflict as the major determinant of psychopathology, into my conception of a clinical common ground that embraces a major focus on psychic conflict and compromise. I do this on the basis of my reading of the clinical material presented by Kohut and other self psychologists, as indeed dealing planfully with the interplay of *conflicted* transferences and countertransferences (see Chapter 2, footnote 3, p. 44; also Wallerstein 1981, 1983b, 1985).

analyse transference amounts to little more than agreeing that we use the same words for whatever it is that we do. . . . (T)ransference cannot be exactly the same word in the contexts of different clinical reports, for close inspection may show that in each case it has been placed in a different network of meanings. Instead of identity of meaning, there will be only family resemblances. One might have to stand far back from individual practices to give mere family resemblances the appearance of identity and then lay claim to common ground" (p. 49).

This imprecision of clinical usage and meaning is indeed a thorny difficulty in the search for common ground, and in relation to a whole host of other complex issues in psychoanalytic conceptualizing as well. It is also not a new observation. I have myself addressed this concern (see Chapter 11) in discussing Sandler's (1983) conception of the 'elasticity' of so many of our conceptions and definitions which become stretched over time and with usage to encompass new ideas and new insights, so that meanings inevitably alter with time and experience, and even very familiar and fundamental concepts come to take on varying (and even multiple) meanings, depending on context. I used this exposition of Sandler's in *support* of my argument about the possibilities for searching out a common clinical ground—based on the disjunction that this kind of elasticity allowed between the prescriptions from theory and the pragmatic requirements of technique, ostensibly directly derived from the theory. That is, the same notion of altered usage and additional meanings can be used in the service of either argument about the feasibility of the search for common ground. We can all agree that, in whatever context, it is a conceptual and technical complexity that must be dealt with.

Schafer (1990) then went on to a variety of methodological problematics. Of the several he described, I highlight the most compelling.

> This problem stems from the recognition that analysts write differently. We should realize that here we have not been sampling analyses [in the three clinical plenary presentations at the Congress]; rather, we have been sampling written narratives of brief segments of analyses. Even though some of the process notes were quite detailed, in every case much has been left out or reduced in order that there could be produced a followable, time-limited, written account of an analytic process. Therefore, we do well to resist developing the illusion that we can hope to draw definite and productive conclusions. [p. 51]

Certainly, a well-taken methodological caveat, but hardly a fatal roadblock. Contained within this caution are all the research issues of the correspondence (or fidelity) of process note accounts, or even of audiorecordings, to the *actual* analytic process (however that is defined or conceptualized), which I have discussed in detail elsewhere (Wallerstein and Sampson 1971). These issues involve the possibility of getting a faithful-enough accounting of the events of an analytic treatment so that it can be helpfully understood and reacted to, upon which, after all, our entire psychoanalytic educational (supervisory) enterprise rests and involves as well the possibility of getting a "good enough" understanding of inner experience, say of the diffuse and affectively charged visual imagery of dreams via the secondary process-constrained words into which they are cast by our patients groping for intelligible recounting, upon which incidentally our entire therapeutic enterprise rests. The methodological constraint Schafer has raised here is therefore no more nor less than the total theoretical and clinical constraint within which we have nonetheless collectively succeeded in bringing our total psychoanalytic knowledge to where it is now, including our capacity to understand our patients as well as we do directly, and even indirectly via third-party reports in our supervisions.

Lastly, and I feel most importantly in terms of his agenda, Schafer (1990) turned to what he called ideological considerations.

> Ideologically, the search for common ground seems to imply a generally conservative value system. It turns us away from the creative and progressive aspects of the struggles between different systems of thought and practice. I say this with all due respect to the progressive intentions of Dr. Wallerstein, but as we know, intentions and consequences are not the same thing. I believe that in the realm of ideas and the practices in which they are realized, conflict can make us both wiser and more creative. Sublimated aggression does have its wonderful uses. . . .
>
> Ideologically, by placing a value on the search for specifically psychoanalytic common ground, one is implying that differences are regrettable, and one is acting on the impulse to level them. Knowingly or not, one is then aiming for a single master text for psychoanalysis. I think it is more truly progressive—and obviously this is my contestable ideological preference—to give up the idea of a single master text and instead to celebrate and study our differences and to continue to grow, as we have, through unsettledness. We should work with the sense that *our differences show us all the things that psychoanalysis can be even though it cannot be all things at one time or for any one person.* The alternative is the blindness of conformism." [p. 52]

This is certainly a clear-cut statement of Schafer's own scientific values and ideological preferences and his rejection of what he feels mine to be. He wants to *celebrate* differences as the road to happier and more productive science and feels that the search for common ground implies differences to be "regrettable." It is also a useful reminder that ideological commitments inevitably do underpin the scientific agendas that we all create and the scientific investigative choices that we all make, for the most part not so knowingly and self consciously as Schafer does, just as values of course also underpin all of life's other significant activities and choices. Having said that, it does not follow that my own scientific values have necessarily been accurately discerned and laid bare, nor—values aside, Schafer's as well as mine—that the quest for commonalities is any more or any less worthy an intellectual goal than the quest for distinctiveness. Both are equally aspects of the scientific investigative enterprise; neither is inherently more *conservative* or more *progressive* (which are indeed value-loaded constructions that Schafer has put on them). Nor need the vision of a comprehensive science of mental functioning with a coherent and unifying theoretical structure be pejoratively dismissed as a simplistic search for a "single master text." The real point, and on this I trust Schafer would agree, is that none of us ought let our value preferences and ideologies cloud or deform our scientific judgments, however much they help shape the kinds of scientific questions to which we assign investigative priority. Nor, incidentally, are the truth-values of our scientific findings affected by the ideological commitments that may have helped shape the investigative strategies that led to them. In a world of enough (re)searchers, all the promising investigative strategies, reflecting whatever ideological commitments, should have their adherents and will be explored. And certainly none should be ruled out on the basis of the value commitments that possibly underlie them.

On the issue of the *possibility* of the quest for a psycho-analytic common ground in a shared clinical enterprise in the face of the diversity of our (proliferating) metapsychologies, we return again to the question (see Chapter 11) of the tightness or not of the fit between theory and technique. I will not repeat that argument here. I will only cite a provocative framing of the issue. When in a discussion-group meeting of the American Psychoanalytic Association a number of years back on the same topic of the relationship of theory to technique—after a detailed exposition of the many advances in theory and in conceptualization of the preceding quarter century—Merton Gill posed the question to the group of mostly very senior colleagues, "Who could specify in any way how his technique in conducting analyses had actually changed with all this enhanced theoretical knowledge?" most were hard put to specify any particulars, or to find it congenial to even rethink their taken-for-granted acceptance of the assumption, originally advanced by Freud, that theory is necessarily indissolubly linked to technique and that the road to understanding and the road to cure are always one and the same.[2]

---

[2]A caveat is in order here. Though many clinicians disclaim knowledge of theory ("I'm not a theoretician; I'm just a practicing clinician" . . . see Chapter 11) and most would be hard put—as Gill concluded—to specify how shifting or enlarging theoretical conceptualization has actually affected or altered their technique, it does not therefore follow that any analyst actually operates without theoretical understanding or that one's theory is in no way reflected in one's technique. My argument here is that the general theory or metapsychology to which one adheres and one's clinical technique are, rather, *loosely coupled* and that the more overriding determinants of technique are to be found in the commonalities of the clinical theory and in the *differences* of individual temperament and style (see my comments with relation to Glover, Anna Freud, and Sidney and Esther Fine in Chapter 11). The concept of loose coupling does not mean that there is *no* relationship of

My own operating assumption is rather, in accord with G. Klein's (1976) (and before him, Rapaport's) distinction between the general theory of psychoanalysis (the proffered explanatory metapsychology) and the clinical (or special) theory (and the Sandlers' [1984] comparable distinction between the present unconscious and the past unconscious), 1) it is the clinical theory—of conflict and compromise, of resistance and defense, and of transference and countertransference—that is experience-near, is linked closely both to technique and to the observable phenomena of the consulting room, and that is therefore amenable to testing and verification by the usual procedures of empirical science; and that 2) the general theory (theories), our overarching explanatory metapsychologies, are experience-distant, not immanent in the clinical theory nor necessarily or logically derivative from it, i.e., are loosely coupled to it, and because of that, with no yet established canons of inference that would enable the kind of hypothesis building and testing that would (or could) link the tenets of the theory to an observable phenomenal data base. That is, the general theories, which I have called our heuristically useful scientific metaphors are, I feel, at our present stage of knowledge and theory-building, beyond the reach of em-

---

theory to technique. However, it does lend support to my conception that the relatively vast differences in metapsychological allegiances can be compatible with a far-reaching clinical commonality that could lead all psychoanalysts to relate reasonably comparably to the psychological worlds of our patients, although we conceptualize those worlds within widely different explanatory languages. Along these lines, a number of Joseph Sandler's students in the Psychoanalysis Unit at University College of London are carrying out doctoral theses under his supervision, exploring, via questionnaire and interview instruments, the implicit and often quite idiosyncratic theories that govern and guide psychoanalysts' psychological understandings.

pirical testing. It is this that allows the diversity of our general theoretical perspectives (our theoretical, i.e., general-theoretical, pluralism) while permitting a commonality at the level of clinical theory and clinical technique, or at least a convergence towards a clinical commonality under the impact of systematic testing and validation of our clinical propositions.

However, the search for common ground need not take these directions. This question of alternative *directions* is the third issue to which I turn. Schwaber (1990), for example, draws the common ground very narrowly, just around our method. "It is this matter of our methodology, how we listen and what we listen for, upon which I will focus in the search for our common ground" (p. 31). Within this (narrow) frame of her conceptualization of the central essence of our method as the arena of common ground, all considerations of theory, general and experience-distant, or clinical and experience-near, are equally set aside: "There is a fundamental question . . . how are we using the differing models of our preference; how are we using even the clinical concepts about which we agree? Addressing this question will, I believe, bring our common ground more directly to the fore, as it invites us to focus on process and aim rather than content" (p. 31). And, further on,

> [there] are times, in this [psychoanalytic] process, that we use our theories—*experience-near or distant*—to infer meaning rather than to discover it. Each of us (and I have in my writings described my own susceptibility to this), in accord with the vicissitudes in our capacities to suspend our assumptions, is vulnerable to remaining grounded to them: a fear really means a wish, a perception really reflects a distortion. Thus we lose sight of the fact they are just that, our assumptions—yet to be corroborated affectively and verbally, with the patient." [p. 34, emphasis added]

That is, meaning is to be "jointly discovered rather than unilaterally inferred" (p. 35) because all inference employs theory, even if very low-level theory, and all theory is to be eschewed in this total subordination to method.

Schwaber's uncompromising and single-minded emphasis on method as a particular way of listening and responding, as the unswerving precept of proper technique, is of course distinctively her own, and most of us, however much we might agree with her on the value and the application of her technical prescriptions, would not choose to draw the search for our psychoanalytic common ground so narrowly around this single aspect of method, no matter how central it is to psychoanalytic technique.

The search for the parameters of our common ground, however, is for the most part, drawn more broadly, and on more theoretical, even philosophical grounds. Richards (1990) is an exemplar of this. Here, he discusses the problem of our theoretical pluralism through a comparative assessment of three approaches to this question, mine, Pine's (1990), and Rangell's (1988). He begins with a philosophical statement about psychoanalytic epistemology and the psychoanalytic conception of truth. In this regard psychoanalysis can be seen in either of two ways, in accord with a correspondence or a coherence theory of truth. (For a detailed recent discussion of this issue by a practicing psychoanalyst, who is also a professional philosopher, see the opening chapter of Hanly's new book, *Ariadne's Thread,* 1991).

In the correspondence theory of truth held to by scientists from Galileo and Newton through Freud, truth consists of a precise correspondence between real objects as they actually exist "out there" and their description. The possibility of scientific testing of theory by observation or experiment rests on this basic premise. In the coherence theory, truth inheres in the coherence of phenomena as they are experienced within a belief system. That is, all observations are ineluctably theory-bound and since multiple vantage points and belief systems exist, so do multiple equally "true" descriptions of the phenomenal world. This is the basis for the hermeneutic as opposed to the natural science conception of psychoanalysis.

Within this framework, Richards placed my response to the theoretical diversity of psychoanalysis and my argument for the common ground to be found in clinical unity, or rather unity of clinical purpose and method, or at least in the (scientific) possibility for convergence toward that unity, as based, he feels, on a correspondence theory of truth at the level of clinical theory and its relationship to the observable phenomena of the consulting room, but upon a coherence theory of truth at the metapsychological level of our diverse theoretical perspectives.

I would put it differently. Our philosophical assumptions cannot be mixed in these ways. My commitments are to a natural science approach to psychoanalysis as a theory of mental functioning, that is, to a correspondence theory of truth, and to the amenability of psychoanalysis, at least ultimately and in principle, to systematic testing in accord with the canons of empirical science. I feel the structure for this to exist now at the level of clinical theory, and the recent burgeoning of methodologically sophisticated, converging psychoanalytic therapy research illuminating normal and abnormal mental functioning through the study of the processes of therapeutic change, and the reach and limitations of outcome achieved, amply attests to this. (See Dahl et al. 1988 and Wallerstein 1991.)

However, I also feel that there is, at present, a significant disjunction between our clinical theory and the observable phenomena of the consulting room that it encompasses, that is all of it amenable to scientific testing, a disjunction[3]

---

[3]This conceptualization of such a disjunction between the clinical theory and the general theory, though conceptually logical and critical to my own argument, is at the same time also an "ideal fiction" in the sense that the separation is not at all points so clear-cut and simple. There are both borderline concepts, which depending on the context within which they are employed, and the connotations that adhere within that context can appropriately be assigned to one realm or the other, and also concepts where the assignment to the one realm or the other is ambiguous or controversial and largely influenced by *which* general theory is being counterposed to the clinical theory realm.

About the scientific value however, in terms of the uses of theory and the requirements of theory building, of keeping this conceptual distinction between the clinical theory and the metapsychology (or general theory), I quote at some length from Edelson (1988). "Metapsychology may not be a substantive theory at all, but a way of talking about and characterizing psychoanalytic theory. The distinction between an object language and a metalanguage is useful here. . . . If so-called clinical theory is an object language in which the psychoanalyst is able to make statements about phenomena, then a metalanguage is needed to make statements about statements in the object language. We need a metalanguage to talk about our own formulations, including our own clinical interpretations. We want, after all, to assign or ascribe qualities to our formulations; make assertions about their relations (not the relations among objects or properties they describe); categorize them; prescribe their form or content; or evaluate or judge them according to various criteria. All these things must be said in a language different from the object language. If the same terms are used in both languages, then they should be used with recognition that they are being used at different semantic levels. (The same injunction applies when a theory of linguistics makes theoretical statements in English about the natural language.)

"Psychoanalytic metapsychology, which often seems to be prescribing what psychoanalytic theory should be like, what it should include, what aspects of phenomena it should pay attention to, what kinds of concepts it should employ, may be such a metalanguage. It can only lead to confusion to suppose one is talking about the object world—the domain one is studying—when one uses metapsychology" (pp. 73–74).

between that and the various overarching metapsychologies, our diverse theoretical perspectives, which in terms of the state of our theory development I have called (see Chapter 2) our chosen explanatory *metaphors,* heuristically useful to us in terms of our varying training indoctrinations and intellectual commitments, in explaining our lower level clinical theories and the primary clinical data of our consulting rooms that they order. And it is these congeries of higher level general theories or metapsychologies, each of which purports to explain *all* of the observed and inferred clinical phenomena discerned in our consulting rooms, and each of which does it in a way that is most congenial and persuasive to its own adherents, that is still to me in a prescientific metaphoric state[4] and beyond the reach of systematic empirical testing. Which is not to say—as is sometimes assumed—that all of them are indistinguishably equal and interchangeable in terms of their potential to *become,* over time, and with refinement and growth, more scientific, in the sense of empirically testable and therefore ultimately with a demonstrably superior truth value in terms of the correspondence theory of truth. It is just that I feel that we are not there yet—are in fact still far from there—and we have no demonstrable basis today, other than our value commitments and preferences, and our scientific hunches and intuitions, to assert that our own theoretical perspective in which we have trained and to which we have committed our allegiance will prove the superior. This is not the same as Richards's imputation to me of a commitment to the coherence theory of truth in the realm of our metapsychologies. I do not feel that the

---

[4]For a discussion of the place of prescientific metaphor in scientific theory-building, see Chapter 2, and for a much more extended discussion, Wurmser (1977).

truth criteria of coherence provide a necessary heuristic or advance us scientifically in our theoretical understandings. In the end I look for the correspondence criteria of truth to be fully elaborated in the realm of our general theory—when it advances to that point—in the same manner as in the realm of our clinical theory. What exact form that more "scientific" general theory will then take, or how much of existing metapsychologies will find place within it, is I feel, beyond present predictive reach.[5]

Richards next considered Pine's (1990) direction of response to the question of psychoanalytic theoretical diversity. Pine, he stated, sees overall psychoanalysis as the sum of four separate psychologies, of drives, of the ego, of objects, and of the self, and feels that the various existant theoretical perspectives fit one or the other of these four molds. Each of the four psychologies is stated to be necessarily inadequate, given the restricted phenomenal domain it encompasses and the limited explanatory strate-

---

[5]I have this same point of difference with Richards's thoughtful critique and overview of the Rome Congress proceedings (Chapter 12) in which he also implies that I adhere (even if only for the time being) to a coherence theory of truth in the realm of our diverse and competing metapsychologies while adhering firmly to a correspondence theory of truth with the possibilities for empirical testing in the realm of our clinical theory, which I see as our common ground. I would rather put it as I have in this chapter, that I adhere totally to a correspondence theory of truth, and that our clinical theory is sufficiently grounded in observable and assessable clinical phenomena to be within reach of scientific testing within that framework, but that our metapsychologies or general theories are at this time still too experience-distant with still too loose inferential links to clinical observables, so that they are at present beyond the reach of adequate scientific test, and that therefore the correspondences between theory and nature that should be there are simply beyond demonstrable reach.

gies that it therefore yields. Since each of the four psychologies is equally valid, but necessarily equally self-limiting outside of its appropriate domain, the analytic practitioner is advised to simply follow the clinical material and its data, and to draw on each of the theoretical perspectives as it appears appropriate or seems to illuminate best the particular event or phenomenon under scrutiny. This may not lead to "theoretical integration" (presumably unreachable) but perhaps "phenomenological synthesis."

Pine's position, of course, runs counter to the claims of each of our general theories, since *each* purports to encompass the *entire* phenomenal realm of psychoanalysis (and further, each purports to do it best, most comprehensively, most coherently, and most effectively in terms of therapeutic explanatory leverage). This is claimed by each whether or not it was originally derived from the study of the particular problems of a specific segment of the psychopathological spectrum, like Kohut's self psychology, which was originally created to better understand and treat the narcissistic character disorders with their particular pathology of the self, but was soon extended to be a claimed more encompassing (and more therapeutically applicable) perspective upon the pathology of all the mentally and emotionally disturbed, whether or not narcissistic pathology plays a significant role.

Pine's position can also be read, as it is by Richards, as the arrival at the end point of theory building in psychoanalysis, assuming that his parceling into four psychologies encompasses the totality of domains of psychoanalytic inquiry. In contrast to my position which Richards states to be one of building towards a future in which there will be a unifying psychoanalytic structure that meets the requirements of the correspondence theory of truth, he finds Pine's position to be an assertion that the future is here, that it provides us with four theories (or groups of theories), that they are distinct, only partially overlapping, each a "truth" from a single limited perspective or vantage point—hence, basically a coherence theory of truth and a clinical therapeutic operation limited to extracting "experiential truths" from each of the four psychologies and drawing on them as clinical circumstances make useful.

But then Richards poses a third response (Rangell 1988) to this same question of dealing with our theoretical diversity. As a major spokesman for the "mainstream" American ego psychological perspective within which he has positioned his own very significant incremental additions to the overall metapsychological edifice, Rangell is a forthright advocate of what he now calls "total composite psychoanalytic theory," a term he finds more felicitous than "classical" or "orthodox" psychoanalysis. The argument is (though it would be vigorously disputed by the adherents of other metapsychologies, for example, most intensively by the Kleinians) that this (American) total composite psychoanaltyic theory represents the most direct line of descent from Freud's own scientific corpus via the contributions of Anna Freud and Hartmann (respectively on the defensive and adaptive aspects of ego functioning) and onto the ego psychological metapsychology edifice created by Hartmann, Kris, Loewenstein, Fenichel, Rapaport, Jacobson, and a host of others. This model, Rangell feels, has room for every emphasis within psychoanalysis and encompasses them all, drive and ego, self and object, pre-eodipal and oedipal, intrapsychic and interpersonal, "here and now" interpretation and "there and then" reconstruction. Each of the other psychoanalytic theoretical perspectives Rangell feels to be a "selective" perspective, with a hypertrophied emphasis on an aspect of the whole at

286

the expense of overall balance and with always the tendency towards a pars pro toto, a part as if it were equivalent in explanatory compass to the whole. Within Richards's frame, he anchors Rangell's position in a correspondence theory of truth with the issue already settled (where in my overview it is still for the science of the future to settle), with total composite psychoanalytic theory to be the one that corresponds best to nature and with all the other psychoanalytic metapsychologies to take their place as selective emphases within this composite whole.

My own comparative assessment of my views and Rangell's as he described them in his paper (1988) was in part a specific response to my Montreal address (Chapter 2), was described in my Rome address (Chapter 11) and is essentially the same as Richards's but without his focus on where our two positions fit in regard to the theory of truth that they assume—where in fact Rangell and I do agree on our shared adherence to a natural science framework for psychoanalysis with its commitment to a correspondence theory of truth. Within that framework, where we disagree is not in regard to the American ego psychological (and now, post-ego psychological) paradigm within which we were both trained and to which we both adhere, but in his assertion that the scientific primacy of that paradigm over the competing psychoanalytic metapsychologies has already been established and my conviction that however much I might want to believe that, it simply has not yet been (scientifically) established and that at the present state of theory development (and of methodological sophistication as well) in our discipline, that it is simply beyond our scientific reach. All of our metaphoric general theoretical structures simply have—none of them—yet matured to the point where they have come within the investigative reach of empirical science, as formal theoretical structures with operationalized constructs amenable to testing by systematic and controlled observation. Within my perspective, Rangell's scientific posture is an imperialism by assertion.

It should be quite clear at this point that I regard our various theoretical arguments—and the various positions in response to the issue posed by the current theoretical pluralism within our discipline, like those just presented, mine, Schwaber's, Pine's, Rangell's, and of course others—to be "resolvable" today only by the persuasive power of rhetoric and not yet by the sounder process of knowledge accrual through proper empirical scientific advance. That the latter can and will happen is an article of scientific faith that I have already articulated in Chapter 11, "that by cohering around our common clinical ground and by building our clinical theorizing incrementally upon that, we will have, we do have, the firm base upon which we can painstakingly fashion a truly scientific theoretical structure that can take its place properly and proudly as a full partner within the array of human sciences."

At this point, given this perspective on the problem of our theoretical diversity in psychoanalysis and the various very difficult proposed roads to its resolution, definitional, conceptual, and scientific-empirical, as well as even the avowed intention—espoused by Schafer—to explicitly eschew efforts at its resolution since the greater "value" is claimed to exist in the continued dialectical interplay of non-reconciled differences in perspective and vantage point, rather than in the building of a coherent and unified scientific theoretical structure, there is still the counterpart issue of the commonality that I feel I do discern in the clinical theory and its technical application in the understanding of the observable phenomena of the consulting room, a commonality that I feel gives all of us under the

psychoanalytic umbrella the warrant to call ourselves psychoanalysts engaged in common purpose and common
endeavor despite the very different theoretical explanatory
languages in which we describe what we do. It is my clinical
and clinical-theoretical answer to the question I posed
initially in Chapter 2. What, in the face of our increasing
psychoanalytic diversity, our pluralism of theoretical perspectives, of linguistic and thought conventions, of distinctive regional, cultural, and language emphases, what in the
face of all this still holds us together as common adherents
of a shared psychoanalytic science and profession?

I have tried both in Chapter 2 and Chapter 11 to provide
convincing enough clinical examples of how a shared
clinical purpose, understanding, and relating appropriately
to the inner psychological world of the patient, can be
pursued in comparably effective and adequate ways by
adherents of differing psychoanalytic theoretical perspectives. In my Montreal address I drew on an example from
Kohut's last book (1984) in which he compared the
interpretive response of a Kleinian colleague from Latin
America to a particular patient that the colleague was
treating, a response cast into a (stereo)typically identifiable
Kleinian explanatory format, with the self-psychologically
cast interpretation that Kohut would have made, as well as
his own formulation of how a "classical" ego-psychological
interpretation might have been made in conflict-
drive-defense terms (Chapter 2). Kohut's point was that
each of the three, distinctively phrased interpretations
might each have been equally helpful in that particular
clinical situation—the patient's silent withdrawal from the
joint analytic work in the hour immediately after notification of the planned cancellation of a pending session—since
each interpretation would have empathically addressed the

same current transference fantasy enacted in this clinical situation, though each interpretation would have been cast in different (metapsychological) explanatory language.

In my Rome address two years later (see Chapter 11) I engaged in a much more extended comparative study of the three major clinical presentations at the Rome Congress, by Hernández, a Latin American trained by the middle or independent (object relations) group in the London Institute, by Feldman, a British Kleinian, and by Kris, within the contemporary American ego-psychological framework. This comparative assessment was facilitated and could be made more meaningful and heuristically useful by the happenstance that the three women patients, selected independently by three analysts of different theoretical persuasions and practicing in three different regions of the world, nonetheless showed striking clinical similarities in the structures of their personalities and the issues that brought them to analysis. I concluded that comparative review with the statement that I had

> tried—I hope convincingly—to demonstrate my own conviction that three representative and respected colleagues, representing the three major regions of world-wide psychoanalytic activity, and trained within three of the major theoretical perspectives within psychoanalysis, have all approached, dealt with, interpreted the clinical material of three surprisingly similar and quite comparable analytic patients, in a clearly identifiably, and contrary perhaps to our preconceptions, surprisingly comparable way. [Chapter 11]

For my purposes of additional clinical comparison at this point, I draw upon a similar happenstance. At its annual meeting in May 1990 in New York, the American Psychoanalytic Association had an all-day panel "Freudian and

Kleinian Theory: A Dialogue of Comparative Perspectives."
Edward Weinshel and Hanna Segal were asked, as major
representatives of the American ego-psychological and the
British Kleinian traditions, to make clinical presentations of
an analytic case giving an overview of the patient and the
treatment course with a process focus then on the detailed
clinical interactions of selected specimen hours. Each of the
cases would be the focus of a half day with the other colleague
discussing the case along with a panel of analytic colleagues
from both the United States and Latin America representing
a variety of viewpoints. In my discussion here I draw on the
two main clinical presentations, together with a statement by
Weinshel pointing out numerous similarities in the two
patients that facilitated the comparison of the analytic han-
dlings from within different analytic theoretical positions,
and also—because his discussion highlighted the kind of
considerations I wish to advance—Otto Kernberg's discussions of both the Weinshel and Segal papers.

Because of the need to protect the privacy of the two
patients whose treatments were presented in such illuminating detail, and since it is not vital to my discussion to
present that detail, I will not draw directly from the two
major presentation texts but establish the clinical base for
my comparative discussion by quoting from Weinshel's
remarks addressed to Segal on the similarities and differences in their clinical presentations. Of the two patients,
Weinshel in an unpublished manuscript (1990) first said:

> In some respects it is advantageous that in many ways the
> two patients demonstrated many similarities. Both women
> were in their 40's, both had been married, and both were
> now living with a man—and both had long histories of
> trouble in their relationships with men. Both are mothers;
> both had significant difficulties with their own disturbed
> and depressed mothers, and both had problems with their

own adolescent children. Both had sisters with whom there was some variety of homosexual feelings and conflicts.

One patient's father died when she was an early adolescent; the other's father had died before her birth. With both, one in regard to her father, the other in regard to the stepfather, there were problems and/or concerns about incestuous, seductive, and exhibitionistic behaviors. Both patients' mothers died during the course of analysis.

Both patients were in the latter phases of their ongoing analysis at the time the reported analytic work took place; and in both cases, the reported sessions occurred just prior to the analysts' going off on holiday. In both, the analytic material included oedipal fantasies and both patients were upset and angry that the analyst was about to be sexually involved with another person during the imminent holiday. Both produced dreams "featuring" the undisguised presence of the analyst during this period. Both had described, in one way or another, a tendency to withdraw in the face of frustration, to act out in somewhat delinquent ways, and difficulties in dealing with the problem of greed and its various derivatives.

Obviously, there were many other ways in which these two women differed, but it is also of interest that the two analysts reported somewhat comparable progress in similar areas; in better relations with the men with whom they were living and with their children as well, in better relations at work, and [I trust that I am using the term in the same way that Dr. Segal does] in a better working alliance in the analysis. In both analyses, a dream triggered at least in part by the transference, played a significant role in the reported sessions.

Weinshel then went on to reflect that these many significant parallels and similarities certainly gave good basis for one to usefully consider comparatively how the two analysts from their different schools each approached the analytic work. His chief surprise, he stated, was that he did not find Segal's work as "alien" as he had remembered from reading Kleinian papers. Having recently closely studied a number of Kleinian papers including Feldman's presentation at the Rome Congress (see Chapter 10), he felt that what the Kleinian analysts were now saying was considerably closer to his own psychoanalytic perspective than had been true in the past. Also, the *differences* he would now describe seemed more relative and subtle than they had appeared to be some twenty years earlier. And he also declared the caveat, that with such a limited sample, one could not be sure if given *differences* reflected significant theory-driven variations in technique or were the product of more personal stylistic and temperamental individuality.

Weinshel then listed some dozen such points of seeming difference that he had discerned, of which I will quote the five that I regard as most salient to technique and analytic work.

1. I suggest that Dr. Segal is bolder and somewhat more positive in her interpretations than I am and—seemingly—less dependent on the *patient's* associations in framing those interpretations. I thought that her patient tended to agree with her much more frequently than my patients with me. I tend to wait longer in making my interventions, look more to the patient's interpretations to support my own, and offer my interpretations in a more tentative fashion.
2. Although we both recognize both sides of the transference/resistance complex, it seemed evident that I emphasied much more the resistance side of the pair while Dr. Segal was more focused on the transference.
3. I believe that I am less likely to come up with a one-to-one relationship/connection between the present and the past.

4. I tend to view the illness as more multidetermined than does Dr. Segal, so that the portrayal of my case seems less clear and even a bit fragmented.

5. I don't think I can prove it, but I have the impression that I make my analysands work harder and have them take more responsibility for the analytic work. In fact, Dr. Segal hardly, if ever, uses the word "work" in talking about the analysis. I depend more on the patient's associations and try to deal with the resistances connected with them. I rarely "interpret" a patient's dream; instead I let the patient associate to the dream material and may interpret the resistances connected with that material or to the dream. I will, of course, contribute some of my own ideas about the dream or ask the patient about it. As best I can, I try to be the Dr. Watson to my patient's Sherlock Holmes; and generally, I try to avoid usurping the patient's "starring" role.

It should, of course, be borne in mind in connection with Weinshel's statement of perceived differences that this is his own view which might or might not be agreed to by Segal, or by the other panel participants, or the audience, and that even if there were a general consensus on Wein- shel's portrayal of the perceived differences, that these might be based more on stylistic and temperamental differ- ences than on theoretically based variation in technique. Certainly, his own well-known proclivity to focus on the systematic analysis of the resistances as the central feature of the psychoanalytic process (Weinshel 1990) lies somewhere on this spectrum from what is idiosyncratic and stylistic to what is theoretically informed and theory-driven. Given all this, we are still left with the impression that the reported differences—as experienced by Weinshel—are in the direc- tion of our usual (stereotypical?) assumptions about the theory-driven differences in technique between the American ego psychological and the British Kleinian schools, but sharply muted from the (exaggerated?) way in which these differences have been traditionally perceived. The question that naturally comes to mind is whether the ways of clinical working of American ego psychological and British Kleinian analysts have come progressively closer together over time—despite the remaining starkly different systems of theoretically conceptualizing the structure of the mind and what "structural change" in its functioning means. This point was experienced in just that way by many of us in the audience that day. Any number in that audience on listening to Hanna Segal's presentation expressed themselves as hard put to discern what made it Kleinian, that is, how did it really differ technically from what they themselves did with that patient.

Among the formal discussants, it was Otto Kernberg who focused most sharply on the kind of comparative assessment that Weinshel essayed and that is the center of my own concern. Kernberg, of course, had his specific points of disagreement technically with each of the presentations. To me the points he made, whether consciously intended or not, were all in the service of further bridging or bringing together the kinds of continuing seeming differences in technique that Weinshel had expressed. In regard to Weinshel's clinical presentation, Kernberg's commentary was in the direction of his feeling that Weinshel could have—should have—interpreted more readily and more *deeply* especially in relation to what Kernberg felt to be the operative more primitive and archaic defense and resistance patterns.

To make his points, Kernberg "translated" Weinshel's drive/structural, that is, drive-defense-conflict, conceptua-

lizations into the language of internalized object relationships. For example, an unhappy "misunderstanding" between Weinshel and his patient in which the analyst had
made what seemed like a very simple and obvious transference linkage, had been responded to with an angry tirade by
the patient in which she had irately demanded to know
how he had reached that kind of farfetched conclusion. She
then complained bitterly that his "playing with words" was
both confusing and unfair. Kernberg described this interchange as reflecting the activation of an internalized object
relationship in the transference, namely the relationship
with the mother played out with role reversal, with the
patient behaving towards her analyst the same way that she
had so frequently experienced her mother behaving towards
her, telling her that it was unclear to the mother how the
patient had come up with something, that it was certainly
not in what the mother had said, and so on.

Kernberg's thrust was that he felt it indicated, or might
be useful, to carry the interpretive work more vigorously,
faster, deeper, in these directions than Weinshel had done—
Weinshel having worked in this way he described, and for
the reasons he gave there, in his own comparative assessment of his work and that of Segal from which I have
quoted. Kernberg then went on to give further examples
from Weinshel's protocol in which he recast the formulations into the language of projective identifications and the
internalized object relationship with the sadistic mother
reenacted in the transference with frequent role reversals of
the kind just illustrated, and how this "could have been
more vigorously clarified, and, with appropriate timing and
tact, . . . interpreted in the context of that vignette." Basic
to Kernberg's overall formulation of the dynamics of this
case was that it was more painful for the patient to think

that she might be behaving like her mother than to project this propensity onto Weinshel and experience him as behaving like the mother with herself as his hapless victim. Painful as it is to be a masochistic victim, it might be less frightening than to be identified with an intolerable victimizer. It is this that Kernberg saw behind Weinshel's patient's "inconsolability."

Overall then, and with an equally detailed discussion of a whole succession of other interactions from Weinshel's protocol, Kernberg pursued his thesis that some of the Kleinian and/or object relational clinical contributions could be used to facilitate a more systematic analysis of Weinshel's patient's characterological defenses in the transference, especially the early defensive operations (in this case, projective identifications), and the activation in the transference of primitive internalized object relations (in this case, the interchange of roles of the grandiose, distant, and devaluing mother and the victimized, "inconsolable" child). In overall intent—as I see it—Kernberg tried to push Weinshel closer to how Segal or a representative of the British object relational perspective might have handled the case.[6]

In his discussion in turn of Segal's clinical protocol, Kernberg acted, as I see it, in counterpart, to show the ways in which this major representative of mainstream contemporary Kleinian technique had moved closer to what has been conceived in America as "mainstream" or "classical"

---

[6]In response to these technical recommendations of Kernberg's, Weinshel's position is that the clinical material was drawn from an early stage of the analysis, at a time that he felt the analytic situation *not yet ready* (deepened sufficiently) for so frontal and direct an interpretive approach.

analysis grounded firmly in Freud's structural model and the ego psychology theoretical development with the concomitant increasing focus on the defenses and the resistances that represent its technical implementation. Using the material from the reported session shortly before the pending vacation where the patient brought a dream, analysis of which revealed the patient's invasive curiosity about the analyst's private life, death wishes against the analyst's husband as well as an implicit attack against the analyst, Kernberg indicated the ways in which Segal's interpretations through this session, though focused sharply on the transference, also integrated information about developments in the patient's life outside the treatment hours into the transference interpretations, and in the process then deepened the patient's awareness of her intrapsychic conflict with the internalized imago of the feared and envied mother, and the mother's "delinquent" sexual license and behavior.

All of this Kernberg felt to be totally "compatible with a contemporary, sophisticated ego psychological approach, although the richness of the analysis of the shifting nature of the dominant object relationship in the transference and its projective and introjective elements are clearly an expression of a major Kleinian emphasis." Along these same lines, Kernberg was also impressed by the absence in Segal's presentation of direct reference to genetic material. For all practical purposes, the interpretations were almost exclusively focused on the unconscious meanings in the "here and now" interactions in the transference, "totally compatible with my own approach to explore very carefully and only very gradually the genetic antecedents of present unconscious conflicts, in order to avoid premature closure by theory inspired genetic reconstructions."

Kernberg went on from this to declare Segal's presentation a particularly lucid and elegant illustration of "mainstream contemporary Kleinian technique," centering on a consistent and systematic concentration on the analysis of actualized internalized object relations in the transference, with a focus on both more archaic and more "advanced" transferences, and aspects of oedipal conflicts, and with transference interpretations including extra-transferential material and actual information about the patient's past in the light of the dominant unconscious conflicts in the "here and now." All this he felt to represent significant shifts from the past "traditional" Kleinian technique, now with a much more careful and gradual approach, from surface to depth, to the transference manifestations, and a concomitant markedly decreased tendency to interpret directly to the "deepest levels" of the patient's anxiety, that is, the assumed developments in the patient's first year of life. Nothing in Segal's presentation reflected that erstwhile dominant emphasis on those assumed earliest phases of development, on the familiar bench-marks of relationships to body parts and to part-object constructions.

Although there are other current developments from the original Kleinian legacy (that is, the different directions of Bion, of Rosenfeld, and of Meltzer), Kernberg stated his main point to be this particular development exemplified in Segal's presentation towards a convergence with the contemporary Freudian ego psychological approach. In summation, he said "I do not think it is a coincidence that in practice, if not in her initial theoretical statement, Dr. Segal should focus so dominantly on the unconscious meanings in the "here and now," pay so much attention to the gradual developments within the patient's associations and immediately observable behavior as well as on her countertransference, avoid symbolic patterns relating the present to the earliest developmental phases, and, in short, pay so much attention to the patient's characterological patterns."

How can we relate these assessments of the Weinshel-Segal comparative presentations, drawn as typical exemplars of contemporary Freudian (ego psychological) and Kleinian practice and technique, to my theme of the common ground of psychoanalysis that I feel exists in the clinical interactions and the interplay of transferences and counter-transferences in the consulting room? Weinshel felt able to adduce a dozen ways in which his technical approach differed somewhat from that of Segal. At the same time he expressed his surprise that these differences he encountered, though all in the direction that we would expect them to be in terms of our conceptions of the distinctnesses of the Freudian and Kleinian approaches from each other, were so very much less than they would have been twenty years earlier. And this was echoed by the prevailing sentiment in the audience that I referred to, again the surprise and the question of what was so Kleinian about Segal's presenta-tion, Kleinian, that is, in terms of the usual conception from America of how Kleinians work.

And Kernberg in turn, while also still seeing an arc of difference, undertook an effort at conceptual bridging by indicating how much he felt that mainstream British Klein-ian technique had moved over those twenty years in the direction of increasing compatibility with the American ego-psychological approach, and at the same time indi-cating how he could have intervened more quickly and more directly with Weinshel's patient, and all, I am confi-dent, in a direction that the Kleinians would feel to be more compatible with their accustomed clinical approach. And of course, both this perception of, and further encouragement

of, clinical technical convergence is in keeping with Kernberg's own agenda in trying to fashion an ego psychological—drive/structural or drive-defense-conflict—theoretical
structure for psychoanalysis in which the building blocks of
the tripartite psychic instances are comprised of internalized
object-relationships, that is, a self-representation, a counterpart object-representation, and the affective valence that
bind them. It is this amalgamation of the object-relational
perspective into the ego psychological metapsychology paradigm that Kernberg would see as yielding the convergent
theory and technique toward which he asserts Freudians
and Kleinians alike are moving.

My own position, though somewhat similar to his and
broadly sympathetic to it, is also somewhat different. It is
rather that despite the still continuing clearly discernible
differences between Freudian and Kleinian technique that
Weinshel could identity—albeit sharply muted from what
they were two decades ago[7]—the seasoned adherent of each
technique would relate equally empathically to the inner

---

[7]In Chapter 11, I reviewed the research study of Sidney and Esther
Fine (1988) in which they did establish that independent analyst judges
could identify the theoretical positions of fourteen analyst participants
(four American ego psychologists, four Kleinians, three self psychologists, and three advocates of Kernberg's amalgamated ego-psycho-
logical/object-relational approach) from detailed accounts of single
analytic sessions at a significantly better than chance level according to
at least one, and in some cases according to most, of six critical factors
or variables. My own question is somewhat different, and that is, what
difference do these kinds of differences really make for our clinical
understanding, clinical method, and clinical work, or for our capacity
to relate empathically to our patient's inner psychological world?
This is the same issue that I discuss in the juxtaposition of Weinshel's and Kernberg's organizing conceptual framework alongside my
own.

psychological state of the patient in terms of the observable and inferable affects and defenses and resistances and transferences and countertransferences, that the patient would be comparably affected, despite whatever different metapsychological explanatory language was employed, or however different the temperament and style of the analyst in consequence of theory-driven or stylistic difference was expressed somewhat differently in the content, pace, or intensity of the specific clinical interventions. Unfortunately, issues of the need to safeguard the confidentiality of the clinical material have precluded the same detailed study here of the precise clinical interactions offered in Weinshel's and Segal's accounts that I was able to do more extensively in relation to the clinical presentations by Hernández, Feldman, and Kris in Chapter 11. Such a more detailed study might shed additional light on how convincingly I could further document my viewpoint.

But like many other theoretical-clinical issues that occupy psychoanalysis during this period of both rapid knowledge expansion and conspicuous conceptual flux, the overall premise of this book concerning where the defining common ground of psychoanalysis is situated, is still an unsettled issue without established consensus. This book has been an effort to advance that argument.

References

Arlow, J. A. (1981). Theories of pathogenesis. *Psychoanalytic Quarterly* 50:448–454.

_____ (1986). The relation of theories of pathogenesis to therapy. In *Psychoanalysis: The Science of Mental Conflict, Essays in Honor of Charles Brenner*, ed. A. D. Richards and M. S. Willick, pp. 49–63. Hillsdale, NJ: Analytic Press.

Arlow, J. A., and Brenner, C. (1988). The future of psychoanalysis. *Psychoanalytic Quarterly* 70:3–28.

Bacal, H. A., and Newman, K. M. (1990). *Theories of Object Relations: Bridges to Self Psychology*. New York: Columbia University Press.

Berger, L. S. (1985). *Psychoanalytic Theory and Clinical Relevance*. Hillsdale, NJ: Analytic Press.

Bergeret, J. (1986). Reflections on the scientific responsibilities of the International Psycho-Analytical Association (unpublished paper).

Brenner, C. (1976). *Psychoanalytic Technique and Psychic Conflict*. New York: International Universities Press.

_____ (1979). Depressive affects, anxiety, and psychic conflict in the phallic-oedipal phase. *Psychoanalytic Quarterly* 47:177–197.

_____ (1982). *The Mind in Conflict*. New York: International Universities Press.

Cooper, A. M. (1977). *Clinical Psychoanalysis: One Method or More—The Relation of Diagnosis to Psychoanalytic Treatment*. Presented at the Fall meeting of the American Psychoanalytic Association.

_____ (1984). Psychoanalysis at one hundred years: beginnings of maturity. *Journal of the American Psychoanalytic Association* 32:245–267.

Dahl, H., Kaechele, H., and Thomae, H. (1988). *Psychoanalytic Process Research Strategies*. New York: Springer Verlag.

Edelson, M. (1985). The hermeneutic turn and the single case study in psychoanalysis. *Psychoanalysis and Contemporary Thought* 8:567–614.

―――― (1988). *Psychoanalysis: A Theory in Crisis.* Chicago: University of Chicago Press.

Eissler, K. R. (1953). The effect of the structure of the ego on psychoanalytic technique. *Journal of the American Psychoanalytic Association* 1:104–141.

Erikson, E. H. (1959). *Identity and the Life Cycle: Selected Papers. Psychological Issues* 1. New York: International Universities Press.

Ferenczi, S., and Rank, O. (1924). *The Development of Psychoanalysis.* Madison, CT: International Universities Press, 1986.

Feyerabend, P. K. (1981). *Realism, Rationalism, and Scientific Method: Philosophical Papers, Volume 1.* Cambridge, England: Cambridge University Press.

Fine, S., and Fine, E. (1988). *Four psychoanalytic perspectives: a study of the differences in interpretive interventions.* Presented to the Los Angeles Psychoanalytic Society.

Freud. A. (1936). *The Ego and the Mechanisms of Defence.* New York: International Universities Press, 1946.

―――― (1954). The widening scope of indications for psychoanalysis: discussion. *Journal of the American Psychoanalytic Association* 2:607–620.

Freud, S. (1910). 'Wild' psycho-analysis. *Standard Edition* 11:219–227.

―――― (1914a). On the history of the psychoanalytic movement. *Standard Edition* 14:1–66.

―――― (1914b). On narcissism: an introduction. *Standard Edition* 14:67–102.

―――― (1915a). Instincts and their vicissitudes. *Standard Edition* 14:109–140.

―――― (1915b). Observations on transference love. *Standard Edition* 12:157–164.

―――― (1915c). Thoughts for the times on war and death. *Standard Edition* 14:273–302.

―――― (1920). Beyond the pleasure principle. *Standard Edition* 18:1–64.

―――― (1923 [1922]). Two encyclopedia articles. *Standard Edition* 18:233–259.

―――― (1923). The ego and the id. *Standard Edition* 19:1–66.

―――― (1926). Symptoms, inhibitions, and anxiety. *Standard Edition* 20:75–175.

_____ (1937). Analysis terminable and interminable. *Standard Edition* 23:209–253.

Freud, S., and Breuer, J. (1893–1895). Studies on hysteria. *Standard Edition* 2:ix–311.

Gadamer, H. G. (1975). *Truth and Method.* New York: Seabury Press.

Gardner, M. R. (1983). *Self-Inquiry.* Boston/Toronto: Little, Brown.

Gedo, J. (1984). *Psychoanalysis and Its Discontents.* New York: Guilford Press.

Gill, M. M. ed. (1967). *The Collected Papers of David Rapaport.* New York: Basic Books.

_____ (1976). Metapsychology is not psychology. In *Psychology versus Metapsychology: Psychoanalytic Essays in Memory of George S. Klein,* ed. M. M. Gill and P. S. Holzman. *Psychological Issues* 36:71–105.

_____ (1982). *Analysis of Transference: Volume I: Theory and Technique. Psychological Issues* 53:193. New York: International Universities Press.

_____ (1984a). Transference: a change in conception or only in emphasis? *Psychoanalytic Inquiry* 4:489–523.

_____ (1984b). Psychoanalysis and psychotherapy: a revision. *International Review of Psycho-Analysis* 11:161–179.

Gill, M. M., and Holzman, P. S., eds. (1976). *Psychology vs. Metapsychology: Psychoanalytic Essays in Memory of George S. Klein. Psychological Issues 36.* New York: International Universities Press.

Glover, E. (1931). The therapeutic effect of inexact interpretation. *International Journal of Psycho-Analysis* 12:397–411.

_____ (1955). *The Technique of Psychoanalysis.* New York: International Universities Press.

Goldberg, A. (1988). *A Fresh Look at Psychoanalysis, the View from Self Psychology.* Hillsdale, NJ: Analytic Press.

Gombaroff, M. Considerations of the psychoanalytic institution (unpublished paper).

Goodheart, W. B. (1984). C. G. Jung's first 'patient': on the seminal emergence of Jung's thought. *Journal of Analytical Psychology* 29:1–34.

Gray, P. (1973). Psychoanalytic technique and the ego's capacity for viewing intrapsychic conflict. *Journal of the American Psychoanalytic Association* 21:474–494.

_____ (1982). Developmental lag in the evolution of technique for psychoanalysis of neurotic conflict. *Journal of the American Psychoanalytic Association* 30:621–655.

Greenberg, J. R., and Mitchell, S. A. (1983). *Object Relations in Psychoanalytic Theory.* Cambridge, MA: Harvard University Press.

Habermas, J. (1968). *Knowledge and Human Interests.* Trans. J. J. Shapiro. Boston: Beacon Press, 1971.

Hanly, C. (1990). The concept of truth in psychoanalysis. *International Journal of Psycho-Analysis* 71:375–383.

———— (1991). *Ariadne's Thread.* New York: Guilford Press.

Harrison, S. I. (1970). Is psychoanalysis 'our science'? Reflections on the scientific status of psychoanalysis. *Journal of the American Psychoanalytic Association* 18:125–149.

Hartmann, H. (1939). *Ego Psychology and the Problem of Adaptation.* New York: International Universities Press, 1958.

———— (1964). *Essays in Ego Psychology: Selected Problems in Psychoanalytic Theory.* New York: International Universities Press.

———— Kris, E., and Loewenstein, R. M. (1964). *Papers on Psychoanalytic Psychology. Psychological Issues* 14:206. New York: International Universities Press.

Holt, R. R. (1976). Drive or wish? A reconsideration of the psychoanalytic theory of motivation. In *Psychology versus Metapsychology: Psychoanalytic Essays in Memory of George S. Klein,* ed. M. M. Gill and P. S. Holzman. *Psychological Issues* 36:158–197. New York: International Universities Press.

———— (1989). *Freud Reappraised: A Fresh Look at Psychoanalytic Theory.* New York: Guilford Press.

Isaacs, S. (1943). Conclusion of discussion 'The nature and function of phantasy.' *Scientific Bulletin of British Psychoanalytic Society* 17:151, 153, 1967.

Jacobson, E. (1964). *The Self and the Object World.* New York: International Universities Press.

Kazin, A. (1957). The Freudian revolution analyzed. In *Freud and the 20th Century,* ed. B. Nelson, pp. 13–21. New York: Meridian Books.

Kernberg, O. (1975). *Borderline Conditions and Pathological Narcissism.* New York: Jason Aronson.

———— (1976). *Object Relations Theory and Clinical Psychoanalysis.* New York: Jason Aronson.

———— (1980). *Internal World and External Reality: Object Relations Theory Applied.* New York: Jason Aronson.

———— (1990). Discussion of the case presentations by Drs. H. Segal and E. M. Weinshel. American Psychoanalytic Association Annual Meeting. New York, May.

King, P. and Steiner, R., eds. (1991). *The Freud-Klein Controversies, 1941–1945*. London: Tavistock/Routledge.

Klein, G. S. (1976). *Psychoanalytic Theory: An Exploration of Essentials*. New York: International Universities Press.

Klein, M. (1948). *Contributions to Psycho-Analysis, 1921–1945*. London: Hogarth Press.

―――― (1949). *The Psycho-Analysis of Children*. London: Hogarth Press.

Knight, R. P. (1953). The present status of organized psychoanalysis in the United States. *Journal of the American Psychoanalytic Association* 1:197–221. Reprinted in *Clinician and Therapist: Selected Papers of Robert P. Knight*, ed. S. C. Miller. New York: Basic Books, 1972.

Kohon, G., ed. (1986). *The British School of Psychoanalysis: The Independent Tradition*. New Haven: Yale University Press.

Kohut, H. (1971). *The Analysis of the Self: A Systematic Approach to the Psychoanalytic Treatment of Narcissistic Personality Disorders*. New York: International Universities Press.

―――― (1977). *The Restoration of the Self*. New York: International Universities Press.

―――― (1984). *How Does Analysis Cure?* Ed. A. Goldberg and P. E. Stepansky. Chicago: University of Chicago Press.

Kris, A. O. (1983). The analyst's conceptual freedom in the method of free association. *International Journal of Psycho-Analysis* 64:407–411.

―――― (1989). Plenary clinical presentation. 36th IPAC, Rome, August.

Kris, E. (1947). The nature of psychoanalytic projections and their validations. In *Freedom and Experience: Essays Presented to Horace Kallen*, ed. S. Hook and M. R. Konvitz, pp. 239–259. Ithaca, NY: Cornell University Press.

Kuhn, T. (1962). *The Structure of Scientific Revolutions*. Chicago: University of Chicago Press.

―――― (1977). *The Essential Tension*. Chicago: University of Chicago Press.

Lacan, J. (1977). *Ecrits: A Selection*. New York: Norton.

―――― (1978). *The Four Fundamental Concepts of Psycho-Analysis*. New York: Norton.

Leavy, S. A. (1977). The significance of Jacques Lacan. *Psychoanalytic Quarterly* 46:201–219.

―――― (1983a). Speaking in tongues: Some linguistic approaches to psychoanalysis. *Psychoanalytic Quarterly* 52:34–55.

────── (1983b). The image and the word: further reflections on Jacques Lacan. In *Interpreting Lacan,* ed. J. H. Smith and W. Kerrigan, pp. 3–20. New Haven: Yale University Press.

Lebovici, S., and Widlöcher, D., eds. (1980). *Psychoanalysis in France.* New York: International Universities Press.

Levenson, E. A. (1972). *The Fallacy of Understanding: An Inquiry into the Changing Structure of Psychoanalysis.* New York: Basic Books.

────── (1983). *The Ambiguity of Change: An Inquiry into the Nature of Psychoanalytic Reality.* New York: Basic Books.

Loewald, H. W. (1980). *Papers on Psychoanalysis.* New Haven: Yale University Press.

Lussier, A. (1991). The search for common ground: a critique. *International Journal of Psycho-Analysis* 72:57–62.

Mahler, M. S., Pine, F., and Bergman, A. (1975). *The Psychological Birth of the Human Infant: Symbiosis and Individuation.* New York: Basic Books.

Merendino, R. P. (1985). On epistemological functions of clinical reports. *International Review of Psycho-Analysis* 12:327–335.

Merleau-Ponty, M. (1965). *The Structure of Behavior.* Trans. L. Fisher. London: Methuen.

Michels, R. (1988). The future of psychoanalysis. *Psychoanalytic Quarterly* 57:167–185.

Modell, A. H. (1968). *Object Love and Reality: An Introduction to a Psychoanalytic Theory of Object Relations.* New York: International Universities Press.

────── (1984). *Psychoanalysis in a New Context.* New York: International Universities Press.

Nasio, J.-D. (1984). The unconscious, the transference, and the psychoanalyst's interpretation: a Lacanian view. *Psychoanalytic Inquiry* 4:401–411.

Norman, J. (1990). The psychoanalytic scene in Sweden. *Bulletin of European Psycho-Analytic Federation* 35:5–12.

Ornstein, P. H., ed. (1978). *The Search for the Self: Selected Writings of Heinz Kohut: 1950–1987, Volume 1.* New York: International Universities Press.

Peterfreund, E. (in collaboration with J. T. Schwartz) (1971). *Information, Systems, and Psychoanalysis: An Evolutionary Biological Approach to Psychoanalytic Theory. Psychological Issues* 25/26. New York: International Universities Press.

Pine, F. (1990). *Drive, Ego, Object, and Self: A Synthesis for Clinical Work*. New York: Basic Books.

Plaut, A. (1988). Letter to the Editors, One Psychoanalysis or Many? *International Journal of Psycho-Analysis* 69:552–553.

Poland, W. S., and Major, R., eds. (1984). French psychoanalytic voices. *Psychoanalytic Inquiry* 4:145–311.

Post, S. (1986). Psychoanalytic rapprochement: a correspondence. *Academy Forum of the American Academy of Psychoanalysis* 30:21.

Putnam, H. (1965). *Studies in the Philosophy of Science*. New York: International Universities Press.

Racker, H. (1968). *Transference and Countertransference*. New York: International Universities Press.

Rangell, L. (1988). The future of psychoanalysis: the scientific crossroads. *Psychoanalytic Quarterly* 57:313–340.

_____ (1990). *The Human Core: The Intrapsychic Basis of Behavior*. Madison, CT: International Universities Press.

Rapaport, D. (1951). *Organization and Pathology of Thought: Selected Sources*. New York: Columbia University Press.

Richards, A. D. (1988). Review of Louis Berger's *Psychoanalytic Theory of Clinical Relevance*. *Bulletin of Psychoanalytic Association of New York* 26:1.

_____ (1990). Introduction to a discussion of the past, present, and future of psychoanalytic theory. American Society of Psychoanalytic Physicians. New York, December.

Ricoeur, P. (1970). *Freud and Philosophy: An Essay on Interpretation*. New York: Yale University Press.

Rosenblatt, A. D., and Thickstun, J. T. (1977). *Modern Psychoanalytic Concepts in a General Psychology*. *Psychological Issues* 42/43. New York: International Universities Press.

Samuels, A. (1988). Letter to the Editors. One Psychoanalysis or Many? *International Journal of Psycho-Analysis* 69:551–552.

Sandler, J. (1983). Reflections on some relations between psychoanalytic concepts and psychoanalytic practice. *International Journal of Psycho-Analysis* 64:35–45.

_____ (1986). Reality and the stabilizing function of unconscious fantasy. *Bulletin of the Anna Freud Centre* 9:177–194.

Sandler, J., and Sandler, A.-M. (1983). The 'second censorship,' the 'three box model' and some technical implications. *International Journal of Psycho-Analysis* 64:413–425.

———— (1984). The past unconscious, the present unconscious, and interpretation of the transference. *Psychoanalytic Inquiry* 4:367–399.

Schafer, R. (1976). *A New Language for Psychoanalysis.* New Haven: Yale University Press.

———— (1983). *The Analytic Attitude.* New York: Basic Books.

———— (1985). Wild analysis. *Journal of the American Psychoanalytic Association* 33:275–299.

———— (1990). The search for common ground. *International Journal of Psycho-Analysis* 71:49–52.

Schneiderman, S., ed. (1980). *Returning to Freud: Clinical Psychoanalysis in the School of Lacan.* New Haven: Yale University Press.

———— (1983). *Jacques Lacan: The Death of an Intellectual Hero.* Cambridge, MA: Harvard University Press.

Schwaber, E. A. (1990). The psychoanalyst's methodological stance: some comments based on a response to Max Hernández. *International Journal of Psycho-Analysis* 71:31–36.

Segal, H. (1990). Presentation at panel. Freudian and Kleinian Theory: A Dialogue of Comparative Perspectives. American Psychoanalytic Association Annual Meeting. New York, May.

Smith, J. H., and Kerrigan, W., eds. (1983). *Interpreting Lacan.* New Haven: Yale University Press.

Southwood, H. M. (1988). A review of 'One Psychoanalysis or Many?' *Adelaide Review of Psychoanalysis* 8:3–16.

Spence, D. P. (1982). *Narrative Truth and Historical Truth: Meaning and Interpretation in Psychoanalysis.* New York: Norton.

———— (1987). *The Freudian Metaphor: Toward Paradigm Change in Psychoanalysis.* New York: Norton.

Steiner, R. (1984). Review of *Psychoanalysis in France,* ed. S. Lebovici and D. Widlöcher. *International Journal of Psycho-Analysis* 65:232–233.

———— (1985). Some thoughts about tradition and change arising from an examination of the British Psychoanalytic Society's Controversial Discussions (1943–1944). *International Review of Psycho-Analysis* 12:27–71.

Stone, L. (1961). *The Psychoanalytic Situation: An Examination of its Development and Essential Nature.* New York: International Universities Press.

Tuckett, D., and Hayley, T. (1990). Editorial: The search for common ground. *International Journal of Psycho-Analysis* 71:1–2.

Tyson, R. L. (1991). The emergence of oedipal centrality. Comments on Michael Feldman's paper 'Common ground: the centrality of the Oedipus complex.' *International Journal of Psycho-Analysis* 72:39–44.

Wallerstein, R. S. (1976). Psychoanalysis as a science: its present status and its future tasks. In *Psychology versus Metapsychology: Psychoanalytic Essays in Memory of George S. Klein,* ed. M. M. Gill and P. S. Holzman. *Psychological Issues* 9:198–228. New York: International Universities Press.

_____ (1981). The bipolar self: discussion of alternative perspectives. *Journal of the American Psychoanalytic Association* 29:377–394.

_____ (1983a). Reflections on the identity of the psychoanalyst. In *The Identity of the Psychoanalyst,* ed. E. D. Joseph and D. Widlöcher. New York: International Universities Press.

_____ (1983b). Self psychology and "classical" psychoanalytic psychology: the nature of their relationship. *Psychoanalysis and Contemporary Thought* 6:553–595. Also in *The Future of Psychoanalysis,* ed. A. Goldberg, New York: International Universities Press, 1983.

_____ (1985). How does self psychology differ in practice? *International Journal of Psycho-Analysis* 66:391–404.

_____ (1986a). Psychoanalysis as a science: a response to the new challenges. *Psychoanalytic Quarterly* 55:414–451.

_____ (1986b). *Forty-Two Lives in Treatment: A Study of Psychoanalysis and Psychotherapy.* New York: Guilford Press.

_____ (1988). Psychoanalysis and psychotherapy: relative roles reconsidered. *Annual of Psychoanalysis* 16:129–151.

_____ (1991). Proposal to Ludwig Foundation for a Collaborative Multi-Site Program of Psychoanalytic Therapy Research.

Wallerstein, R. S., and Sampson, H. (1971). Issues in research in the psychoanalytic process. *International Journal of Psycho-Analysis* 52:11–50.

Weinshel, E. M. (1990). Further observations on the psychoanalytic process. *Psychoanalytic Quarterly* 59:629–649.

_____ (1990). Presentation at panel. Freudian and Kleinian Theory: A Dialogue of Comparative Perspectives. American Psychoanalytic Association Annual Meeting, New York, May.

Winnicott, D. W. (1949). Hate in the counter-transference. *International Journal of Psycho-Analysis* 30:69–74.

_____ (1953). Transitional objects and transitional phenomena. *Inter-*

national Journal of Psycho-Analysis 34:89–97.

Wurmser, L. (1977). A defense of the use of metaphor in analytic theory formation. *Psychoanalytic Quarterly* 46:466–498.

Zetzel, E. R. (1955). Recent British approaches to problems of early mental development. *Journal of the American Psychoanalytic Association* 3:534–543.

―――― (1956). An approach to the relation between concept and content in psychoanalytic theory (with special reference to the work of Melanie Klein and her followers). *Psychoanalytic Study of the Child* 11:99–121. New York: International Universities Press.

―――― (1970). *The Capacity for Emotional Growth: Theoretical and Clinical Contributions to Psychoanalysis, 1943–1969.* New York: International Universities Press.

Index

Abrams, S., 64, 211, 212
  on analytic interaction, 76–78
  on classification of disorders, 72–73
  on normal development, 70–71
  on psychoanalytic process, 73–76
Active therapy, 31
Adelaide Review of Psychoanalysis, 206
American Psychoanalytic Association, 13
  self psychology and, 15
  as a common forum, 43
Analytical psychology, 28
  Jungian, 45
Appy, G., 64
  on limits of common ground, 81–94
Argentine Association, the, 22
Arlow, J., 222–223, 260
Aslan, C., 64, 215
  on aims of clinical process, 95–108
  on common ground, 103–106
  on frames of reference, 106–108

on identification, 100
on progression upward, 216
on psychoanalytic babel, 98–100
on truth and pluralism, 106
Attachment theory concept, 12

Bacal, H., 20
Berger, L. S., 264
Bergeret, J., 34
Bion, W., on projective identifications, 101
Birth trauma, 144
Bowlby, J., on attachment theory concepts, 12
Brenner, C., 222–223
  and ego psychology, 15
  on theory-dependent technique, 260
British Object Relations school, 6
British Psychoanalytical Society, Klein and, 6
  pluralism and, 7

Chestnut Lodge, 13
Clinical technique
  active therapy, 31
  aims of, 95–108